GOING APES#!T

Born in Australia in the 70s, Phil Slade spent his early years on a wheat and sheep farm in Central New South Wales before moving to Brisbane, Queensland where he still lives today. A successful musician and composer for theatre and film, a registered psychologist and renowned behavioural economist, Phil co-founded Decida in 2017 dedicated to improving the decision-making capability of people all over the world.

"Books are not here to show how intelligent and cultivated you are. Books are out there to show your heart, to show your soul, and to tell your readers: You are not alone."

–Paulo Coelho

THANK YOU

First and foremost, I would like to thank you, the reader, for being curious enough to pick up this book and open the front cover. I promise if you continue with me on the journey through these pages, I will do my best to reward your curiosity with entertaining insights that will hopefully lead you to a more harmonious and successful life. Without curiosity we are nothing.

I would also like to thank all of the people who have made this book happen. First, a big shout-out to my Decida partners, Roshelle Weir and Peter How. Roshelle, you know how important you are. Tirelessly listening to my many theories, helping refine many concepts, patiently suffering through my ever-vigilant analysis of life and keeping my feet on the ground. I am eternally in your debt. Pete, whether it be your health routines, your view on life or your quirky sense of humour, you are a true inspiration. The fact the universe brought us together to build a world-changing company is something I'm forever grateful for!

To my editor, Suzanne Oxford. Your sharp intellect and savvy editing skills make me look so much better than I really am. Your fingerprints are indelibly printed throughout the text of this book and I am lucky to have you in my world.

I'd also like to thank many of the people who have influenced my thinking and helped shape who I am today: Chris Cohen, Faye Crane, Kim Chandler, Michael Futcher, Andrew and Liz Buchanan, Scott Oxford, Craig Proudley, David Walters, Professor Alex Haslam, Professor Arthur Poropat, Stacey Parker, Russell and Eva Kaye, Tim and Mandy Burns, Isabelle Baines, Ros Mills, Mike Townsley, and all the FOGTs past and present. Not only did you feature in many of the stories in these pages, but our many scotches and philosophical discussions continue to fire my curiosity and challenge my thinking.

Last, but by no means least, to my ever-patient and understanding family—particularly my boys, Ethan and Liam, and my gorgeous, patient and brilliantly intelligent wife, Ali. Choosing to do life with me for so many years is definitely an adventure, and I am constantly amazed and inspired by your love, resilience, compassion and insightfulness. Writing can, at times, be a very selfish endeavour, and without your trust, grace and support, this would never have eventuated.

Thank you.

Phil Slade

GOING APES#!T

Mastering your reactivity in a highly reactive world

Decida
Australia

Published by Decida Digital 2020

01

Copyright © Philip Slade 2020. All rights reserved.

Philip Slade has asserted his right under the Copyright Designs and Patents Act, 1988 to be identified as the author of this work.

Photos on page 13 by Guy Frederick & Dunedin Multidisciplinary Health and Development Unit, University of Otago.

Photo on Page 121, Australia v South Africa - The Rugby Championship by Cameron Spencer; Image #:1029132770; License type: Rights-managed; Collection: Getty Images Sport

This book is sold subject to the condition that it shall not by trade or otherwise, be lent, resold, hired out, or otherwise circulated without the publisher's prior consent in any form of binding or cover other than that in which it is published and without a similar condition including this condition being imposed on the subsequent purchaser.

First published in Australia in 2020 by Decida Digital Pty Ltd.

Decida Digital Pty Ltd
ABN 52 625 164 927
PO Box 3007, Chermside West Qld 4032

For all feedback and correspondence email hello@decida.co or visit the website at www.decida.co/goingapes#!t

ISBN 978-0-646-82563-2

Printed and bound in Australia by InHouse Printing, Queensland.

*In some cases several real-life stories have been combined to protect individuals identity, and make clearer the moral of the story.

To my boys.

May you leave this place better than when you entered it.

CONTENTS

Introduction   **1**

Section A
All about Apes

Chapter 1
What is this 'Ape' you speak of?   **8**

    Killing me with Big Momma's hot sauce: part A. 8
    A happening in Dunedin.. 11
    Two Israeli-Americans walked into a psychology lecture.......... 14
    If our Ape is so destructive, why do we have one?...................... 23
    Chapter snapshot 26

Chapter 2
You and your Ape   **28**

    Guns and seatbelts... 28
    OK, but I think I'm pretty in control of my Ape, aren't I?.......... 34
    Activity 1: The cow and the toaster 34
    Activity 2: Invisible shapes... 36
    Activity 3: What's in a picture?... 37
    Activity 4: Stochastic stimuli... 39
    Activity 5: The stroop test... 41
    Rules of thumb—cognitive bias: part 1 43
    Chapter snapshot 51

Section B
Going ApeS#!t

Chapter 3
Apes behaving badly — 54

- Killing me with Big Momma's hot sauce: part B 54
- From the stage to the page 62
- The artistic temperament 65
- Politics, psychopaths and the power of the group 68
- Chapter snapshot 80

Chapter 4
Cognitive Bias: Part 2 — 82

- Rules of thumb and tricks of the mind 82
- Loss aversion 84
- Confirmation (and information) bias 87
- Sunk cost fallacy 94
- Anchoring 97
- Chapter snapshot 101

Chapter 5
So what can I do about it? — 103

- A theory of cognitive influence 103
- Chapter snapshot 112

Chapter 6
Is it ever OK to go ApeS#!t? — 114

- The dishwashing incident (justifying reactions) 115
- The bar fight 119
- The problem of 'resulting' 121
- The Steve Jobs effect 122
- JR and the law 125
- Love, love me do 135
- Chapter snapshot 141

Chapter 7
Emotion, spirituality and the group   **143**

    The case of the teetotalers and the golden teeth 146

    The sound of hell 153

    Emotions for good 157

    The healing power of emotion and belief 163

    Chapter snapshot 167

Section C
Apes in packs

Chapter 8
Running with the pack   **170**

    The power of belonging and identity 170

    What is social identity? 173

    Ingroups, outgroups and irrational Ape behaviour 179

    Who am I and who are you? 182

    Chapter snapshot 188

Chapter 9
Are Apes tribal?   **190**

    The theatre of thespians 201

    We're all individuals... kind of. 205

    Tribe 1: The Groupies 208

    Tribe 2: The Authoritarians 210

    Tribe 3: The Purists 213

    Chapter snapshot 216

Chapter 10
Living with your Ape   **218**

    Switching between you and your Ape 218

    Sex and money 226

    Grieving Apes 230

    Chapter snapshot 240

Section D
Influencing Apes

Chapter 11
We're all going Apes#!t! — 243

- Helping others switch 243
- Parking lot 244
- Active listening 245
- Respond 245
- Experience nature 246
- Debating Apes 247
- Nudging 254
- Chapter snapshot 263

Chapter 12
Creating new habits — 265

- Simple rules 268
- Reduce resistance 270
- Keep it front of mind 272
- Share it 278
- Transparency and the nudge dilemma 282
- Chapter snapshot 288

In conclusion — 290

Reading list — 293

If we all make slightly better decisions today than we did yesterday, the world of tomorrow will be immeasurably better.

So superior that yesterday will seem like a bizarre dream, an almost implausible reality.

Introduction

Never in history has there been a time when it has been as critical to take control of our reactivity. The digital media and instantaneous mass communication have fundamentally shifted the way we think and behave. Mix this with significant advances in weaponry, science and globalisation, and we have a perfect mix for potential disaster. With all of the benefits that technological advancements give us, we need an increased maturity of mindset to make the most of this digital revolution. If we don't, the darker side of human nature—greed, lust, envy, power and control—will lead us into social situations that could have devastating consequences.

This book isn't about deep-diving into your past to pick at wounds or explore your experience. There is a place for that, but not in this book. My starting position is, whatever your experience (and we all have some pretty crap experiences), each of us has the power to do something today to make tomorrow better. Sins of the past are immutable and we cannot change them. What we can control is whether or not we let those past experiences dictate our future. In this way, we avoid becoming a slave to our experiences and become the master of our destiny.

In this book, I hope to give you the tools to make sure your past doesn't dictate your future.

My journey on this little planet has been one full of varied experiences, unfortunate events and fantastic opportunities. Like most people I know, I have learned life lessons mainly through my failings and misfortune. In this book, I use many of my own experiences as cautionary tales and humorous anecdotes with which to highlight key psychological insights.

In my heart of hearts, I believe that if we all become a little less reactive and improve our decision-making capability—even by the smallest increment—we will solve most of the political, social, economic and environmental problems that exist today. This isn't just about the powerful few whom we blame for the state of the world. We can all take responsibility for our actions and be a better influence on those around us.

As the musings of an apparently unknown monk from around 1100AD articulated:

> *When I was a young man, I wanted to change the world.*
>
> *I found it difficult to change the world, so I tried to change my nation.*
>
> *When I couldn't change my nation, I focused on my town.*
>
> *I couldn't change my town and so, as an older man, I tried to change my family.*
>
> *Now, as an old man, I realise the only thing I can change is myself, and suddenly I realise that if, long ago, I had changed myself, I could have made an impact on my family.*

> *My family and I could have made an impact on our town.*
>
> *Their impact could have changed the nation, and I could, indeed, have changed the world.*

I'm not entirely sure if this was really the work of an unknown monk at the turn of the first millennium (which I think is highly unlikely) or the ramblings of a tripping stoner circa 2000 that became an internet meme. I also don't care. There is a lot of truth in it.

Change ourselves so we can change the world around us. Understand why it feels so good to go Apes#!t at times, how we justify it… and why it never ends as well as when cooler, more responsive heads prevail.

It's probably also worth mentioning I tackle some pretty meaty topics in this book in quite a light way. Many, many books have been written on any number of issues that I spend only part of a chapter on. I apologise in advance if you find this irritating but this is intentional. Think about it like learning to drive a car. If you want to become a race car driver, then by all means follow your curiosity and spend the time to develop your passion. But most of us just need to get to places. This book is designed to simply get you driving, and driving more safely.

You'll also notice I use a lot of humorous and interesting stories from my own life to highlight how our reactive Apes work. This is also intentional.

Scientifically, we know the brain learns best through storytelling. Many studies and experiments have shown the dramatic uplift in people's knowledge retention when they're told the information in a story. I'm not going to get caught up in why stories have such an impact—a simple internet search will guide you toward many interesting and diverse points of view. All we need to know here is it's the way our brains work. It's why we dream. Dreaming is a way our brains collect events and feelings into a story so we can file it into our memory and quickly retrieve it later.

A great example of storytelling trumping detailed explanation can be found in the work of Professor John Paul Kotter, author of *Leading change*. This is one of the most influential books on human psychology and change management in the past century. Ten years after he wrote his seminal and massively influential book in 1996, he discovered a lot of people who were buying his book weren't finishing it. Or, if they had finished it, they only understood the eight key steps of change at an intellectual level rather than actually implementing them. He found this incredibly frustrating. However, instead of writing another book or revising the original text with more examples and research, he did the exact opposite. He got together with co-author Holger Rathgeberger and wrote a simple picture book where the eight steps were embedded into a simple allegory about penguins. The book is called *Our iceberg is melting*. It will take you less than an hour to read and you will retain more practical insight after reading it than ploughing through his earlier, lengthier tome.

I know this from my personal experience. I studied *Leading change* as part of my undergrad degree, making copious notes and spending a couple of months reading and studying the book each night. But after all of this study, I still struggled to remember and apply each of the eight steps in an organisational setting. Then I spent 45 minutes reading

Our iceberg is melting, and it all clicked. That was almost 15 years ago now and I can still remember and recall what I learned. However, I can recall no examples or research used in the more-acclaimed *Leading change*. Now, I'm not as smart as others, but I suspect from the volume of feedback and comments on sites all over the internet (including Kotter's homepage) that I am not the only one who's had this experience.

This is the simple power of story.

As the goal of this book is to help you gain insight into the way the brain ticks and be able to apply it in real life, it only makes sense we take this journey through my stories. To not do so would be to ignore how our brains work. By telling stories of my own life, I hope you're much more likely to be able to remember the how, the why, and the so what, to improve your decision-making.

Plus, stories are much more fun for me to write. So there.

By the end of this book you should be able to better:
1. Identify your Ape
2. Control your Ape
3. Help others control their Ape
4. Understand how emotion and social identity can influence your judgment
5. Realise not all science nerds like me are entirely boring.

To start our voyage, let's first have a look at what behavioural economics is and how your instinctive reactions, primal instincts, emotions and experiences shape your decisions and your destiny.

Let's meet your Ape.

"Holding on to unforgiveness is like drinking poison and then expecting the other person to get sick."

– Grandad (who was told it by his Grandad)

Section A

All about Apes

Reacting and responding

Chapter 1
What is this 'Ape' you speak of?

> *"Life is 10% what happens to me and 90% how I react to it."*
> *–Charles Swindoll*

Killing me with Big Momma's hot sauce: part A.

Once I went completely Apes#!t and, to be honest, I was lucky not to have ended up in a cell in Guantanamo Bay.

In the late 2000s, following a decade of terrorist attacks across America and the world, I was recording and composing music and sound for film. Craig and Shawn, a great Brisbane writer/director duo, were creating a documentary about conspiracy theories and they asked me to tag along to capture sound. I jumped at the chance. Five weeks in the States chasing down conspiracy theories and crazy people on the fringes of society sounded like fun.

L.A., San Francisco, Elberton, Atlanta, Austin and many places in-between. We met the most amazing and diverse corners of society, and heard many funny and insightful stories I still tell to this day. I truly treasure the experience. Even so, I was emotionally, physically and mentally exhausted by the end of the trip. I had nothing left in the tank. Which meant that on the final leg home at LAX, when a security guard challenged me about something that I thought was ridiculous, I simply had no energy to control my Ape. My Ape went completely Apes#!t.

As fun as the trip was, it was long, hard and sometimes painful work. Freezing cold 2am shoots in graveyards, downloading and editing sound and video every night, up at 6am to get ready for the day's shoot, driving hundreds of kilometres to get to hard-to-reach places… Day after day, week after week, it was relentless. I had two young boys and a wife at home and, by the end of the five weeks, I was missing them terribly. I couldn't wait to get home.

Toward the end of the trip, on the plane from Austin to Phoenix and flying over terrain that looked remarkably like central Australia, I was flicking through photos of the kids when the Tom Waits song, *Tom Traubert's blues*, started to play on my iPod. For those familiar with the song, you'll know it's a lilting orchestral lullaby, voiced by the earthy, gruff tones of Tom Waits' beautifully pain-filled voice. The song is about lonely travellers, with the chorus a stirring and melancholy rendition of *Waltzing matilda*. At the time, I wasn't even aware of the song and definitely not cognisant of the lilting Australiana-inspired chorus. As the orchestra swelled and burst into the surprising and searing rendition of the ironically Australian anthem, I simply couldn't contain the tide of emotion. It was all too much. I was a blubbering mess. I just burst into uncontrollable weeping. Snot bubbling out and everything, it was my emotional cracking point. I was more than ready to go home, and couldn't wait to get there.

But as much as I wanted to head home, there was a problem: I hadn't been able to find a meaningful gift for my wife, Alison, and there was no way I was going home empty-handed. The problem was that getting a uniquely American gift you can't get already in Australia (that isn't simply tourist kitsch) is very difficult. However, I was determined to find something unique and meaningful. Five weeks of searching in the small breaks that we'd had in shooting had resulted in nothing. I had been able to find quite a few gifts for my boys—football and basketball shirts and little airport trinkets—but nothing had resonated for Ali.

As the days wore on, the pressure to find a meaningful gift mounted. Finally, on the last day of filming, I found myself in Austin. What a great town: home of Texas University and the SxSW festival. At one of the last stops on our tour, we were filming a notorious conspiracy theorist and radio host, Alex Jones. At the end of the interview, I confided to him about my failed mission to procure a meaningful gift.

"Ya know what, son?" he said, in a typically big, gruff, Texan accent. "If I were you, I'd go down to Big Momma's House on the corner and get some genuine TexMex sauces. You can't get them anywhere else in the world and Big Momma makes the most divine, tantalising sauces. It's a sure-fire winner, guaranteed to turn any dish into pure joy. Give her that and she'll love you forever!"

I was sold. This was it, the final chapter in my quest to find the perfect gift.

Little did I know it wasn't to be the final twist in this tale, a twist that would trigger my Ape to come out in the most dramatic of ways…

We'll finish this story in chapter three, but for now, let's take a short detour from LA to New Zealand.

A happening in Dunedin

Sometime long before the internet and PowerPoint presentations, two post docs in psychology named Terrie Moffitt and Avshalom Caspi met when they had adjacent displays at the poster session of a conference in St Louis, Missouri.

Now, I don't know if you've been to a science poster session before, but it's basically a big hall where people can put up a display of their research and others can walk past and ask questions if they're interested. The people presenting their research on these posters stand and wait next to their displays for long periods of time, waiting for someone at the conference to be curious enough about what they did and found. Needless to say, it can get very tedious after a few days.

However, in a stroke of good luck for the rest of us, this gave Moffitt and Caspi plenty of time to build a strong friendship as they were tending their displays. To stave off boredom, they talked to each other about their research and found they were curious about many of the same things. It was a truly beautiful nerd connection that blossomed into one of the most significant scientific and personal love affairs of all time. It was the start of a journey I'm sure they had no idea would be as adventurous as it turned out to be.

Maybe it was the unbridled optimism of young love but, not long after meeting, Moffitt and Caspi decided to join one of the most ambitious studies ever conducted: The Dunedin Multidisciplinary Health and Development Study, or The Dunedin Experiment for short. The research was a longitudinal study that would engage 1000 young children who lived in Dunedin, New Zealand, and then measure and track everything they could think of over the course of their lives. The purpose of the study was to see if there was anything that could predict a healthy or successful life.

Knowing what they might find could be controversial, they knew they had to look for a way to study lots of people from very diverse backgrounds to make sure their results were generalisable and not attributable to some quirk of the experimental design. This is why Dunedin was such a perfect setting for the experiment. In the early 70s, Dunedin was one of the more culturally, socially and economically diverse cities in the world. It was a population that had just about everything you'd want in a study like this.

The incredible thing about this study is that it has continued for more than 50 years. An extraordinary 96 per cent of all living, eligible members of the original 1013 three-year-olds remain in the study. In most studies like this, you'd expect a 30–40 per cent drop-off. So a drop of just 4 per cent is incredibly impressive, almost unbelievable.

Participants were examined at ages 3, 5, 7, 9, 11, 13, 15, 18, 21, 26, 32, 44 and, most recently at 50. To be assessed, participants are brought back to Dunedin from around the world for a comprehensive set of interviews, physical tests, health examinations, and digital questionnaires.

The study has measured everything you could possibly imagine, including all aspects of their health (physical, mental and social), physical characteristics, behavioural choices, socio-economic status of the families and cultures, IQ and general attitudes to see if there were any factors that predicted a more successful life.

The wealth of information and insight into the human condition that researchers have gathered is nothing short of stunning. More than 1200 papers have been published, with results impacting many aspects of life as we now know it.

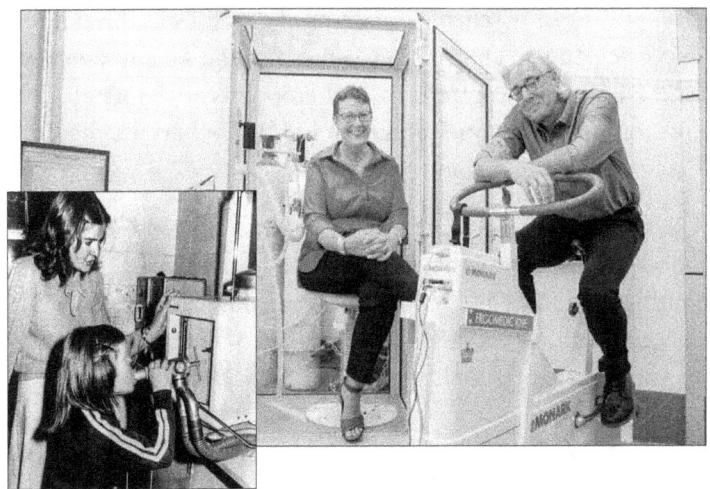

Terrie with one of the participants early in the study (inset) and Terrie Moffitt and Avshalom Caspi in 2018. Photo: Guy Frederick.

There were many incredible discoveries uncovered and many myths busted. One of my favourites is they've proven that not everyone is born equal. Some people really do have more talent for certain things and others really do struggle right from the beginning. Despite how much you nurture, nature has more to say than we'd like when it comes to aptitude.

Even more intriguing was what they found to be the only significant predictor of success. What would you think it is?

- Socio-economic status?
- Diet?
- Sleeping habits?
- Cultural background?
- IQ?
- Level of education or school you went to?
- A mixture of all of these?

Nope. The only reliable predictor of success was the ability of participants to control their emotions. Put simply, people who are better at controlling their emotions are better at controlling their money and their life, and others are more likely to help them along the way.

What subsequent studies have continued to prove is people who learn to control their emotions, and can delay immediate gratification for bigger pay-offs in the future, are reliably more successful. The good news is this trait can be learned. It's not an immutable personality trait. It's a skill.

But like most things in psychology research, real life is a little more complicated than the controlled environment of a lab. Simply assuming that becoming more emotionally intelligent is the answer to life would be incorrect. It's a significant part of the answer, sure, but not the whole story. To understand the story, we must first understand something of behavioural economics. We must understand more about you and your Ape.

Two Israeli-Americans walked into a psychology lecture...

Around the same time the study in Dunedin was kicking off, two researchers in Israel named Amos Tversky and Daniel Kahneman met and started another revolution in the understanding of human behaviour. Unlike Moffitt and Caspi, Tversky and Kahneman seemed to be opposites with almost no natural chemistry between them. Those close to them would say they were the most unlikely of acquaintances. Kahneman was a pacifist, Tversky a trained warrior. Kahneman was introverted and aloof while Tversky was much more personable and outgoing. Either way, it seemed their different approaches to life made for great intellectual debate and both were fascinated by why people seem to consistently make decisions that are not in their best interests, particularly when it comes to money.

You see, the more respected and popular economic theory of the time was that people were rational 'actors', making decisions that served their own best interests. Indeed, most of the current economic system and democratic philosophy is still built on this principle—and it's not such a bad one. People want to survive and thrive, so making decisions to improve their lot in life seems to make intuitive sense, right? This is why most democratic governments encourage people to own their own home. If you own your own home and land, then you're more likely to want its value to appreciate and increase your personal wealth, and you're more likely to take care of it. You're also likely to care more about what your neighbours are doing because good neighbours will make for a good neighbourhood, which again increases the value of your asset and your wealth. You're also likely to be invested in the health of your community and participate in the political process in order to protect the value of your asset. All because you invested in a home and you personally benefit from it accruing value. This is you making decisions for the benefit of your own self-interest.

There's a lot of evidence to support this point of view when you look at the behaviours of people who do not own their own home. Renters are much less likely to care for properties, and less likely to invest in maintenance because it doesn't serve their self-interest. They also show less concern for neighbours and the broader community because they reap no benefit personally from such endeavours (apart from personal reputation for living in a particular area).

The theory at its most basic level holds true, but Tversky and Kahneman observed numerous situations where this theory didn't seem to pass the pub test. People were acting in irrational ways all the time. To do our own pub test, look at the below pictures and think for a moment if all of the decisions linked to those pictures are rational.

Not sure we're always such self-interested and rational decision-makers anymore? Neither were Tversky and Kahneman.

Their big observation from thousands of hours of research, argument and experimentation was that we seem to have two systems or ways of processing information. The first system (creatively called system one) is a largely unconscious, automatic and emotional system, built on rule of thumb instincts we've developed as a result of experiences and genetics. The second way we process information is creatively called (drum roll, please…) system two. It's more rational and slower, and it's activated when we encounter anything novel or new. This system takes time and energy, so we only activate it when we need it. Once our brain's limited bucket of energy is used up, we revert to our system one automatic reaction to get us through the day.

If you're anything like me, remembering which is system one and system two, what they do and the relationship they have with each other is hard to recall. For this reason, I looked at what system one does and realised it's largely related to areas of the brain that are first developed in the womb: our primal brain, our automatic motor responses and our survival instinct. This is the area of the brain linked to the amygdala, deep inside the centre of the brain and commonly referred to as the fear centre. This emotional part of the brain is believed to trigger our fight, flight or freeze responses. Interestingly enough, it's also the part of the brain that shares eerie similarity to our tree-swinging evolutionary cousin, the chimpanzee. It's primal, automatic and unconscious. That's why, instead of calling it system one, I call it our Ape.

We seem to have developed our primal automatic Ape in order to survive in a complex and dangerous world. It allows us to learn rules of thumb to reduce cognitive load and instinctively respond to emotion. As humans, we've evolved an ingenious way to survive by quickly assessing the millions of pieces of information our environment throws at us every second of every day. As Kahneman states in his seminal book, *Thinking fast and slow*, our system one Ape is a purpose-built machine for jumping to conclusions that helps us to safely navigate a dangerous world. It is our learned, fast, intuitive, automatic behaviours, and it works really well for us most of the time. System one reacts, and does it well. However, when these rules of thumb (which scientists call our cognitive biases) are applied in incorrect contexts, we get problems.

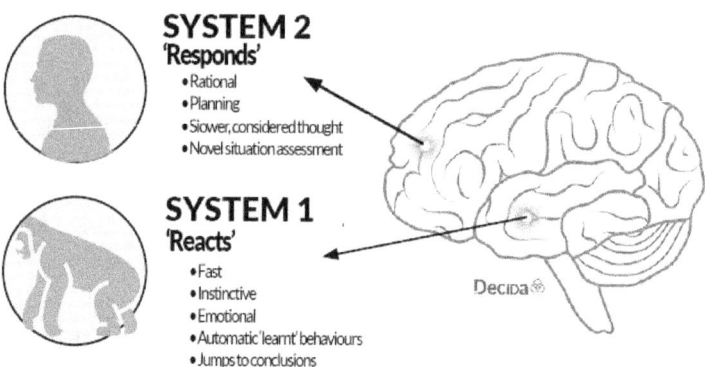

The two systems of the brain, according to behavioural economics, and key traits of each system.

As intelligent-thinking humans, we like to believe our decisions employ a more conscious, rational, system two style of thinking. The reality is our Ape actually makes most of our decisions. The reason for this? Well, the answer for me is two-fold. First, we trust our Ape more than we trust ourselves. I mean, we've survived this long, right? Going with our gut can be the right decision a lot of the time, particularly if it's in an area where we have experience. Second, we default to our Ape a lot of the time to conserve cognitive energy. Our brains are finite things, having to deal with a seemingly infinite barrage of information, so our brains are hard-wired to conserve energy, to take short-cuts, to make sure we have enough brain power in our rational bucket to assign to really important things.

System two thinking is hard and cognitively demanding, so we avoid using it when we can.

While our system one Ape reacts, our system two responds. We're more conscious of our system two thinking, while our reactive Ape sits more in the unconscious recesses of our minds. As our system two is more conscious, we often incorrectly assume we are making rational system two choices, when in fact we're actually using our system two to justify our Ape's snap judgments. The smarter you are, the better you are at rationalising irrational behaviour. It's one of the reasons that high IQ and high EQ (emotional intelligence) are not correlated.

Our reactive Ape is there to help us through life by jumping to conclusions so we can quickly respond to danger and get out of harm's way. As cave-dwellers, if we saw someone go into a cave and get eaten by a bear, we'd approach the next cave with caution—as if there's a good chance there's a bear in there. Our Ape jumps to this conclusion in order to keep us safe. In that moment, we're not thinking, 'Well, there are millions of caves and only thousands of bears, so we only have a 1 in 10,000 chance there's a bear in there, so as probability goes it should be fine'. No, we go, 'It's a cave, bears live in caves, bears can kill', and then we're surprised and relieved when it's empty. Naturally bad statisticians, but we're alive. Those who don't take enough care get eaten, natural selection does its work and humans evolve to heed the instinct of the Ape. The thing is, while our Ape makes snap judgments that protect us from bears, it can equally lead us to irrational assessments of situations that put us in harm's way.

This fact was highlighted when I was a first-year psychology student at the University of Queensland. Like most students I used to take the 169 bus that terminated just north of the

Brisbane River. Then, as the buses arrived in unison on the hour, hundreds of students would migrate in a silent herd along the long path between the bus stop and the university buildings. Students of all shapes and sizes, most of them with earphones playing previous lectures, music or talking to friends as they walked. This slow procession is made all the more dramatic because the path for the most part runs along a ridge that drops away to two beautiful lakes on either side. As universities go, it's one of the more beautiful entrances. Not that many students would take much notice, distracted by their devices and lost in their thoughts as they walked.

There are lots of automatic Ape behaviours observable in this situation. We don't have to think about walking as we learned that skill of balance and movement long ago. We know from the direction the crowd is walking and the fact we've walked the path hundreds of times that we don't need to spend mental energy on it. So, we just follow the herd. We also know that, as long as the crowd in front of us doesn't deviate from the path, there are no obstacles in the way. So there's no need to waste any awareness on that. In fact, as people are marching from the bus stop to the university, it's one of the few places to observe people in a complete Ape state. That's why most students are able to listen to podcasts, watch videos or read study notes as they walk, because their Ape has almost everything else sorted. Automatic, learned behaviours. Our Apes are helping us focus our energy on solving problems or learning new things. Because of this we are heavily reliant on our Apes being ever-vigilant, constantly keeping our peripheral senses active to look for danger. It was this vigilance to peripheral vision that didn't end up so well for me one evening.

It was just on sunset as I was walking back from class. The sky was silver black and the shadows were starting to look less defined in the encroaching night. There weren't many people leaving that late so I was almost on my own. As I was walking toward the buses on the path between the lakes, I was focusing on my phone and not giving much attention to the path in the dimming light. Then, out of the corner of my eye, I saw something long and shimmering in the light. My Ape instantly leaped to the obvious conclusion: a snake on the path! Everyone who's grown up in country Australia like me knows many snakes are deadly and to be feared, and our Ape is trained by our parents with truisms like 'the only good snake is a dead one.'

Startled, my Ape sprang into action and I immediately leapt backward off the path. So far, in fact, I clipped the edge of the embankment and lost my balance over the other side. As I rolled my ankle and went head-over-turkey down the hill, I got a glimpse of the large stick on the path that I had, in a split second, identified as a possible snake. My Ape had made a snap judgment to save my life, but instead all I got was a twisted ankle, a cracked phone screen and some dented pride. My Ape had reacted, thinking it was helping me before my more rational self had a chance to respond and make a better choice.

This idea of reacting and responding was explored in a fascinating way a few years ago by former US Treasury Secretary Robert Rubin. At the time, he was on a bit of a crusade to highlight the effects of the prison system on the cycle of poverty. If you search his name, you can find a fantastic TED talk where he details this experience. During his investigation, almost accidently, he discovered something astounding. Among the 28 prisoners they were studying, they were able to identify they'd all ended up in prison because of a collective 4 minutes and 26 seconds of reactive decision-making. For a share of fewer than 10 seconds each, their Apes had taken over and they'd lost control of their rational decision-making. Ten seconds of madness to flip their lid and go Apes#!t—and just enough time to turn an argument into physical abuse, robbery into murder, or for an impulsive drag race to kill an innocent bystander.

A screen shot of the TEDx talk given by former U.S. Treasury Secretary. Robert Rubin. www.youtube.com/watch?v=s4GFOczg0Gw

Across the 28 prisoners, how many years of incarceration do you think those short passages of madness turned into? The answer: 715 years. Less than 10 seconds of reactive behaviour for each prisoner collectively landed them in prison for 715 years! The consequences of going Apes#!t are simple to see when it results in illegal behaviour as the consequences are easy to track with jail time.

Until Moffitt and Caspi's Dunedin experiment, there was no way of measuring the true impact the reactive, impulsive, emotional Ape had on our lives, where the consequences may in fact be the absence of success or lost opportunities as opposed to the addition of a constraint. We can only assume the loss of opportunity we experience when we go Apes#!t is somewhere in the magnitude of the loss of freedom experienced by the prisoners. This is why the Dunedin study was so amazing. It was tangible evidence that the more you can control your Ape, the more likely you are to experience a more successful life.

Control your Ape and you will be immeasurably better off. Learn to ask yourself if you feel your Ape get triggered: Am I about to react or respond? If you react, chances are you're about to make a poor choice.

If our Ape is so destructive, why do we have one?

Our unconscious, automatic Ape helps us to avoid spending precious mental energy on irrelevant things so we have more mental energy for things that matter. For instance, learning to ride a bike is hard in the beginning. We can't do anything but focus on our balance, pedalling, steering and speed. But once we get the hang of it, our Ape starts to take over and we are less conscious of what we are doing. Now, we can have a conversation while we ride, or listen to a podcast. Interestingly, when we start to think about balance, pedalling, steering and speed again, we often start riding like a beginner. Once our Ape gets the hang of something, it seems like it's actually much better at it than we are. Our Ape loves learned behaviours and familiar routines because it protects our cognitive energy.

One of the most complex, and energy-sapping situations we find ourselves in is social interactions. We know social connectedness is key to survival but maintaining connectedness and trust can be hard work. So our Ape strives to find predictable rules and processes to guide interactions to simplify things. Manners, opinions, appropriate behaviours, cultural practices… these are all rules and processes we've created. We call them social norms and our Apes love to conform to them.

Our Apes get very upset when we challenge these social norms because we unconsciously perceive the challenge as a threat to our survival. It's why debates about what is socially acceptable and what isn't are so heated, and why people react so intensely when we say something that goes against popular opinion. Their Apes come out and go Apes#!t! We will discuss politics and the impact of social identity on behaviour later.

An American economist and cognitive psychologist in the 1940s named Herbert A. Simon contributed greatly to our understanding of our Apes. For instance, he coined the term 'bounded rationality', which describes the observation that we have a limit to the amount of information we can rationally process at any given time. Simon was concerned the popular economic understanding of motivation and human behaviour was flawed. His insight was that, in order to focus on the things that matter, humans tend to simplify as many things as possible into 'administrative tasks' and processes to conserve mental energy. But for all of his great insight, there was one thing that he underestimated. This oversight, and the basis for Kahneman and Tversky's work, was the strength of influence our unconscious Apes have over our conscious rational decision-making. Simon's term of 'administrative behaviour' implies we are in control of our Ape—that our Ape serves our more rational state. Kahneman and Tversky argued the opposite, saying our Ape—our instinct, our learned behaviours—actually control us in many instances. An unfortunate many times, we're the marionette that thinks it's controlling the puppeteer. Kahneman and Tversky's genius was to construct experiments that helped expose when it was actually our Ape pulling the strings. This insight led to the development of behavioural economics and propelled the science of decision-making into prime time. The more we learn about our Apes, the more we can recognise when we are thinking in reactive 'Ape' ways.

Remember the Dunedin experiment. The more we can control our Apes, the more likely we are to succeed. The more we can see our Ape, the more we are likely to tame it.

What we now know is Ape-taming is more than simply regulating emotion and delaying gratification. We need to know how our Apes work to know how to make better decisions. We need to know how our Apes are influencing, or biasing, our thoughts. Discovering, labelling and understanding these cognitive biases has been the basis for thousands of experiments since the 1970s. Controlling and influencing Apes toward better decision-making is today's evolution.

But first, you need to feel your Ape, see it, sense it as a real thing before you can tame it. Often, we can approach the topic of out-of-control Apes as if they are other people's problems. Even if we do have an Ape, surely we're less likely to be influenced by it because of our superior intellect or breadth of experience. If you think that, then you're most likely to be the most controlled by your Ape. I am often amused by the observation that the least self-aware people are often the ones who declare themselves to be very self-aware.

So with this in mind, let's remember that, as humans, we all have unconscious Apes and conscious selves. It's you and your Ape. So let's meet your Ape.

Chapter snapshot

Key take-aways

1. Controlling our emotional reactivity is the only scientifically proven predictor of financial success and better health.

2. We all have an automatic, unconscious, sometimes emotional, reactive system of thinking (system one) which we call our 'Ape'. Controlling our Ape's reactions, and learning to respond rather than react, is key in making better choices and improving our cognitive performance.

3. We also develop a more rational, conscious system of thinking (system two), which focuses on new and novel information and experiences.

4. Our Ape makes most of our important decisions in life, with our more conscious system often rationalising our Ape's irrational decisions.

5. Our Ape is not bad or good, it just is. It helps us navigate the world safely, but sometimes gets us into trouble.

Things I can do to practically apply this insight

- Start to notice things that you do automatically, like riding a bike or walking while you talk on the phone. Start to think about doing these activities and see how your performance drops! Now do the same activity, but in reverse. Start to notice the things that you are overthinking or you feel you are underperforming in. See if you can put some simple automatic rules in place to allow your Ape to take more of the repeatable tasks on so you can focus on the things that really matter.

- Start a daily journal to help record your moments of emotional reactivity and consider ways you may be able to respond more constructively. At Decida, we have created a journal you can purchase at decida.co that breaks this process down into a series of Q&A sections to help focus your energy on what is important.

Thought-starters

- When was the last time you were emotionally triggered?
- Why do you think the event or person you are thinking of triggered you so much?
- Was there a better way to handle the situation?

Chapter 2

You and your Ape

"On one level, wisdom is nothing more than the ability to take your own advice."
–Sam Harris

Guns and seatbelts

People playing poker machines rarely display any rational decision-making. They will experience a significant losing streak and instead of their Ape saying, 'Enough is enough mate, this is a really dumb investment!', their brain instead says, 'We've already had so many losses, the next one has to be closer to a win! How stupid would I feel if I left this machine and the next schmuck rolled up and won the jackpot?' And so people play another round, unable to reconcile they are no closer to a win than they were before they started playing.

What we fail to realise is every pull of the handle has just as much chance of winning as the previous 20, and the next 100. In no way do we increase our chances of winning simply by sticking at a machine. Worse still, when we do win a small random amount, even though it often doesn't even cover our initial investment, it makes the whole thing even stickier, often post-rationalising actions and outcomes to confirm our poor choices. We think. 'A-ha! If I hadn't stayed here this long, I wouldn't have won anything', and then keep pulling the lever until we're broke.

This is classic Ape behaviour. Terrible at probability and magnetically drawn to the prospect of winning after you've already invested or lost so much. The pokies are purpose-built brain-candy machines designed to fleece you of your cash in a way that actually feels good for your Ape and, as a consequence, millions of people are addicted to them. There it is in living colour—people behaving in ways that rationally make no sense, and not at all in their own self-interest. It is my personal view that pokies are evil. There is a special place in hell for them.

The point here is there is something else driving our decision-making other than our rational selves, something stronger than our rational brain. There is an automatic and emotional driver that works in a way that does not follow rational logic and often hurts us—and yet it still feels good. The observable nature of poor decision-making is why gambling games was the initial focus for Kahneman and Tversky. Whether at the poker table, in the share market or investing in property, gambling is a gold mine of irrational decision-making.

If you still need proof we're not entirely rational decision-makers, take the gun control debate that often plays out in America. As an Australian, I must admit I am simply befuddled as to why people need weapons of such murderous power. I mean, simple guns that can be used for hunting or simple deterrents, sure. But automatic weapons that are specifically designed for mass human murder?

The primary argument I hear from gun lobbyists is one of individual rights and civil liberties, rooted in a deep (and I might say well-founded) fear of oppressive governments. However, in that last statement is a clue as to the irrational decision-making process going on in this debate. Do your own analysis and you'll find countries with tighter gun control have greater freedoms, live more peacefully and have a much lower murder rate. However, if you are a gun-lover, this won't mean anything to your Ape. I can produce all of the statistics of dramatically lower death rates in other countries. That statistically your child is much more likely to be murdered in America than in any country with gun control. That our survival as a species is much more likely without these tools of enablement for the psychologically disturbed and politically unhinged. This argument would be unlikely to change anyone's mind, however, because of one simple four-letter 'f' word. Fear.

Fear of being disempowered, fear of authority, fear of being made the fool, fear of losing what you think is rightfully yours. Remember we are all terrible at probability, and what I see in America is fear mixed with statistical errors. The fear of death seems unlikely in your estimation because no-one you know has died. No-one you know has died, so it feels less likely to happen to you. You also feel with a personal firearm you have an element of control, so you discard the likelihood of dying because you feel more in control of the situation than you really are. The more powerful the firearm, the more you feel personally in control. As with the poker machines, bad decision-making actually makes your Ape feel good and traps you in poor logic. This Ape logic make us feel safer—even though it actually puts us at greater risk of death and injury.

Our Ape is massively susceptible to the influence of fear, and incredibly poor at judging risk and probability. For a race that has evolved with a sharp instinct for survival, it's incredible how lightly we can treat real risk when we assume we have more control over a situation than we really have. It's the curse of complacency, and it's what gun control and seatbelts have in common.

The discount of personal risk with gun ownership is similar to the discounting of personal risk that fed into the resistance to wearing seatbelts in the 70s. To illustrate this further, allow me to take you back to my childhood, growing up on a wheat and sheep farm in central New South Wales—in a particular part of Australia where, when it's hot, it's burning hot. Dry, searing and unforgiving. Regardless, we still went to church every Sunday afternoon at 3pm.

My family had a light green Valiant station wagon, one of the ones where you could wind down the back window. I thought that was the coolest car in the churchyard. On the way home from most hot summer Sunday services at Trundle Baptist, my brother and I loved nothing more than to sit in the boot with the back window wound down as Dad tore through the country roads, leaving a dust storm in our wake. There was something magical about it, watching the dust dance and curl in the car's wake, and on those hot summer days, my parents were very happy to have the car aired out as quickly as possible after being parked in the hot sun for a few hours. Happy parents, happy kids, happy days.

Now, of course, there were some seatbelts in the car but out in the bush no-one even thought about putting them on. We were free from constraints and confident the car (the potential weapon of death in this story) was being driven responsibly and carefully. We didn't wear seatbelts because we drove all the time, had never had an accident, nor had we really heard of many people we knew having had an accident, so it didn't seem important. I mean, there was our cotton-farming friend, Mr Butler, who was in a wheelchair because of a run-in with a cow on a country road, but we discounted that as just being extremely unlucky, and we were much better drivers than he was. The fun and freedom in the moment was more valued than acknowledging or mitigating any risk. We were complacent.

This scenario seems absurd now. These days putting children in that type of perceived danger would be decried by some safety campaigners as child abuse. Low perceived likelihood of an injury and high complacency toward wearing seatbelts meant a devastating catastrophe when an accident did happen (and fortunately for my siblings and me, this circumstance never eventuated). Accidents happen, gun deaths happen, but the magnitude of the impact is significantly reduced by the mitigation strategies put in place to protect human life. When seatbelt legislation came in, there was an outcry that it was nanny state-ism, an assault on our individual freedoms and rights in our own cars. The perceived loss of freedom and rights when simply trying to enforce seatbelts to help protect life was absurd. It's the same mental fallacy playing out with the gun control debate.

Savings and investments can be seen as financial seatbelts. They help protect us when unforeseen bad things happen. In many ways, complacency toward financial security is even riskier than driving around without a seatbelt. But the loss of things in the immediate, seems to outweigh the need to create financial seatbelts. I know I should invest but I want [insert new shiny thing] now, and I can buy now and pay later! Invest in something that won't pay dividends for a long time, or buy [insert new shiny thing] now, which will make me feel good and be the envy of all my friends? I wonder which one most people choose most of the time??

I want a new car now, and I can get it with a loan with small repayments. Invest in something that won't pay dividends for a long time, or buy a car now that will make me feel good and the envy of all of my friends.

Whether it's gambling, sex, investing, consuming or wearing seatbelts, taking risks when we shouldn't and not taking risks when we should seem to be an inherent and never-ending part of the human struggle. As a human race, we seem to make decisions that have negative impacts on us all the time—primarily because we fail to realise it's our automatic and emotional Ape that's doing the decision-making, and our conscious selves working hard to reconcile and justify our choices.

The invisible automatic forces or rules of thumb our Apes use to make decisions is what scientists label as cognitive bias. You have a rule to close the door after you walk through. That's a bias that not only makes you close the door behind you, but also judge those who fail to follow this rule. You have a belief that a fit body indicates a fit mind, then that bias will drive you to fitness regimes and judging others who are overweight. You have a rule that you don't trust or talk to strangers, and that will be a bias that impacts your judgment and perception of new people.

These biases that we create to keep us safe and to help us succeed can also be the very rules that hold us back. We, as individuals, have literally thousands of rules that are constructed and maintained by our emotions—a complex myriad of biases built into our neurology that can leads us to all sorts of incorrect conclusions, poor decisions and negative outcomes.

The maddening thing is it always feels good to follow our bias, our Ape's rules of thumb, because our brains give us a little hit of dopamine every time we comply with the rule. Our brain assumes we learned this Ape rule in order to survive, so we keep on letting our Ape direct us.

OK, but I think I'm pretty in control of my Ape, aren't I?

Often when I talk about going Apes#!t to leaders, I get a sense they feel like it's interesting but more applicable to their staff than to them. What these leaders fail to realise is we all have an Ape and we cannot escape its influence on our decision-making. We can just control its influence a little better when we clearly see it. Just because you can't see it doesn't mean it's not there. It just means you haven't been looking in the right places.

In order for people to feel their Ape and see a little of the Ape's influence on decision-making, I take them through a few simple activities. Below are the five I use the most (and I think are the most fun).

Activity 1: The cow and the toaster

The first activity is simple. Take note of the very first word that comes to mind when you answer the following question. Don't think about it too much. Just note what word instinctively pops into your mind when you read the question. The test is to see how fast you can answer the question. Ready? Fast as you can. Go.

What do cows drink?

If you intuitively thought the answer was milk, you're not alone. Rationally, we all know the real answer is water but, for 90 per cent of us, the immediate conclusion that jumped to mind was milk. Your Ape did what it normally does and jumped to a conclusion that felt intuitively correct. Remember, we are hard-wired to limit the amount of cognitive energy our brains use, and so we rely on our Ape to help us think in the most efficient way possible. So, in the first split-second when we look at answering a question like, 'What do cows drink?' our Ape doesn't actually read the whole sentence. It just reads 'cow' and 'drink' and then, in an instant, your Ape searches your brain to pattern-match the words. We link cows and drinking to drinking milk. So cows/drink/milk seems like a more intuitive match then cows/drink/water. So before our responsive, slower brain answers the question at hand, our faster, intuitive brain stands up and confidently shouts, 'Milk!'

Welcome to your Ape hard at work. It's fast, intuitive and actually impressively smart. It's just wrong some of the time.

But if you're one of the very few people that report you didn't think of milk (maybe because your experience growing up didn't include lots of references to cow's milk), I'd hate for you to feel left out. So let's try another question. Everyone else: you know what it feels like now, so you should do better this time, right? Let's see.

Remember, answer the below question as fast as you can, and take note of the first word that pops into your mind. Ready? Speed is the important thing here. Go.

What do you put in a toaster?

Toast? No, it's bread of course! Your Ape is at it again!

Still think you're in control of your Ape?

Maybe it's just a word thing… What if this penchant for pattern-matching isn't just limited to words? What about pictures?

Activity 2: Invisible shapes

Look at the picture below. What is the shape that sits at the centre of the picture?

Did you think of the white triangle? It's obvious, isn't it? Problem is there is no white triangle in the picture at all. It's just that the shapes on the page suggest a pattern that indicates a white triangle. The strange thing is we can't not see the triangle, even though it's not actually there. Look at what happens when I rotate all of the elements in the picture.

Now, it's just a random mess of shapes and lines on a page. Same elements on the page, and it seems as though the white triangle is nowhere to be seen. There is no sense to make of the picture. Our Ape has nothing to compare it against so all you see are the actual elements on the page.

But what happens when our Ape has to decide between multiple truths? Multiple conclusions when we look at the same lines on a page?

Activity 3: What's in a picture?

Take a look at the pictures on the following page that are popular visual illusions.

A – Is it a dashing cowboy, or an old man?

B – Is this a young woman with a fur coat, or an old woman with a head scarf?

C – Is this a bearded man, or someone sitting on a grassy knoll overlooking the countryside?

D – Man's face or naked woman?

E – Girl or artist?

F – Duck or rabbit?

The answer, of course, is both. (If you can't see all the images, give it some time and you'll see them all.)

All of the interpretations of the information (the picture) on the page are true. There are two truths in each of these pictures. But what if we were trying to make sense of human behaviour, or situations where the information is less obvious than in a line drawing? It might be drawing meaning from

Going Apes#!t

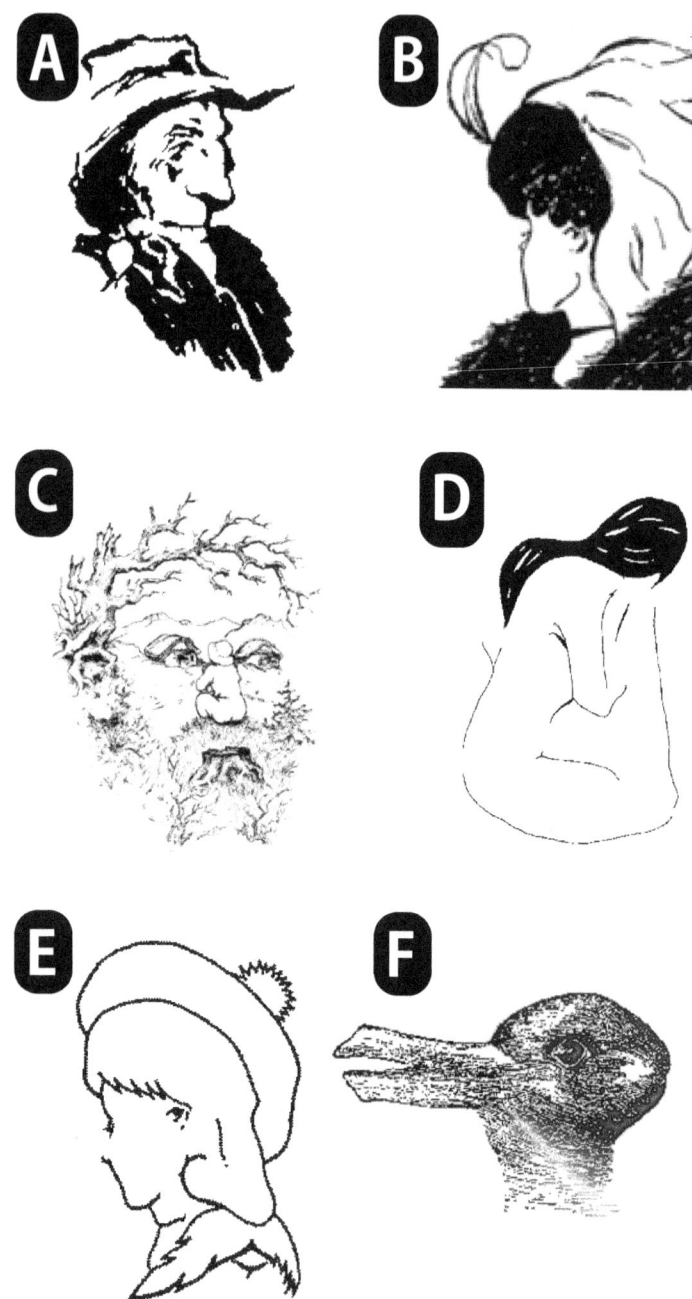

another person's actions or comments, or predicting what the likely future actions of someone might be.

We jump to conclusions to make sense of others' behaviours all the time. We do this because our Ape is a conclusion-jumping machine, and we often fail to see there could be multiple truths or interpretations of the same information. People fighting over which interpretation is correct are often bickering over two truths, but they just can't see it. By the time the disagreement lines are set, Apes are out defending honour and no-one is getting any wiser.

How are you going? Getting the general drift? Well, let's see if you can hold on for a few more activities.

Activity 4: Stochastic stimuli

This compulsion for our brain to make sense out of the world can also lead to us see things that aren't real at all. Our Apes can often make sense out of noise, even white noise. Have a look at the picture of white noise on the next page—stare at it for a bit and see if any patterns or pictures emerge.

(Go on, turn the page and give it a stare for a few minutes.)

Multiple scientific studies have shown that if you put people in front of a screen filled with stochastic stimuli (random white noise) and ask them what they can see, many people swear they can see images—even though it's just random dots on the page. This is said to be linked to something called 'magical thinking', and it's something we humans seem to be very good at doing.

We often do the same thing when navigating the complexity of the world around us. Our Ape helps us to make sense of the world, and it does this by creating logic patterns and compiling an experience matrix with which to compare what's expected, to what is before us. It fills the gaps and helps us come to conclusions that feel logical. As soon as we find a pattern that helps to make sense of the random world around us, we latch on to it. Making sense of things makes us feel in control, and being in control of our environment is seen as critical if we are going to successfully navigate life. It is a core function of a most basic survival instinct.

But if you can see your Ape—as most of you can by now through these simple tricks and fallacies—surely that means you can better control its influence?

Well, let's see if that's the case. Let me see if I can make you fight with your Ape. Let's try this out with a couple of tests we psychologists like to call Stroop tests. There are hundreds of these tests online but the ones below are the ones I like to use the most.

Activity 5: The stroop test

Ideally, try to find a space where you can speak out loud. If you can't, a close second would be to visualise yourself saying each of the below words out loud. The point isn't to skim read; I need you to try to keep your rational responsive brain in control. This test requires you to do a number of activities based on the two following lists:

First, read the list on the left only. However, instead of reading the words, if it's in upper-case, say 'upper' and if it's in lower-case, say 'lower'. Fast as you can. Go.

LEFT	upper
left	lower
right	
RIGHT	**LOWER**
RIGHT	upper
right	**UPPER**
	lower
LEFT	**LOWER**
right	upper

Easy, right? Now looking at the same list on the left, read it out loud. But, this time, if the word is on the left, say 'left', and if the word is on the right, say 'right'. Fast as you can. Go.

Ok, let's try a little harder but still a pretty simple exercise. Let's have a look at the second list on the right. Like before, if the word is on the left, say 'left', and if the word is on the right, say 'right'. Fast as you can. Go.

Simple. Now, let's look at that second list again but, this time, if the word is in lower-case say, 'lower', and if it's in upper-case, say 'upper'. Fast as you can. Go.

Hard, isn't it! I imagine some of you went a bit Apes#!t and didn't even finish the list.

Why is this so hard?

It's hard because your Ape has been trained to read English, and hours of reading millions of words has trained our Apes to see the word 'upper' and say 'upper'. So when I've tired your brain out a little with the first three steps, cognitive fatigue steps in and controlling your Ape instincts to say the word rather than its case state kicks in. Your Ape escapes out of its controlled cage and doing the exercise becomes much harder.

Seeing and feeling your Ape in action is easy with these little tests of cognition, but recognising and making decisions that go against our Ape instinct in real life is much harder. Controlling your Ape is the key to growing into your fullest potential.

With the pattern-matching and word activities we have just done, I have highlighted some inaccurate or unhelpful thought processes. These thought processes are the things that guide what we think is logical and correct. They are cognitive biases.

Rules of thumb—cognitive bias: part 1

So what is cognitive bias? My favourite way to explain this is to take you back to my own childhood. Back to a small farming community on the outskirts of a town in central New South Wales, Australia. Just outside a small Australian town called Parkes. A place where I learned a safety rule that almost killed me.

Parkes is named after the highly influential Australian politician, Sir Henry Parkes, who is credited with being the architect of federation for Australia. This is one of three things that true Parkes people are proud of, along with being the location of a large (65m) radio telescope that played a crucial role in relaying footage of the moon landing, and home of one of the biggest Elvis Presley festivals in the world. This is the proud town I grew up in.

During the early 80s in country NSW, it wasn't common for parents to drop their kids at school like it is nowadays. Back then, we walked to the bus stop and caught the bus to school. To get to the bus, my older brother Steve and I had to cross the Parkes-Orange road. This was a major road that carried many road trains (trucks with two or more trailers) travelling at more than 120 km/h. Mum was quite concerned about this, so she drilled a simple rule into our heads: Stop at the side of the road, take hold of your brother's hand, look up and down the road both ways and, if there are no cars coming, cross the road. There was even a song on children's television that reinforced the rule: Look left, then right, then left again, before you cross the road. It was a great rule and we took it very seriously as young boys.

Unlike later in life, following the rule to the letter of the law was very important to us as kids. You did exactly what

Mum said or risk the wrath of your Creator. We would quite enthusiastically correct each other if we thought we didn't follow the rules exactly. You can see it now, a six- and eight-year-old standing on the side of a wide-open highway at 7.30 in the morning, not a vehicle to be seen for a hundred miles. Yet Steve and I would argue if we'd done the 'stop, hold hands, right, left, right, left' rule properly before we attempted to cross the menacing Parkes-Orange road. We literally thought we'd die if we didn't follow the rule properly. It's no wonder kookaburras laugh in the morning in Australia. The ritual of small humans getting to school is enough to send any small-brained kingfisher into hysterics.

My older brother (Steve) and I in our early school years when we lived on a wheat and sheep farm just outside of Parkes in central NSW.

However, in time, we slowly learned the entire rule wasn't actually necessary... particularly the part about holding hands! As we grew up, we found a shortcut for the rule that worked just as effectively: 'Look right, start crossing, then look left'. It worked well for us, and it was shorter, easier and less cognitively demanding. We practised this rule almost every day of our lives. It became an automatic cognitive heuristic, a cognitive bias, a mental shortcut. Our Apes had learned this new simpler rule was enough to keep us safe and we were pretty satisfied with that.

That was until the day I won a competition in my early 20s. Part of this competition's prize was a trip to L.A. I was so excited. Even after the 18-hour flight, I was so enthusiastic. This was the land of the Blues Brothers, home of a huge portion of musical and pop culture icons, land of burgers and coke. This was a dream. I remember I was so excited I didn't sleep a wink on the flight. But it was almost a very tragic story. From the moment I got out of the airport and stepped out onto the road, my Ape took over: 'Look right, start crossing, then look left'. Small problem: in the States, the cars travel on the other side of the road and, as I stepped out onto the road looking right, I was almost taken out by a bus whizzing past from the left. I can still feel the wind whipping past my nose to this day. I literally almost died.

The interesting thing was my initial instinctive emotional reaction wasn't relief. It was anger. And not anger at myself for stepping out onto the road in a dangerous way, but anger at the bus driver for almost taking me out! Why the heck would this crazy American be driving so recklessly? Then the bus driver stopped and gave me a piece of his mind as well! It was quite the welcome.

So, what happened? There was a rule, and my Ape, in an attempt to conserve cognitive load, applied the rule I'd learned for crossing roads. Then, when the context changed and I was almost hit by the proverbial bus, my Ape jumped to the conclusion that it wasn't the rule that was at fault, but the bus.

It's easy to articulate this problem when discussing road rules and buses. But what if the rules are to do with interpersonal communication and the bus is other people's reactions? How often have we delivered information in a way that's worked in the past, watched people go Apes#!t—and then blamed the people going Apes#!t for the mess rather than the way we applied the rules of interpersonal behaviour?

In my road-crossing debacle, there was a more complete rule for crossing the road that would've allowed me to cross any road safely anywhere. My mother's initial instructions told me to look both ways before I crossed the road. And if I'd followed this, I would have been perfectly safe. It was the shortcut that was the issue.

It's the same with interpersonal behaviour. As we're growing up, we learn all sorts of shortcut rules to navigate our early life—a very large number of these before we even hit puberty. Then we take these shortcuts and reapply them when we're older, in all sorts of contexts where people seem to be operating under different rules. And then we get angry at them when they go Apes#!t. We keep telling ourselves, 'They just couldn't handle the truth', or 'They're just immature', or any number of other excuses. But maybe it's not them at all. Maybe our shortcut rules don't work in this context. Maybe we need to relearn and practise the full rule in order to better navigate these similar situations next time.

We all do it—and it really does have a lot to do with the way we learned to survive growing up. The rules we learned for survival as young children tend to be the rules we apply to life.

****

So, a quick recap of what we know so far.

1. The core framework of behavioural economics suggests we have two pathways of processing information—creatively called system one and system two. System one is linked to parts of the brain that are developed first in the womb and the parts of the brain that are most closely linked with our evolutionary cousins still swinging in the trees. That's why system one is our Ape.

2. Our Ape brain is intuitive, unconscious, faster, instinctive and reactive. Our system two brain is more conscious and rational—it's the you that you recognise. It's slower, conscious, thoughtful and more responsive, and it's linked to parts of the brain that don't fully develop until our late teens or early 20s. It holds our ability to plan, to assess probability and to inhibit our compulsive behaviour. As humans, we get our Ape at birth, but only get our Ape-tamer after 20 years on this rock.

3. Cognitive biases are the brain's rules of thumb we use to navigate and compute the constant barrage of information the world throws at us. As humans, we have limited cognitive capacity, a finite bucket of mental energy with which to navigate the world. Once this bucket is empty, it's empty, and it takes time to fill it up again—time we don't always have when we need to survive. Therefore, conserving the cognitive energy we spend on irrelevant things becomes vital for survival, and we do this by creating cognitive biases so we don't have to think about things. We can only absorb so much information before we become overwhelmed and send ourselves into a state of decision paralysis. In order to triage this information

and retain clarity of thought, our Ape brains act like a shortcut-creating machine, establishing rules and pathways that make it easier to make sense of the world. While these shortcuts make our lives easier, they can also lead us to incorrect judgments. These incorrect judgments are the focus of behavioural economics.

4. Our brains are naturally set up to automate as much as possible so we have the cognitive energy to focus on the important, novel and complex situations deserving of our attention. This is why we hate change or anything that causes us to divert cognitive energy to a task we've previously not had to think about, or a problem we thought we'd already solved (i.e. Big Momma's hot sauce).

While using the personal Ape is a nice analogy to understand what system one does, it doesn't really talk to the relationship system one and two have with each other. A really nice way to explain the relationship between these two systems comes from American author and psychologist Daniel Siegel. In his book, *Mindsight*, he talks about an exercise called 'the hand brain' as an example of how these systems work. The activity is simple.

a. Put your hand palm-up in front of you.

b. Roll your thumb into the centre of your hand (your thumb represents your amygdala, your fear centre, your feel-good chemical distributor. It is your Ape, your system one reactive self).

c. Close your four remaining fingers over your thumb and turn your hand over (these fingers represent the brain folds that are your system two, your emotional

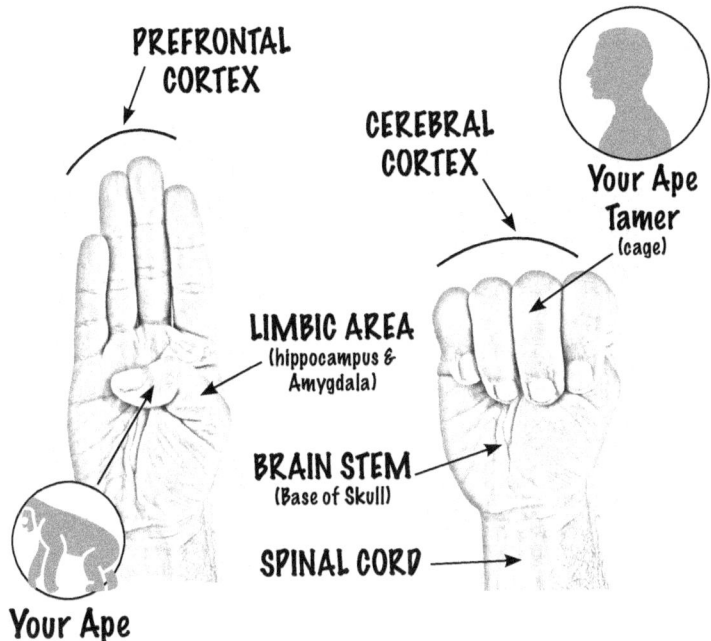

Your Ape

regulation, your mirror neurons, your planning and risk assessment centres. I like to think that this looks like a bit of an Ape cage. When you are in control, your Ape is in its cage.)

When you get emotional and reactive, it's often talked about as 'flipping your lid'. Lifting your four fingers from your thumb represents the action of flipping one's lid—letting your Ape out of the cage. What happens when you do this? Your Ape is exposed, released. Your Ape is now running the show and your rational, conscious self has lost control.

Behavioural economics is the study of our Ape and the rules of thumb we learn and then misapply in other contexts. Caging the Ape is the first step to getting your s#!t together but it's not the whole story. Understanding the influence your

Ape has on your judgments and behaviours when caged and uncaged is the next level.

In the US, I stepped onto the street applying an incorrect rule of thumb, which created a blind spot to the bus careening toward me. To this day, I still don't know how that bus missed me. The rules we learn to survive as children are the same we apply to survive the world as adults.

The rules we develop to save us can create our biggest blind spots.

Chapter snapshot

Key take-aways

1. Emotional reactions to perceived threats and 'rules of thumb' that have been learned over time in order to survive are the key drivers for your Ape's decision-making process.

2. Overriding your Ape's instinctive choices and logic can take a lot of cognitive energy.

3. 'Rules of thumb' that our Ape learns to help us to navigate life as simply as possible—but, when our context changes, we often find ourselves applying the same mental rules incorrectly, which gets us into trouble.

4. Our brains love to make sense and create patterns when there is no sense or patterns to be made. Our Apes love to create order out of chaos, even if that order is completely made up (we're not very good at handling things that are truly random).

5. Using the hand brain on page 49 is a great way of remembering how your Ape brain works. When you 'flip your lid', you uncage your Ape, allowing your Ape to run the show rather than your more rational, conscious self.

Things I can do to practically apply this insight

- Explain to someone how the brain works by using the hand brain analogy. The more you practise saying it, the more you will learn to recognise when you are about to 'flip your lid' and therefore you'll be more likely to keep your Ape in its cage.

- Think about the areas of your work, your health, and your social relationships. Write a list of assumptions you have about you and those around you for each area, and ask yourself if these assumptions are actually true (i.e. I am not good at detail; I'm too old/busy/tired to exercise; people are out to get me).

- Think of some simple daily routines you can set up to lessen the choices you have to make (i.e. have a few outfits that you always wear on workdays; have the same breakfast each day) and save cognitive energy for the things that are important.

Thought-starters

- How has the way you learned to survive the world in the first 15 years of your life impacted the way you see the world today?

- Are there things you can do to set up your environment in ways to help you make better decisions (i.e. don't keep junk food in the fridge).

Section B

Going ApeS#!t

Rules and consequences

Chapter 3
Apes behaving badly

*"The world is changed by your example,
not your opinion."*
–Paulo Coelho

Killing me with Big Momma's hot sauce: part B.

The next morning, after receiving the recommendation from the slightly over-zealous Texan conspiracy theorist, I raced down to Big Momma's store and was able to pick up a three-pack of sauces made just that week. I told them the story of my plight and who it was for, which inspired them to specially wrap the gift for me with a little handwritten note from Big Momma. The present looked awesome. I was saved! I got on the plane and headed to L.A. with an overwhelming sense of peace. Looking out the window as we flew over the Arizona desert, it started to look like home again.

At LAX, we had to repack our bags to comply with the different overhead and undercarriage baggage limit requirements between domestic and international flights. The weight ratio of cabin luggage to undercarriage luggage is different when transferring from a domestic American flight (where carry-on luggage can be quite large) to an international flight to Australia (where carry-on luggage is much more restricted). Adding to the mayhem of 500 people repacking bags in the airport walkways at 11pm was the fact they were renovating this part of LAX, so we were forced to lug all of our gear about 1km outside to a temporary building they were using during construction. Through the cold rain. At 11pm. After a four-hour flight from Austin. It wasn't ideal.

So there we all were in the terminal, repacking our bags for all the world to see. Tired, wet and desperate to get home. Add to this the weeks of non-stop sleep deprivation and I wasn't very conscious. I definitely wasn't that conscious during the re-packing of my bag. During the re-pack you have to decide what stays in your hand luggage and what will get packed underneath. When I got to the sauces, I did have a good thought: That I wouldn't put them in the hold because they could break with the cold and pressure. So I put them in my hand luggage. It was a decision I was later to regret.

It was about 11.45pm when around 150 cold, tired, frustrated Australians strewn out across the waiting area were told to start checking in. As the crowd slowly groaned to life, kids started crying and families got agitated with each other as they organised who was taking what bag through security. It was a mess. I wasted no time heading to the check-in counter, checked in my larger bags and then proceeded to the scanners acting as the golden gateway to the boarding area.

As I approached the army of security guards surrounding the scanner, I can remember feeling utterly exhausted. Unbelievably shattered. I was literally using the last of my will and strength to drag my carry-on luggage to the sanctuary of the plane.

As I approached the scanners, I saw only one of the three makeshift scanners was open, which made the queue slow and long. Perfect. I hadn't had more than five hours' sleep in a single stretch for five weeks, and we'd been constantly on the go for 34 days straight. As I looked in the reflection of the stainless steel walls, I noticed I also hadn't shaved for five weeks and my last set of clean clothes wasn't exactly matching—cleanliness and comfort were obviously much more important than fashion. When I finally got to the scanner, I looked at the over-sized American security guard on the other side with a sense of being out of body. He looked eight foot tall. Catching a reflection of myself, I thought, "And I look like a homeless terrorist". I smirked. We were only a few years post 9-11 and the World Trade Centre crisis was still very raw in the global consciousness. However, I was tired and my appearance as an unshaven homeless bum with no fashion sense amused me. This was the last time I would feel amused in LAX.

As my bags were being scanned, I looked forlornly at the cluster of concerned officials gathered around the scanning screen as my bags passed through. There was a sudden flurry of pointing and shaking of heads. Something had obviously attracted their attention in my luggage. I initially thought nothing of it, thinking that they were probably looking at all the hard drives and recording equipment I had in my bag that were too fragile to be checked into the hold. It always tends to attract attention.

Somewhat predictably, the eight-foot security guard walked up to my bag and motioned to me with a commanding and slightly condescending tone, "Is this your bag, sir?"

"Yes it is," I replied politely. Without pausing to wait for a follow-up question, I continued, "I'm travelling with a film company and the bag is full of all sorts of slightly unusual recording equipment."

Ignoring my comment, he turned my bag to face him and asked if he could look inside. Carefully, with his extra-large blue latex gloves on, he opened my bag and started to pick through it.

It was at this point I became aware we were holding up the rest of the line. Hundreds of tired Aussies just pining for a broad Australian accent and a decent coffee.

To my surprise, the guard pulled out my recording gear and simply put it to one side. Instead, he reached for my specially wrapped and personally signed Big Momma's three pack of hot sauce, my long sought-after gift for my long-suffering wife. He looked at me commandingly and said, matter-of-factly, "I'm going to have to get rid of these, sir."

The world kind of stood still for a moment. My Ape stood to attention in bewilderment.

"What?" I replied in a somewhat direct tone. "Why on earth would you need to throw away hot sauce?".

He retorted sharply, "I can't let you take these on the plane. They are each 50ml over the allowed the liquid volume limit for containers. The limit's 200ml, and these bottles are 250ml each."

Somewhat shocked, I changed tone to try a more light-hearted approach replying, "No, I'm sure there is a mistake. I was able to take them on the plane from Austin to here. They are a precious gift for my wife that has taken me five weeks to find. I need to take them home with me or someone is going to die."

Realising my gaff, I quickly followed with, "Me, of course, my wife is going to kill me if I come home empty-handed. No-one here is in danger. No-one."

It was an unhelpful comment in an airport so close to 9-11. The security guard looked at me, obviously trying to figure out if I was a homeless muso bum or a dangerous terrorist. He started to repack my bag without the sauces in it and I started to feel myself getting really irritated. In my exhausted state, I was definitely struggling to keep my Ape in its cage.

"How could a few bottles of handmade hot sauce that are only 50ml over the limit possibly be a problem?" I said a little too loudly, the crowd in the line starting to take more notice. The officer started to get sterner, more commando-like, and told me he'd have to destroy them.

My Ape was rattling the cage door pretty hard by now.

"Destroy them? You're bloody-well kidding me, right? There is no need to throw out my wife's present. It is just hot sauce!" I said, in a very loud and pointed manner.

Stony silence. We both froze. All chatter in the line behind me by this stage had stopped. Even the scanners seemed to go silent. Mexican stand-off time. Maddening, illogical and heartless bureaucracy vs man with gift for his wife.

There was no keeping my Ape contained anymore. It became a matter of principle. I no longer cared that I was in an airport only a few years after 9-11 looking like a homeless terrorist. I was so close to being home. I went Apes#!t. Completely. Ape. S#!t!

"What do you mean it's 50ml over the bloody limits?" I said with a quiet violence only reserved for the most serious of times. "This is bloody bureaucracy gone completely bonkers. This is a gift for my wife that I have procured from the bowels of Texas!"

I was in full flight now and nothing was stopping me!

"It's hot sauce, hot-@!*#-ing-sauce! What the hell am I going to do with hot sauce? Threaten to mess the white shirts of the pilots? Burn the eyes of the hostesses? This is crazy! What could I possibly do with 250ml that I couldn't do with a 200ml bottle? This is stupidity at its all-American finest. It's the only present I have for my wife, and you're telling me 50ml of hot sauce is some earth-shattering security risk?"

I could feel the crowd behind me rallying to my cause. Aussies tend to hate bureaucratic heavy-handedness. I had the crowd, so I continued.

"How on earth does the extra 50ml of hot sauce possibly pose any threat to the safety of the plane? Tell me exactly how I am going to take down a plane with an extra 50ml of Big Momma's hot sauce!"

At this point, the crowd was about to revolt with me, getting right behind the cause of the poor Aussie homeless-looking bearded man being oppressed by Uncle Sam. Officers in the background, I'm sure, were unclipping their weapons and reaching for radios to call for back-up at the slightest sign of physical escalation.

I must have been nanoseconds from a holding cell in Guantanamo. I didn't care. Screw the oppressive system and its Orwellian ways! A cell in that moment seemed an honourable price to pay for the unjust stealing of the specially wrapped and personally signed bottles of Big Momma's Hot Sauce. But the most surprising thing happened next.

The 8-foot behemoth of a guard wilted. Retreated. Possibly sensing a near riot, he completely changed his tone and body position to being completely submissive. It was like I was speaking to a seven-year-old boy.

"I am so sorry sir," he said. "It's not me. If I don't throw these away, I'll lose my job".

He literally started to cry right in front of me. Pause. I shared an awkward moment of looking at the other security guards, who were as confused as I was. The sauces were still on the bench next to the bins.

It was at that point I felt a gentle hand on my shoulder and the calming Texan voice of my friend, Shawn, who was behind me in the line: "Come on mate, let me buy you a Guinness to calm down while we still have a chance of getting on a plane."

Maybe it was the promise of Guinness, maybe it was the second of pause that made me think of home, maybe I was just floating in a complete daze of exhaustion. Whatever the reason, my Ape gave up and I stood down. Stand-off was over, crisis dissipated.

As I picked up my bag and walked to the departure lounge, I watched the guard put my hot sauce in the large bin beside the scanner.

I took my bags and went for that promised Guinness to calm my s#!t. I was still incensed. My Ape was not getting back in its cage and I didn't want it to. A gross miscarriage of justice had been served. I didn't want to tame my Ape—I wanted my Ape to rage. It felt good for my Ape to rage. It felt just.

I was halfway through my glass of Guinness when I realised how serious the situation could have become. The guard had the authority to detain me simply for hearing some trigger words, of which I am sure I said plenty. I could've also earned a black mark next to my name for future trips, flagging me as a person of interest whenever I travelled in the future and creating all sorts of inconveniences. I am only lucky the giant American guard was as understanding as he was. It wasn't his fault. He was doing his job.

No doubt his eventual conciliatory response had been part of his training for tired travellers like me. I'm glad it was. Things could have gone very differently if I'd chanced upon a tired, power-hungry guard.

On reflection I realised that, despite part of me feeling justified in going Apes#!t, the outcome hadn't changed. The sauce was still destroyed and I was on my way home sans present. The only things my Ape had managed to accomplish was to create a tense scene, delay my fellow passengers, ruin the shift of a guard simply doing his job, and cost my mate two pints of Guinness at an overpriced airport bar. It could have been much, much worse.

I actually wonder if I had kept my s#!t together, responded rationally and negotiated an outcome that served us both that I might have gotten on the plane with some of the sauce. Maybe I could have taken a photo of the bottles and then put 200ml into a plastic bag? Maybe there was another solution? After all, it was the sauce that was the present, and getting something home would have been better than nothing. However, as soon as I went Apes#!t, any possibility of a negotiated solution was gone. The guard was backed into a corner defending a position he didn't really care about and I turned the hot sauce issue into a debate about Orwellian-style oppression. Instead of negotiating a solution, my Ape all but sealed my fate—and the fate of the sauce. Going Apes#!t might have felt good at the time but it did nothing to serve my actual objective.

In the moment, going Apes#!t might feel good, feel justified, feel righteous. Going Apes#!t rarely ends well for you because it doesn't consider the repercussions. You simply become blind to other alternatives. When you flip out, you no longer have any planning or inhibition, no cage to tame or contain your Ape. Your Ape just runs riot for all to see.

Sure, there are times you should be upset. But most of the time, it just ends up harming you in ways that might not be obvious to you. How are you to know the extent to which your reactive outbursts have led to missed opportunities? Your Ape might have steamrolled you right past an opportunity that you never even knew was there.

This raises an interesting question: How can we look at potential losses when they haven't happened yet? How do you measure the absence of something when you have no idea of what could have been? One way to attack this issue is by looking at what happens to other people when they go Apes#!t. I found myself in this situation in my theatre days.

From the stage to the page

My own journey with storytelling and the human condition comes from years of work in the film and theatre industry in Australia. Well before my journey into psychology and behavioural economics, I was a composer working with all the major professional theatre companies in Australia. This was a charmed and much beloved part of my life, working with a beautiful community of the most nuanced and talented storytellers. Bards such as Michael Attenborough, Michael Futcher and Bille Brown, and some particularly genius lighting and set designers (David Walters, in particular, was a great inspiration). These great raconteurs, along with an army of amazing actors, artists, theatre workers, writers and musicians, taught me volumes about group psychology and the human condition. I am forever grateful to have been a part of their story. A live audience in a darkened theatre is an amazing place to experiment with influence, persuasion and herd behaviours.

I remember one moment in particular that had a lasting impact on me. In the Queensland Theatre Company production of *The glass menagerie* by Tennessee Williams, there is a scene where Jim (played by James Stewart) and Laura (played by Helen Cassidy) share an intimate dialogue that lasts about 10 minutes. Over the course of the scene, we were able to craft the music and lights (again, David Walters) to slowly fade away to a single candle in the centre of the stage with the faintest hint of suspension in the music. At the end of the scene, the faint music was abruptly cut as the candle was blown out, and each night there was a collective gasp of emotion that instantly swept over the audience. It was an incredible moment. The astonishing thing for me was how the length of that scene seemed irrelevant to the audience. I mean, for 10 minutes they were motionless, almost breathless. Completely hypnotised by what was before them. Through simple tricks of sound, lighting, direction and acting, we were seemingly able to create a kind of group tunnel vision, a social phenomenon of sorts. It was simply electrifying.

It wasn't just artistry and storytelling that I learned about human behaviour. The people who make up the industry itself were a fascinating petri dish of human interaction. Put a group of highly competent, highly strung individuals into the pressure cooker of an intense show and the result is extremely entertaining! Actors and artistic teams in Australia usually only have around five weeks from meeting each other for the first time, to opening night. Five weeks to create a great show and tell a great story that will be reviewed by every critic around the country. Hugely diverse groups of heavily outcome-focused people with massive issues around power and professional identity. Add to this some economic pressures and the boom and bust nature of the industry, and you have almost the perfect microcosm of the human condition to observe and from which to learn.

It is hard to know the adrenaline rush and pain associated with making a profession out of being so vulnerable. I am ever so grateful for those thespians who, night after night, bare their soul for the benefit of us all, portraying the stories that are often cautionary tales of what happens when we succumb to reactivity. They go to the 'dark side' of human nature for us so we don't have to.

Added to the great privilege of working with great artists was the amazing experience of working with incredibly insightful scripts. One way to really understand the human psyche is to look at the stories that have survived the test of time. Shakespeare, Marlowe, Chekhov, Tolstoy, Mozart and Brecht had some of the greatest ever insights about human psychology. If you want to really learn about the human condition, study *Macbeth, Faust, The Cherry Orchard* and *Caucasian Chalk Circle* before you touch a psychology textbook. Really get under the text and drink the wisdom within the words. Within the pages of these three scripts is some of the best exploration of power, human desire, motivation, social identity and decision consequence ever written. And they're in storytelling form, which means you're more likely to remember their lessons.

The artistic temperament

Creating theatre productions in Australia is the ultimate pressure cooker. As mentioned earlier, you have just over a month to create, produce, rehearse and put on a show. If it's not any good, it gets talked about in every media outlet that matters to you—and a whole lot more that don't. Opening night is booked so there's no chance for an extension, and the budget you're working with tends to be about a quarter of what it should be in order to succeed. And yet somehow, year on year, hundreds of beautiful shows are put on, telling hundreds of incredibly powerful human stories.

Every artist knows they're only as good as their last show, so every show could make or break their career. I know of no other working context like it.

Now, if that isn't enough, add to the mix the fact that many of the actors, artists and theatre workers have been told their whole lives they're special, they're unique and their artistry deserves worldwide recognition. This tends to force artists to create a 'presentational self', which is different from what they believe their real self to be. As artists are exposed to more and more adulation, often the gap between their presentation and real selves grows. As a result, many of these artists' Apes have a deep fear of being unloved, of being exposed as unworthy and detestable. Their Apes become ready to react at a moment's notice to protect their real selves from being exposed.

You can imagine how much of a hit artists get from the adulation of an audience, the constant praise of critics and the long-suffering love of those who attempt to get close. The only way many of these unique wallflowers know how much someone loves them is by pushing them away, just to see if the other person comes back. The harder they reject, the more the other has to work to come back, and the more they know they love them. It's a vicious circle, but a common one in the glamour industries. I love a lot of these artists dearly but some can be highly strung and completely unstable. This mix of a high-pressure environment with erratic personalities makes the rehearsal room a fascinating study of human behaviour.

When Apes go Apes#!t in the rehearsal room, it usually evidences itself by someone flatly refusing to do something or to work with someone. They might block another person's ideas, irrespective of merit. All simply because they feel disrespected or overlooked. Ironically, this can often be a cry for love and affection because the artist deeply fears they're not loved. After they go Apes#!t in one of these ways, they'll hear people say, "We love you, darling, you're the only reason this show will work and everyone knows it". But what they're really thinking is, "Just suck it up and get on with it. Grow up for once in your entitled, self-indulgent life".

Inevitably, the true repercussions of these narcissistic individuals going Apes#!t come months later when new positions are being decided upon for new shows. The people who had to deal with the Apes going Apes#!t are often the same people who are in a room making decisions about upcoming shows. When choosing between people of equal talent, all it takes is for someone to say, "Oh, they were a real piece of work on a show I worked on", or, "They were trouble, total high maintenance, almost derailed my show in production week". And just like that, the opportunity for people perceived as difficult disappears. They never even knew they were in the running.

I've often found myself in the room when these conversations happen. The artists never see these missed opportunities because they're never even offered to them in the first place. I don't think this is a situation that's confined to the theatre. It happens in the workplace all the time, hidden within large bureaucracies of ambiguous responsibilities and red tape, or in future business and career opportunities.

Our lives are filled with people and opportunities that pass us by because we go Apes#!t, and we're then avoided or passed over for subsequent opportunities. People who even celebrated the righteousness of your Ape in the moment still avoid offering you a future opportunity because they don't feel as confident in your ability to keep it together. To them you become unpredictable, a potential management problem, a risk to their own reputation. As somebody who is known to go Apes#!t, you're seen as painful—and our brains are hardwired to avoid pain.

Keeping your Ape in control isn't just about avoiding the consequences you can see. It's about making sure you avoid the missed opportunities you'll never know.

There is a slight variation to this story—and that's when you let your Ape make unethical decisions you know are wrong but you seem to get away with them, so you keep giving in to your Ape and becoming more and more skilled at justifying your actions to yourself. It's a situation commonly found in stories of sports cheats (one famous American cyclist comes to mind). However, it's not limited to drug cheats. It's a behavioural pattern that can also be found in politics or any pursuit where the line between winning and losing can be severe and the consequences of losing potentially devastating.

But what if a workplace bully gets promoted into leadership or a psychopath is voted into public office? Isn't that people being rewarded for going Apes#!t? What happens then?

Let me retell a story of my own experience in a highly political environment, where Apes grouped together to destroy a psychopath. It is a common story of silent Apes, revenge, glamour, ego and betrayal.

Politics, psychopaths and the power of the group

It's a strange feeling walking into a local meeting of a political think tank in Australia (which is a polite term for a lobby group) for the very first time. There is that moment when you get to the doorway of the meeting room, full of nerves and anticipation, and wonder who exactly is going to be on the other side of the door and what opportunities await. Will they all be high-flying businesspeople? Pensioners with too much time on their hands and opinions to match? Young activist types who paint placards and are ready to go to jail for justice? Or, even worse, maybe they're all members of a secret society and I'm about to walk into some weird ritual where everyone wears red sheets and dead animals on their heads? I mean, what on earth do you wear to such an event?

Confronted by this last question, I had gone the safe option—bone-coloured pants, a sharp white shirt and a dark blue sports jacket. Typical late-Nineties/early-Noughties smart casual wear. Able to mix easily with suits or boardshorts or anything in between. I remember looking at my watch, seeing 7.45pm and wondering if I should loiter in the carpark for a bit so I wouldn't be too early for the 8pm start. I despise those early awkward conversations or standing in the corner pretending to read something interesting. However, on a 30-degree hot summer night, the promise of air-conditioning was more attractive than the fear of being awkward. I took a deep breath and decided to continue. As I approached the door I was already feeling the beads of sweat starting to form, and regretting the jacket. I wished I'd gone for my board shorts, a T-shirt and my 'going out' thongs (flip-flops for all those not familiar with Australian vernacular).

As I cautiously opened the door, all of my fears were completely put to rest. There were about 20 men and women standing up around a long boardroom table, all happily chatting and making coffee. No red sheets, and no placard-painting activities going on. As I poked my head into the room, I caught the eye of a portly gentleman who seemed to be scanning the room for newcomers. Boldly, he bounded over to me and enthusiastically thrust his hand out and said, "Phil?".

"That's what my Mum keeps calling me," I replied, instantly regretting the first impression I just made.

"Excellent! My name's Jamie, we talked on the phone I think last week?"

We had. In fact, it had taken quite an effort to try to find out where and when they were meeting or how to get involved. I had a friend of a friend on the other side of the city who was able to get me a phone number. I had no idea who I was ringing or if the person giving out the number was reputable. Other than that, I'm not sure how anyone finds out about these things.

The meeting started just after 8pm and I was instantly glad I was there. Sitting with business leaders, ex-members of parliament, prominent social identities, intellectuals and young activists, all discussing in some depth administrative, community, political and upcoming election issues—I slotted straight in. After a very short time it was as if I'd been part of the group forever.

As a psychology masters student, I was fascinated by social psychology, the impact of social identity on behaviour and what happens when groups of Apes go Apes#!t together. Exploring this curiosity within the walls of the university was interesting but it wasn't enough. I had to find a place where I could immerse myself in a situation where it would be easy to study all of these things at once. And then one day it came to me: the perfect place to scratch my curious itch and learn about the best, and worst, of Ape behaviour. I had to get into politics, but not just a political party. What I needed to find my way into was the real power base: a political think tank.

At that very first meeting, I happened to sit next to the woman who was leading a large and complex project for the state health service. Let's call her Leanne for the purposes of this story. It turned out she recognised my name as, in my previous music career years earlier, I'd helped her daughter out by giving her some free studio time and connecting her to some influential industry networks. To her, I was already a trusted friend, and when I told her about my interest in social psychology and political engagement, she got very excited.

Within three months, I was leading the engagement portion of her project, with a sizable budget and many volunteers and medical staff involved. While I'd gone to the meeting to understand the power-plays of politics, health was much more complex than any political party could ever dream to be. You have the CEOs of the hospitals, the clinical leads (i.e. mental health, surgery, allied health), medical practice boards, the health departments, the Health Minister's office, the unions, the facilities managers, the media and, of course, the nurses (who actually run things). All of this is a cluster of political muck the project must wade through in order to get anything meaningful done. Leanne may have been running the logistics of the project—but I had the keys to its success in my hand. It's no wonder she needed an outsider that she trusted to come in and help steer the ship. It was an eye-opening and crazy time in my life, and I met some amazing people whose friendships I still treasure to this day.

While it was a deeply enriching experience, it also taught me a bucket-load about social identity, communication, influence, in-group behaviour and the psychology of decision-making. It also taught me things I was not expecting. One of those things was how people can silently go Apes#!t and how herds of silent Apes kill other Apes who are behaving badly.

At the very first engagement and key stakeholder meeting, I met a man who was sitting across from me at the boardroom table. Let's call him, Paul. Paul was dressed in a tailored suit, had a pleasant smile and confident demeanor. He was a prominent surgeon who had significant career aspirations, but I didn't find myself thinking much of him at the time. He felt a bit abrupt, almost a little unempathetic or insensitive—all of which I thought were odd characteristics for someone wanting to endear himself to leadership. He definitely didn't seem to have much time for some blow-in psychology nerd. When it was announced during the meeting that I was going to manage the engagement project, he was the first to offer help. I was grateful. I mean, what did I know about politics in a complex health environment? I had helped pull together hundreds of theatre shows, musical productions and albums, but this was a completely different beast. Paul wasn't as helpful in the end as I thought he would be. Turns out he was a textbook psychopath.

Fortunately, and somewhat surprisingly, while Paul was technically proficient, he was not emotionally intelligent—so he didn't take out too many innocent bystanders before his eventual demise. If he'd happened to be an intelligent psychopath, it could have been a very different story and I may not have survived. This, however, isn't an exploration of workplace psychopaths. This story is about how people around psychopaths silently and politely suffocate them over time. It's the passive-aggressive way Apes deal with a member of their group going Apes#!t—and it all began with me accepting an offer of help from Paul. With psychopaths, it always seems to start there.

It was an unusually chilly march morning when the newly formed team I had pulled together gathered over breakfast at a local café to discuss the upcoming project. It was going to be a complex one, with many in the media already starting to question the cost, and unions already making noise about the impact on the quality of healthcare during construction. 'Quality of care' is the one big trump card in health. If you don't want to do something, you just assert it's going to adversely impact patient outcomes and the whole thing comes to a grinding halt. We needed to raise millions in private investment before government funds were released, we had to keep all of the specialist clinical colleges and unions onside— not to mention the trigger happy and hostile media waiting at any moment to get a juicy story of unrest and budget blowout in the months leading up to a state election. In this context, I needed all the help, connections to money, influence with the medical professionals, and general experience we could muster.

I needed Paul, or so I thought, even though I was warned by Leanne that he was a little unhinged.

In the beginning, Paul was enthusiastic and seemed to be pulling strings and helping the project get ahead with his influence and connections. As soon as I was officially appointed engagement manager, however, something changed. Paul went from being an enthusiastic helper to an anxious neurotic, afraid of being undermined or losing control. Text messages that were small essays were sent to Leanne at midnight, with follow-up texts every 10 minutes or so if there was no reply, and then a call at 2am to ask why he was being ignored. He was a high-ranking medical professional with key links to contributors and medical clinicians, and he expected you to jump whenever he wanted. He needed control. He booked catch-ups for myself and Leanne to meet with powerbrokers, and would 'accidentally' send me the wrong address for the meeting so I'd be late to the actual venue. He would phone around staff and union officials to seed questions about my ability to manage an engagement program. The text messages to Leanne were constant, and increasingly paranoid and abusive. As it turns out (I didn't find this out until much later), Paul had actually offered to run Leanne's engagement program for her. He saw it as the perfect platform to further his own career aspirations. However, Leanne (sensing the controlling psychopath below the surface) politely refused and decided to give me the opportunity instead. This did not sit well with Paul.

All of this being said, he was still a very well-connected member of the medical and political community, and so I had grand delusions of being able to harness his energy and connections and invited him to be part of our team. At the very first meeting, at the aforementioned café, I began to lay out the overall strategy, initial budget allocations and key engagement themes. About five minutes in, Paul interrupted with a long speech that basically said, "Phil, that all sounds great, but I'm more experienced and more senior than you and so I've done up my own engagement plan that we should follow. I've spoken with the Health Ministers office (which he hadn't; I'd literally just gotten off the phone to them minutes before the meeting) who are all very good friends of mine (they didn't really know him). If you want my connections, financial contributors and experience, then you will follow my plan instead."

OK, this was interesting. Not exactly subtle. Not even five minutes into the first meeting and the game was on. I'd tried many times to connect with him in the lead-up to the meeting to bounce my strategy and ideas off him, but he'd always been "way too busy". Now, in front of the core team, he decided to flex his muscles and take command. At that moment, this was not about help. This was about power and control. I shot a look at Leanne, who was looking at me like, "Well, you invited him, you deal with him." I knew Leanne detested many elements of Paul's overly simplistic plan, which was actually terrible, and was fearful Paul might intentionally scuttle the project for his own political gain, I had to do something quickly to avoid things derailing. Paul's Ape was well and truly out, and so was mine, to be honest. In fact, everyone's Ape in that meeting was on high alert at that moment. In hindsight, this would have been the perfect time for me to keep my Ape in check. Unfortunately, I didn't. I fought fire with ice.

Fortunately I had a lot of competent friendlies at the table with lots of experience and strategic brilliance. Even better, at Leanne's request, I'd resisted Paul's earlier suggestions to include some of his old clinical friends in our team who didn't have great reputations. This is probably why he was so unimpressed with me in the first instance; I had already shown him I wasn't a pushover. He wanted control—but I had the room. Still, for some reason, my Ape couldn't resist letting him know how little control he actually had. As he finished his self-important monologue behind the noise of the coffee machine and clatter of morning commuters, and before someone could ask a question, I quietly thanked him for his input and used the agenda to throw to the finance manager to go through the figures based on my plan that we'd already worked through. The meeting thus quietly ignored him and focused on the next matter to be discussed. This small, passive-aggressive move may have felt good at the time, but I had made an enemy of a power-hungry paranoid android, and from that moment on, he would be a persistent pain in my side. Paul's Ape was furious and offended at being so easily dismissed, and my Ape was incensed at his sense of entitlement. The whole meeting was intense. For the next couple of hours, my Ape was no longer simply focused on completing a successful project.

At the end of the meeting, Leanne came up to me to let me know she was happy with how the meeting ended up and added, "Remember, we're here to navigate a complex environment to deliver a vitally important project. Small 'p' politics shouldn't distract us from the main game". It was a warning, and fair enough.

What I learned over the ensuing months was that I didn't need to compete with Paul for control of the group. They already respected me—and they already disliked him. Passive aggressively dismissing him actually poured fuel on an unnecessary fire, and gave him a target in need of destruction (me). Instead of quietly influencing him and focusing his energy on a common goal, I now had a motivated saboteur who ended up being constant trouble for the entire project.

I found out soon after the meeting this wasn't Paul's first time going Apes#!t, and playing power games where he wasn't entitled. He was known for bursts of rage when he thought people were disrespecting his power or positional authority.

In his little kingdom, he was king, and demanded to be treated as the all-powerful, all-conquering demi-god he thought he was. There were stories of him going Apes#!t everywhere—from unleashing a public tirade on unsuspecting visitors who unknowingly parked in his carpark, to tearing shreds off nurses in front of patients, claiming they had done something wrong when they hadn't, to keeping medical students up for days on end with deadlines that were completely fictious, to having one of the highest turnovers of administration staff and loudly boasting to people about the incompetence of the people working for him.

But it was also known he 'up-represented' very well. To the hospital leadership, he was well respected. He came across as charming, clear, concerned and hardworking. Stories of some evil character seemed at odds with what they saw, so they were dismissed as the rantings of jealous people who just wanted to score political points by taking someone else down. Whenever anyone complained about him, it was the complainer who was sidelined and the complaint almost seemed to strengthen his position. People learned to remain silent and he maintained the ability to run around in his psychopathic ways.

Silent, however, does not mean inactive. Groups of Apes have a way of dealing with this type of thing. It just tends to take some time. The downside of the extra time is it means people unfortunately get caught in the crossfire—collateral damage. The longer the time, the more dramatic the fall, and the more pain it causes. But it will be dealt with. We are herd animals at heart and the herd will eventually move to protect itself from the poison of a psychopath. I didn't need to assert power over him. The more I let go, the more the group did it for me.

After a few weeks of Paul's power-obsessed Ape going Apes#!t, the group started to act in some really interesting ways. Official decision-making meetings became informal gatherings from which he happened to be excluded. Even the core engagement team became smaller and unofficial so there were no minutes or agendas, and decisions we made appeared only in a spreadsheet kept close by the finance manager and fed through to decision makers for governance and accountability purposes. The official engagement campaign meetings that Paul was invited to were large events everyone attended, including volunteers, staff, media and community representatives. This meant they became more like rally meetings than a strategy and decision-making forum. On paper, though, they had agendas and minutes and looked like official engagement meetings. Our real decision-making team had gone underground. Paul had tried to assert control—but, in effect, he'd cut himself out of any influence at all.

This reminds me of the 'holding sand' analogy. If you hold your hand open, you'll be able to hold a lot of sand. The more you close your hand in order to try to hold the sand and not lose any, the more sand you actually lose. Close your hand in a tight fist of control and you only end up with a few grains that are unable to escape. Paul's Ape had tried to close his fist and assert control but all he actually ended up doing was losing any influence he had, except for few lost souls who lived in fear of doing anything to upset him.

All of the secrecy and ostracism happened totally without any co-ordination. The group just naturally did it, and no-one did anything to discourage it. It was classic passive-aggressive group behaviour.

The engagement program rolled on for months and eventually he took his small band of loyal supporters and refused to help (which was finally something the executive noticed was odd, particularly for an engagement campaign that was, in their view, doing remarkably well). We were happy with this because, by that stage, we had hundreds of people and donors eager and willing to help, and Paul's absence was met with a collective sigh of relief across the entire team.

This wasn't, however, the end of the group administering its own brand of mob justice. Some time later, Paul finally decided to make a play for a seat on a reigonal health service governing board (a quite powerful and public position which has a large element of popular campaigning). However, when the call went out for support, hardly anyone put up their hand to help. Fellow clinicians would send through apologies for not being able to show up to meetings but wished him all the best. Eventually the entire effort was left to Paul, a few loyal supporters and a couple of student die-hards who didn't know any better.

It also turned out a couple of Paul's former employees were now working in the state health department, and had risen to places of considerable influence. It was interesting how some political resources were reallocated to priorities other than Paul's. The mob was acting out, working as antibodies to expel something toxic out of the body. Apes were quietly working together to rid themselves of psychopathic poison.

Needless to say, Paul did not get the seat on the influential health governing board, in fact, he hardly even raised a vote. For him it was a public humiliation, and one he never really recovered from. After he lost, he tried to remain relevant and hang on to some influence, all to no avail. The group had spoken. Eventually he left the hospital and moved inter-state in an attempt to start again.

People now only talk about him with eye-rolls and smirks. He's a cautionary tale of what happens when ego, fear, paranoia and power combine. His story shows how short-term actions that feel good, and even justifiable to your Ape, can have long term consequences. Paul wasn't denied an opportunity because he was incompetent—it was because he couldn't control his Ape. Who knows what he could have become and what opportunity he squandered?

It's quite a sad story, really. To think what could have been. I learned a lot about group Ape behaviour during that project.

Controlling your Ape is more important than money, IQ, education, cultural heritage or who your family is. Our success is more tied to the collective than we realise—and the collective simply doesn't trust Apes who go Apes#!t.

Chapter snapshot

Key take-aways

1. Going Apes#!t can feel good, like the 'right' thing to do, even when it puts us in danger or works against our overall objective.

2. Keeping your Ape in control isn't just about avoiding the negative consequences you can see; it's also about the missed opportunities.

3. When under threat, Apes often work in packs to deal with poisonous elements in the group, or people believed to be making the group look bad.

4. Short-term actions that feel justifiable to your Ape can have long-term consequences.

5. Big Momma's hot sauce bottles are too large for international hand luggage restrictions.

Things I can do to practically apply this insight

- Practise controlling your Ape in moments where you are being challenged, undermined or threatened. Do thought experiments where you visualise these reactive moments beforehand, and take note of what it feels like. The more practise you do, the more your Ape will instinctively help you react more constructively in the moment.

- Download the *Decida switch* app to get some handy suggestions as to how you might switch yourself or others into a more responsive state of mind when your Ape wants to go Apes#!t.

Thought-starters

- Think of someone who regularly troubles or annoys you. Is there another approach you might take to more harmoniously collaborate with them?

- Does that approach feel unjust because of what they have done to you?

- Is it your Ape that is preventing you from collaborating with this person?

Chapter 4

Cognitive Bias: Part 2

"I am not a product of my circumstances. I am a product of my decisions."
–Stephen Covey

Rules of thumb and tricks of the mind.

I've mentioned earlier the discovery of cognitive bias, and how its irrational influence on our decision-making is one of the great leaps forward in the science of decision-making in the past 50 years.

Where the psychologists Tversky and Kahneman demonstrated their genius was in observing specific, irrational everyday behaviours. If they could repeat and manipulate the behaviours in an experimental setting, they gave it a name. Once they had a name, the behaviour could be explored in a whole new way because we had a brand new set of conceptual keys to unlock new areas of insight.

Loss aversion, status quo bias and sunk cost fallacy are all behavioural constructs that came directly out of their research. More than 350 separate biases have been identified to exist at the time of my writing. Their world opened a whole new world of insight and birthed an entire field of study called behavioural economics. Their revolutionary efforts earned them the Nobel Prize for economics in 2002 and continues to attract accolades more than 50 years after their initial research.

This isn't the study of the individual differences between Apes, this is the study of how irrational all of our Apes can be. As we use the language of cognitive bias, the conceptual keys at our disposal, we can identify many areas of our lives where these irrational biases are influencing our decision-making. Behavioural economics makes the implicit explicit, illuminates the hidden areas of our Ape's decision-making, and gives us specific areas we can focus on to improve our decisions.

However, it's simply impossible to be constantly aware of all 350 biases all of the time. The very reason we developed these biases in the first place was to make it easier to navigate the world with our limited cognitive capacity. To try to bring them back into our conscious behaviour all the time is, in and of itself, counter-intuitive. So what we tend to do is just look at the top 3–5 biases that impact us the most and focus on training our Ape to better handle these influences. However, there is another way we can mitigate the effects of cognitive bias. It was an insight we discovered as part of my master's thesis, a theory of cognitive influence, and it continues to be a large focus of my work to this day.

In short, all biases tend to be reduced by one of three things: emotional regulation, increased awareness, or designing our environment in better ways. In order for me to explain this more clearly, I am going to need to momentarily dig deeper into four biases. These biases are four of the most influential biases we see play out every day in decisions impacting our finances, our relationships and our health. They are loss aversion, confirmation bias (and its close bedfellow information bias), sunk cost fallacy, and anchoring. Forgive me if my inner nerd pops out a little too much in the following but I find each of these biases continuously fascinating. I hope my boyish curiosity and passion is enough to engage your Ape to keep reading. It's worth the ride, I promise.

Loss aversion

Loss aversion was one of the very first cognitive biases to be uncovered and it remains one of the strongest influences on decision-making to this day. Basically, it's the observation that we weigh potential loss more than opportunity. The pain of taking $50 off you is greater than the joy you get from receiving $50. For instance, imagine you have $5000 worth of travel benefits that you use each year as part of your job (a perk that a lot of university professors use as they travel to conferences). Now, imagine I offered you a pay rise of $7,500 if you were willing to give up the travel benefit. Would you accept that deal? Rationally this seems to be a no-brainer. You're better off with the pay rise, right? But when this exact scenario was offered to a group of university professors in California, almost all rejected the pay rise. The pain of losing something drives decision-making.

In their classic 1972 gambling experiment, Tversky and Kahneman showed people only tended to risk the loss of $50 if their potential winnings were at least $100. This showed us the expected hurt from a loss was roughly twice as strong as the expected good felt by an equivalent gain (see figure 1). This is an incredibly robust effect that has been replicated many times in many situations.

Behavioural economics proposes a revolutionary framework for analysing why people make irrational decisions, often to the detriment of themselves and others (Tversky & Kahneman, 1979, 1981).

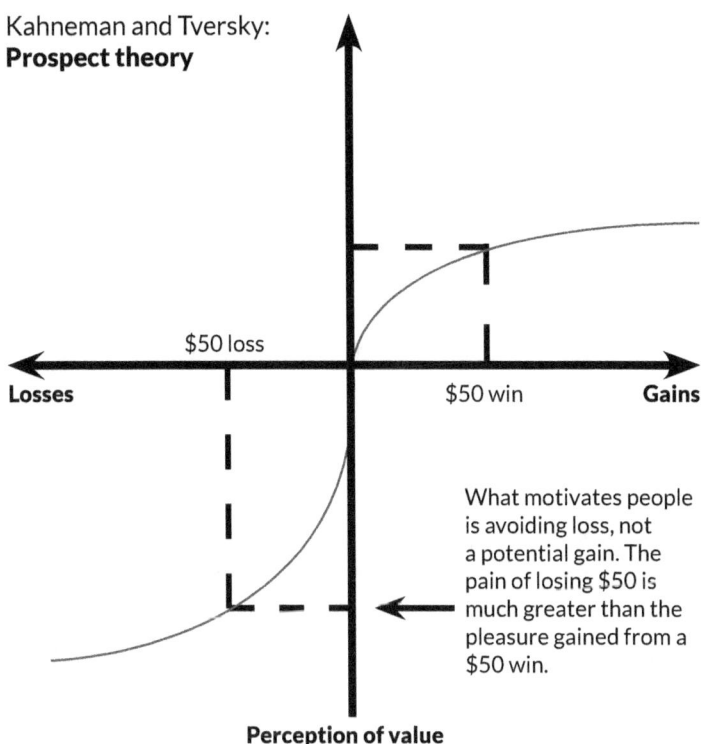

A diagrammatic representation of Kahneman and Tversky's prospect theory (1974)

What's really interesting is when people did experience a loss, the very real pain of that loss actually reversed this effect. So when people lose $50, they're more likely to take a big risk in order to regain what they've lost. They double down on the next bet, even if the odds are stacked against them, and often end up losing even more. It's as if we say, "It's already hurt so much, what does it matter if I hurt a little more?" We see this in companies all the time when money is lost on a speculative innovation. Rather than learning from the experience and cutting their losses, they double down on the average idea and end up losing even more.

Another way we often explain loss aversion to executives is by running an experiment I borrowed from Richard Thaler's book, *Misbehaving* (another great book on behavioural economics from another Nobel Prize-winning psychologist). Put yourself in the room with these executives as I talk through this experiment, and think about what you would choose in their situation.

Usually, we're in a boardroom of a top tier company with, on average, 12 executives sitting at the table with the CEO. Each of the executives are given a piece of paper and asked to simply mark *Yes* or *No* to whether they would accept the following proposition. Imagine I will go to each executive in private and offer them a deal that could instantly earn the company $2 million, all on the toss of a coin. If the coin lands heads, I transfer $2 million to your account immediately. However, if it lands on tails, you owe me $1 million, which would come straight out of your budget's bottom line. If you were an executive, would you take that offer?

Unsurprisingly, 9/10 executives do not take the deal. They have reached where they are by being cautious and only investing in sure bets. In this scenario, the decision that feels rational to the executives is completely irrational. If you look at the actual probabilities of the room as a whole, you'll realise that if half won and half lost, the company would have made $6 million. Not a bad day's work, really. In fact, the chance that the coin flip would actually land tails enough for the company to lose money is 1:3200. That's right, if all the 12 executives in the room took the deal, there is only a 1 in 3200 chance of experiencing a loss. Usually we turn and ask the CEO if he's comfortable with the risk appetite of his executive—which they're obviously not! This is classic loss aversion, and it undermines innovation and creativity in companies every day of the week.

Loss aversion is based on the survival instinct to avoid pain. It is a deeply emotional bias, rooted in fear and reactivity. Often, in the search to justify poor, loss-averse decisions, we fall prey to another decision-making bias: confirmation bias.

Confirmation (and information) bias

When I was in high school, I decided I wanted to be a musician, and not simply a gigging muso—I wanted to be a composer. At age 14, I was captured by the melancholy of Anton Albinoni's *Adagio in A minor* and Anton Dvorak's *New world symphony*, the majestic sound of Edge's soaring guitar-playing in U2, the raw passion of Miles Davis' trumpet, the sheer energy of the Seattle grunge movement, and any artist that was in The Blues Brothers. It was an eclectic mix and something I knew was unusual for a boy growing up in the Nineties that were so defined by genre—but it was me.

At 14, I was playing piano for my church. At 15, I started writing pieces for the school choir and concert band, was playing French horn in the Queensland Youth Orchestra, and started getting paid for writing 30- and 60-second jingles. At 16, I co-wrote my first musical. At 17, I was asked to tour with Australia's most popular country music artist as the keys player and also toured my musical to 12 cities across four states. Music was my life. I was going to be a world-famous composer. At that point, however, I had to make the decision whether or not to accept an offer into the prestigious Conservatorium of Music in Brisbane (affectionately called the Con). You would think that this would be a no-brainer. I should have just gone and learned from other composers to further my craft, right? Well, not exactly.

Before I accepted the offer, I attended a concert that showcased pieces from that year's graduating cohort. I was so excited. I had dreamed of being a part of this community for most of my high school life. This concert was going to illuminate the pathway to the glittering and celebrated career that awaited me. A celebration of great artistry and all that was good, passionate and beautiful.

It was a disaster. A cold, intellectual, mathematical disaster. For example, in one piece, the student composer had borrowed more than 100 alarm clocks from every person he could find and set all of their alarms to go off within a three-minute period. And that was it. Three minutes of random alarms going off on stage. Another piece had someone banging a gong incessantly while a poetry student read random passages out from some obscure philosophical text. I could go on but you get the drift. It was an ode to the absurd, a blatant abuse of the language of music and complete intellectual wankery. In that moment, I wanted nothing to do with any of it. I made a snap judgment. My Ape was not going to let me be anywhere near those fools.

From that point on, I noticed every reason under the sun that justified my decision to snub the pretentious self-indulgence that was in every sense of the word, the Con. I counted all the successful artists that never studied at an institution. I made a list of all of the students I knew that did go to a music institution and never made it (and there are a lot of those). I made fun of the fact that I, at 16, was already more prolific and making more money out of music than most graduates were years after they'd graduated.

I looked at all of the lecturers that were teaching in the course and found all of their failings—and even realised I was already more prolific than half of them. To everyone else, this must have looked like part of the decision-making process. After all, I hadn't officially rejected the offer until the last moment. It wasn't really, though. I'd already made up my mind months earlier in that concert. Those alarm clocks were the wake-up call I needed. All I was doing in these months was searching for information that already confirmed my decision, and ignoring or dismissing any evidence that would suggest an alternative.

This is confirmation bias and information bias in action. I make a decision, then give more weight to information that confirms that choice, less weight to anything contradictory, then feel more confident with my decision simply because I collect more information—irrespective of whether or not that information was right.

Was I right to snub the institution? Well, I suppose we'll never know, but the rightness of my decision isn't the point. My argument was very compelling. It made me feel like I was making the right choice. For me, not only was it the right decision to snub the institution, it would have been absurd to go.

Confirmation bias and information bias, it happens all the time… everywhere. To help people see what it actually feels like, I often run a little experiment to get people to *feel* these biases in action. It's a simple experiment, called 'the best boss', that I created while in my masters of organisational psychology. Try to play along as you read this. It's fun.

Picture yourself as part of a technology team in a large company. You know they've been recruiting someone who will be your boss. One day the powers-that-be come to you with a proposition. Through an extensive recruitment process, they have whittled hundreds of candidates down to a final four. From their perspective, all four are worthy candidates and they've asked you to help choose who you'd prefer to have as a boss. Rather than give you all the information relevant to their jobs, all they've done is show you the differentiating information—the interesting piece of information that sets them apart from each other. On the picture below, read through the candidates and put a mark on the candidate you think you'd prefer, and then put another mark on the scale at the bottom of the page from 1-10 to indicate how confident you are that your decision is the best choice.

> *A new manager is about to be hired as your supervisor. You have been asked to give your opinion on which person you may prefer.*
> **Which one would you choose?**
> *All applicants are equally qualified and represent the final 4 out of more than 100 applicants. The information provided presents the differences between the candidates.*

Applicant A

Is in his mid 40's, has three teenage children and has worked as a project manager for five years after changing careers from a professional football coach.

Applicant B

Is in her late 20' and is newly married. She only has an undergrad degree but has worked successfully as a project manager for nine years.

Applicant C

Is in his early 30's and was a successful manager at a technology company for many years, until three years ago when the company he was working for was bought out and he started working as business manager.

Applicant D

Is in her late 50's, during her working life she has been a history teacher and a linguist, and has been working as a project manager for 15 years, although only more recently as an IT project manager.

Rating out of 10, how confident are you in this decision?

Cognitive bias: Part 2

Once everyone has done that, I let them know we now have some more differentiating information. I hand out another card, which I have provided on the next page, with one extra sentence at the bottom of each candidate's description. Take the time now to read the extra sentences and mark on the picture your choice of candidate (it can be the same or you can change) and then, once again, mark on the bottom how confident you are in your decision.

Now let's have a look at what you did. The first thing to know is it doesn't actually matter who you chose, or whether or not you changed your choice between the two pictures. In this experiment, I'm only interested in the confidence ratings at the bottom of the card. If you gave a rating at the bottom of the first card that was more than 2.5, then you are exhibiting over-confidence bias. You know nothing of these candidates—most of the information shown is practically irrelevant—so you actually only have a one in four chance of making the best choice. That's 25 per cent or 2.5 out of 10. Anything more than that's simply over-confidence.

Now you might be one of the few that did pick around 2–3 and are feeling pretty good about yourself right now. Have a look to see if your confidence rating went up from the first and second card. Even if you rated the first card a one, the likelihood is your rating increased on the second card. I gave you more irrelevant information, and your confidence rating in your decision increased. This is information bias. More information must equal a better decision, irrespective of the quality of the information given. Consultants play on this bias all of the time. It's why presentation packs at the end of projects are so long. People feel better about paying for something that generates more information, particularly if it confirms some things they believed all along.

After digging a little deeper you discover some more differentiating information.

Applicant A

Is in his mid 40's, has three teenage children and has worked as a project manager for five years after changing careers from a professional football coach.

He also runs his own IT consulting company on the side.

Applicant B

Is in her late 20's and is newly married. She only has an undergrad degree but has worked successfully as a project manager for nine years.

She was debating champion of her university.

Applicant C

Is in his early 30's and was a successful manager at a technology company for many years, until three years ago when the company he was working for was bought out and he started working as business manager.

He also develops mobile apps for the food industry.

Applicant D

Is in her late 50's, during her working life she has been a history teacher and a linguist, and has been working as a project manager for 15 years, although only more recently as an IT project manager.

She is also studying an MBA part-time.

Rating out of 10, how confident are you in this decision now?

But there is a strong caveat to this tale. It's a conundrum I first saw play out when I was doing a workshop in Sydney for a group of high-powered industry executives and emerging business owners. I knew one of the up-and-coming business owners, who owns a company called Conversion Kings that A/B tests changes to websites to help convert more web traffic into paying customers. He was a very excitable and passionate person in a room full of largely conservative executives from the financial sector. I did the best boss experiment with the room and, really, to lighten the mood as I started to debrief, I asked people to put up their hand if on the first card they gave a '10'. Sure enough, up went his hand, confident and bold. I instantly felt terrible: I felt as though I was setting the guy up to be embarrassed in front of the whole room. On I went through the whole debrief—and then he stuck up his hand again for putting 10 on the second card. My heart sank.

At the end of the session, I searched him out straight away and started to apologise if the experiment had caused any embarrassment. He said, "Are you kidding! I was the only one in the room who didn't fall prey to information bias!" True, one can't get any more confident if you've already maxed out the scale. "Furthermore," he continued with a smile on his face, "if I recruited you, would you perform better if you knew you were randomly selected as one of the final four and we'll just have to see if you were the best candidate, or do you want me to be over the top with confidence that I chose you, that you were the best candidate and I have no doubt that you are the one that will take us to the next level as a company?" He has a point, right? He might have not actually made the best decision, but does his over-confidence actually work *for* him, and turn his decision into the best decision? I'd been doing this experiment for years, celebrating and poking fun at the absurdity of people's decision behaviour—could he be right?

My head was spinning and I needed guidance, which I got in the most random of places.

One month later, and by completely random coincidence, I found myself in a room with a world-famous, highly successful entrepreneur and about 30 others. It was a quick-stop promotional thing and we were asked if we had any questions after he spoke briefly. I asked him about his decision-making process and quickly outlined the scenario with the Conversion King guy. He said something I thought was very insightful. He said, "When we are in the process of making a decision, particularly if it's one we are really wrestling with, I try to ward against things like overconfidence and information bias, and I make sure those around me do the same. However, once I make the decision, I double down on it, I lead with confidence as if it were the only reasonable decision to make. All the struggle of the decision-making process is left behind and we move ahead with speed and confidence". He also went on to add that he always creates an easy out if it's a bad decision, which helps mitigate status quo bias and the sunk cost fallacy, which are the next biases we're going to quickly explore.

Sunk cost fallacy

Nineteen-fifties America. Eisenhower is president, Elvis is shaking his pelvis, Martin Luther King is in full voice, Marilyn Munroe is bursting onto the silver screen, and Route 66 is the most popular road in the western world. The road was an ode to the car and everything that made America great. It was more than just a highway. It was a destination; a microcosm of American culture. The road linked the main streets of hundreds of towns across the states, and the resulting traffic was a boom for entrepreneurs up and down the length of the highway.

In 1956, a wiry man by the name of Clive Orchid was sitting at his desk of a successful accounting firm in Chicago that his father had started and he now owned, dreaming of a better life. Inspired by the economic boom that Route 66 was enabling, he sold his accountancy practice and, with his wife and young family, moved to a small town on Route 66 to start a simple bed-and-breakfast. It was wildly successful and with so much demand that Clive eventually decided to build a 100-bed hotel right there on the most popular road in America.

This was a significant move. He sank all of the money he had left in savings into the project and, to save on costs, he also project-managed the entire build, which led to a serious drain on his time and his marriage. Two years into the four-year project, things were looking good. The building was out of the ground and you could really start to see what the end result was going to look like. Then it happened. The state announced it was going to build a new interstate that was going to bypass the town.

Clive faced a big decision. Did he stop the build, sell the land and start again somewhere else? Or did he double-down on advertising and trust America's love affair with the car and the road would continue to draw travellers? He knew the first option made more sense but he had invested so much time and money into the venture that it felt right to just keep going and make it work. On top of that, they'd spent a lot of time building relationships in the community, and his building project was a source of employment for many of the young men of the town. It would seem unconscionable to stop now. Clive and his wife had simply sunk too much of their time, money and emotional energy to stop now. There was too much sunk cost.

I think you can see where this story is going. The classic American tragedy. Two years later, the hotel opened with as much fanfare as optimism but, soon after, the interstate was also opened. It was a slow death. First the service stations began to disappear, then the frozen custard shops, then the diners started to throw in the towel. As land prices plummeted and occupancy rates took a steep dive, Clive continued to advertise more, spending their last savings on a series of ads in newspapers around the country and advocating the virtues of the great American highway to anyone who would listen. The fact was that the main streets of America were dying. So was Clive's dream.

This classic tragedy isn't limited to 1950s America. It happens all of the time all over the world. Clive was a smart guy but he wasn't able to change his plans when the context shifted. He was suffering from sunk cost fallacy: the idea that we're bigger than the contextual shift. Our thinking is: we've made it this far on our own smarts and sunk so much into the project… surely we can make it work? The loss of everything invested so far, seems so much greater in the moment than the potential loss at some point in the distant future.

I believe one of the big industries suffering from the sunk cost fallacy at present is large, prestigious universities. The reality is the interstate highway of micro-qualifications is coming, but the investment in PhD programs and long-term study pathways is so strong that universities think they're smart enough to trade off their trusted brands and offer some online alternatives. Time will tell, of course, but the sunk cost of time, history and personal relationships may be too much for many to notice the slow transition of many sandstone institutions into ghost towns, until it's too late.

This leads us to our final cognitive bias we're going to explore and, to be honest, one of my favourites. It's one of the most robust effects ever seen in behavioural economics and never ceases to amaze people when they see it in action. It's called anchoring.

Anchoring

Anchoring is the process when our value of one thing is influenced by preceding the assessment of value by another number. When we have to estimate a value that we don't know, our Apes grab onto some unrelated number as a reference.

There is a very simple activity that I do with people when trying to explain the concept of anchoring. I simply hand out a card that has two questions on it. What is unknown to the participants is, while the cards on the surface all look the same, they have one crucial difference. On half of the cards, the first question reads, "Do you think Gandhi was older than 35 when he died?", and the first question on the other half reads, "Do you think Gandhi was older than 105 when he died?" The second question on both is the same: "How old do you think Gandhi was when he died?"

After everyone has written down their estimate, I get each group to meet together to figure out the average age of Gandhi's death. Of the thousands of times I've done this experiment, it's never failed.

The 105 group's average is always 10–20 years higher than the average of the 35 group. They have been anchored to the number presented in the first question. They think they're making a completely uninfluenced guess but, in the absence of knowing the real answer, their Apes are using whatever numerical information they can access in order to make what they feel is the best choice. This is anchoring and it's fascinating. If you search online for different anchoring experiments, you'll find a treasure trove of ideas and most of them are pretty simple to do.

As you can imagine, Kahneman and Tversky did a lot of experiments investigating this weird quirk of anchoring. In fact, they were the first ones to recognise this effect. In one of their most famous experiments, they had participants spin a wheel that had many numbers on it. Secretly, they'd rigged the wheel to land on 10 or 65. Once they'd spun the wheel, they were asked to estimate the percentage of African countries that are members of the UN. The people that had spun a 10 on average estimated 25 per cent, and the ones that spun 65 estimated on average 45 per cent. They didn't know the real value, so they were unconsciously anchored to the number they'd spun earlier.

This effect has also been studied in supermarkets where they were selling cans of soup. The experimenter set up two conditions. One had a big sign that advertised a limit of 12 cans per customer, and the other had a simple sign saying the cans were on sale, but did not indicate a limit to the number of cans that could be bought. In the no-limit condition, customers bought an average of 3.3 tins, but in the condition with a limit of 12 tins, customers bought an average of seven. You can also see this effect in stores when the price for an item one day is $2.50, and on the next day, the price tag reads $6 reduced to $3. When people are anchored to the $6, it flies off the shelf, even though the day before it was cheaper.

You find anchoring everywhere. Where I find it most fascinating is during financial negotiations. Whether it be second-hand goods you found online, the value of a piece of art or the final price of a house, anchoring is being employed. My 17-year-old son is big into guitars at the moment and is trying to fund his ever-growing collection of guitars, pedals, amplifiers and recording gear. As nearly all of this is bought second-hand, it's the perfect way for me to teach him the importance of anchoring as a technique in negotiation. For instance, the other day we bought a Vox wah-wah pedal (for those unschooled in the art of rock, this is a real thing) that was in near-new condition. It's currently worth about $250 brand new and around $100 second-hand.

We went around to the seller's house to try one out that was listed for $110—and it was perfect. Eventually the conversation (he was quite the conversationalist) shifted to the price and the seller made a crucial negotiation mistake. After we'd said we'd been looking at other cheaper ads, he asked my son what we'd be prepared to pay for it. My son looked at me with the fear of someone who doesn't want to offend another by doing what his Dad had instructed earlier to do in this situation. I piped up and asked, "Would you take $30?" Silence. Deathly silence. Both my son and I knew not to break this moment, for the one that did was going to lose. Eventually the guy looked at my son and said, "How about $50?". Deal. He was happy because he thought he'd talked us up from the abomination that was $30 and we were happy because, simply by anchoring the seller to an absurdly low number, we had bought it for less than half his asking price.

When I was at university, I was fascinated by cognitive bias and, in particular, loss aversion and anchoring, which are two of the most robust of all decision-making biases. I was also a budding psychologist interested in other influences on decision-making like emotion and personality. What I was particularly interested in was if some people were more susceptible to cognitive bias than others, and if the effects of bias overall were amplified when people were more emotional. The results of my study were fascinating and led to me developing my theory of cognitive influence.

Which we will explore in the next chapter.

Nerd alert.

Chapter snapshot

Key take-aways

1. When you experience a loss, don't 'double down' in order to make up for your losses

2. Confirmation bias is when you look for evidence to support the decision you've already made, and information bias is feeling more confident about a decision simply by increasing the amount of information you have (irrespective of the relevance of the information).

3. Always create a clear exit strategy for any major decision you make. When context changes, or you have more information to hand, you need to be able to course correct.

4. Anchoring is one of the key tools in any negotiation. Knowing how to recognise or use it, and having as much knowledge about the relative value of what is being negotiated, is key to leveraging or mitigating this bias.

Things I can do to practically apply this insight

- Never make a decision when you are grieving the loss of something. The bigger the loss, the more time you will need to pause before making another decision.

- When you don't know the true value of something, never let someone else set the value for you. Make sure you have a clear idea of value before you enter into any negotiation.

- If you want to convince someone of a particular argument, always provide more information than those with competing arguments.

- In the face of loss, look at what you have right now, rather than what you've lost, in order to make the best decision.

Thought-starters

- Are there situations, or projects that you know are lost causes, but you are continuing them simply because you have invested so much time or resource into them?

- Why are you doing this?

- What would be the worst outcome if you stopped it now?

- What could be the result if you didn't?

- How do you handle loss? When you lose money, status or power, what are the risks that you are likely to take in order to account for the feelings attached to that loss?

- Are you doing yourself long-term damage in order to make your Ape feel better in the now?

Chapter 5
So what can I do about it?

"You're braver than you believe and stronger and smarter than you think."
–Winnie-the-Pooh

A theory of cognitive influence.

How can we use our understanding of cognitive bias, emotions and personality to influence better decision-making?

My master's thesis explored if emotion, personality or an interaction of the two had any effect on susceptibility to anchoring bias. The personality model I was using was the standard five-factor model of personality commonly referred to as OCEAN (openness, conscientiousness, extroversion, agreeableness and neuroticism). Basically, I was trying to answer three questions:

1. If I am more emotional at the time of making a decision, does that make me more susceptible to a bias like anchoring?
2. If I test high in one of the big five personality types, will I be more susceptible to a bias like anchoring?
3. Is there a correlation between personality and emotion such that an emotionally neurotic person would be more susceptible to anchoring than an emotionally conscientious person?

Previous research had shown strong correlative links between these elements and biases (such as loss aversion and the endowment effect) but not so much with anchoring bias. This was too good for my curiosity to ignore. I had to explore.

Cool, right? So what did I find?

Nothing. Not a scrap of anything. While anchoring itself as an effect was shown to remain incredibly strong (I used the Gandhi test), there was nothing that I did with participants that increased or decreased their susceptibility to the bias.

The weird thing is this isn't the case for all biases, just for some it seems (like anchoring). In light of previous research, what my study did suggest was that increased awareness and active regulation of emotion aren't always a precursor to better decision-making. Sometimes, as humans, we are more influenced by our environment than we think, irrespective of our IQ, personality, age, or emotional state.

A plausible explanation for my results may have to do with anchoring not being an emotive bias in the first place, unlike a bias such as loss aversion where fear and pain avoidance are major drivers for activation. My work suggested we may be susceptible to some cognitive biases (in particular, anchoring) in our system one Ape thinking, irrespective of our emotional awareness or regulation. What was also interesting was that, even though I explained what anchoring bias was before the experiment and I tested it on some really smart people, the anchoring effect remained strong. This isn't the case when you look at other biases that don't seem to be highly emotionally driven, such as information bias (simply seeking more information irrespective of its relevance to increase your confidence in a decision). Anchoring was like the Jedi master of cognitive bias; it was simply immune to the impact of any mind tricks!

So, taking what I found in light of incredible researchers who have gone before me, it seems fair to suggest the impact of emotional regulation and awareness may change, depending on the type of cognitive bias that's being accessed. Some cognitive biases may be relatively immune to the way emotional or personality factors can influence cognitions, while others aren't. It was this thinking that spawned my theory of cognitive influence. This theory is a framework that helps guide us as to what we should do to mitigate or leverage cognitive bias. It hopefully starts to shift our focus away from the specifics of individual biases, and more towards effective ways we can nudge the behaviour of ourselves and those around us.

My theory is simply the observation that the things you can do to help mitigate or leverage cognitive bias fall into one of three categories (or a mix of all three).

1. Develop your emotional regulation and intelligence.
2. Increase your awareness, familiarity and experience of particular cognitive biases.
3. Design your environment.

Take a moment to look over the below picture, which plots on a graph the four biases we've discussed, depending on how susceptible they are to either emotional influence or awareness.

As you can see, loss aversion (the circle) is deemed highly susceptible to the influence of emotion but it's less controlled or influenced by awareness. In other words, even though I might be very aware of loss aversion, it's still very easy for me to feel the impact of losses as weightier in a decision—much more than than the impact of an equivalent gain. It's highly emotional. Therefore, one of the most effective things to do

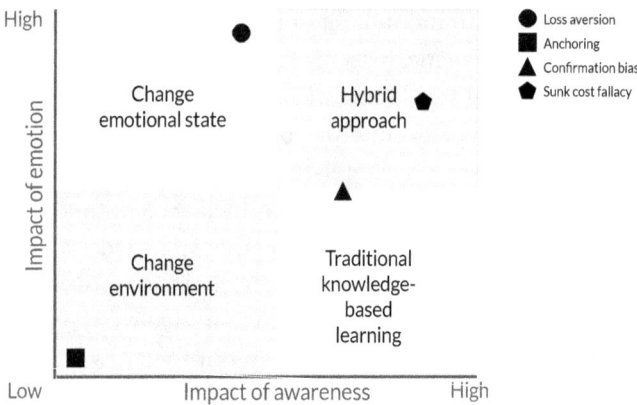

The impact emotion and awareness have on an individual's susceptibility to different cognitive biases

to mitigate loss aversion is to engage in emotional regulation activities every day (such as mindfulness, using the *Decida 10 minute journal*, or exercising). Awareness does indeed help, but emotion wins the day with loss aversion.

On the other hand, confirmation bias (the triangle) seems to be more influenced by awareness and experience than emotion. Emotion still plays a large role, but here awareness packs a bigger punch. Therefore, learning more about the bias, how to identify it at work in your everyday decisions, creating exit strategies and visualising yourself enacting on those strategies, are all examples of activities that help increase awareness and experience to mitigate against confirmation bias.

What about when emotional regulation and awareness training won't work? This is where the third group comes into play, in particular for things like anchoring.

My study showed that we remain susceptible to the effects of anchoring regardless of our emotional and awareness levels. The only way to change this bias is to control our environment: making sure we see relevant and timely information. A great example of this is to look at buying houses.

Back in the early nineties when we bought our first house, it was hard to get a good sense of the market. The agent was the expert you relied on to give you good information so you knew the relative value for a property. However, the agent got a higher commission if they sold the property at a higher price. Over time, agents learned if they anchored people to market value (what similar properties actually sold for), they got a lower price than if they anchored people to the listing price of similar properties. Agents were incentivised to use anchoring to sell, in order to drive higher prices, and over time the good agents became masters of anchoring. Often, they'd tell you the prices of the biggest houses selling for the most astounding prices, before they showed you your potential buy. They'd joke about living in other expensive cites or even talk about things that seemed utterly irrelevant but gave them a chance to mention big numbers. Things like, "Did you know 50,000,000 people around the world ran marathons last year?" or, "Did you know the population of China is now 1.4 billion?". All of these things are examples of anchoring and agents were having a field day. Then the environment changed. Along came the internet.

Online real estate sites have dramatically reduced agents' ability to use anchoring to leverage a better price out of you because we now have relevant information available to us in the moment that we need it. A simple search on our phones can cut down the impact of any anchoring techniques. Anchoring only works in a vacuum and sites like domain.com.au and realestate.com.au take the guesswork out and arm you with the correct information before you even talk to an agent. You mitigate against anchoring by knowing factual data. In the Gandhi experiment, no-one who actually knows how old he was when he died is impacted by the anchor. That's why agents get so upset when a house in the area is sold cheaply due to a relationship breakdown or some other factor. It anchors all the other buyers in the area to the lower price.

According to the model, decisions and behaviours highly influenced by conscious thought and emotions would include things like charitable giving, values-based judgments (such as leaving a job because of a clash of principles) and explicit prejudice. These are all behaviours strongly driven by emotions but are also highly cognisant of our thought processes. The cognitive biases in the lower quadrant are potentially less susceptible to emotional influence and, as one moves up the model, the influence of emotion on the triggering or functioning of the bias becomes stronger. Therefore, anchoring bias is down in the far bottom left, relatively impervious to emotional or informational influences. On the other hand, loss aversion (where the pain of loss is twice as bad as the joy received from an equal gain) is often coupled with fear and has been shown to be subdued through emotional regulation and conscious awareness (Fenton et al., 2011). On the model, it would be represented high on the emotional influence axis and higher on the conscious influence axis than the anchoring effect. Conscious awareness of the bias has the ability to mute its effects (but not get rid of them completely) so the bias sits high on the emotional influence axis and closer to the midline between conscious and unconscious influence.

So, once you've identified what cognitive biases are influencing decisions in your organisation, your team, or even at home with your family, the theory of cognitive influence tells you what to do in order to mute the negative influence of the bias, or what to leverage in order to influence behaviour in more desirable ways. But many times it's just too overwhelming to think of all the biases involved. We have limited cognitive capacity, right? So, what's the shortcut? What's a mental rule of thumb I can rely on that can improve my decision-making? You simply need to do something in all three areas: emotion, awareness and environment.

For instance, say you wanted to lose weight. To do this, you need to change your eating and exercise habits, but making these decisions is difficult because there are so many cognitive biases you've built up over time working against you. So, rather than getting lost in the scientific detail of sunk cost fallacy, in-group biases, stereotype effects, loss aversion or any of the hundreds of other biases, simply address the three areas of emotion, awareness and environment.

Here's how it helps me to keep control of my weight. Keep in mind, this is just a snapshot of what works for me—different things work for different people.

Emotion is a big one for me. I find ways to feel good about losing weight. I celebrate with others when I lose a kilogram or reach a weight milestone. I keep low carb treats easily accessible to give me a feel-good option when I need it. I look at inspirational stories on the internet of people who have lost and kept off weight. When people compliment me on any weight loss, I make sure I say something like, "Thanks, that means a lot. I'm working hard to keep myself in shape, so it's nice to know it seems to be paying off", which gives me permission to feel good about the compliment. I also diarise how good I feel after each run, so my emotional Ape can remember the good feeling in the afterglow, rather than focus on the pain throughout the exercise.

For awareness, I use scales every morning and apps to track weight and exercise. Many apps are really well gamified and do a great job of tracking and measuring things in ways that nudge better behaviours. Use of scales is very contentious, I know, but it works for me—maybe because I'm so innately curious. I also make sure I read articles on health and fitness, and watch videos to learn how to easily prepare good food so I don't default to easy, less healthy options. I also work a lot in the city so I research good places to get a healthy snack, so when I'm mentally fatigued and hungry, I don't need to think about where to grab a bite. I know where I can go so I can avoid the fat burger or the chips that my emotional Ape so wants to consume.

Finally, I control my environment by not having anything in the fridge or pantry that will cause me to slip up. This is really important for me because, after a long and hard day, my Ape is running the show, and controlling my choice environment is important to help me make good choices. The other thing I do is lay out my exercise gear the night before so it takes the least amount of effort possible to get dressed and go for a run when my alarm goes off at some ungodly hour. Literally, I lay out my shoes and clothes, layered in the order that I will put them on. This leverages my sunk cost bias to my advantage because I've already invested effort in laying out my clothes. So I really should keep going and go for a run when that evil alarm goes off.

This works for me, and whatever your health goal is, I encourage you to do this for yourself and watch how this makes it easier to get into good habits. Once you've done this for health, try it for your financial goals as well. The Decida Universe (free on decida.co) will help you articulate your goals and the theory of cognitive influence will help you change your behaviours in service of those goals. Emotion. Awareness. Environment. Train your Ape so it works for you, not against you.

It can be easier to implement changes in all three areas at home than at work. In the organisational context, the complexity of the system can make it much more financially and physically impractical to effectively change all three areas simultaneously. But organisations are built in the image of humans, in the way we work and understand the world. So what works for the individual will work for the team and, in turn, will work for the organisation. The only thing that changes is the scale, complexity and level of investment (finance, time or effort) required to make it work. Therefore, first identifying the major influences driving decisions is important in order to direct investment into the programs and changes that will have the greatest impact. Prioritise effort on the biggest influences and work down the list from there.

Our Ape is something we all have. The trick is not to demonise it or to love it too much. It's there to help us through life, and whether it's a help or a hindrance depends largely on how we decide to use it. Our past experience may have shaped our Ape to date, but we have the power to design our future experiences and train our Ape in new ways every day. We aren't simply an expression of our past or our context. We have the power to change our story, to guide our own journey and to live a more fulfilling life. Keep your Ape in mind and start making better decisions today that will create a better future.

Chapter snapshot

Key take-aways

1. There are three things you can do to mitigate the negative impact of popular biases (lower your emotion, increase your knowledge and change your physical environment.)

2. Your personality doesn't seem to have a significant impact on how susceptible you are to common cognitive biases.

3. There are some biases where no amount of emotional regulation or learning will have an impact. Designing your environment to nudge you toward better decisions is the best way to train your Ape to make better instinctive decisions.

Things I can do to practically apply this insight

- Pick a particular behaviour you would like to change, or outcome that you would like to achieve.

- Make a list of what emotions could be leveraged or are currently encouraging poor decision-making. Think about how you might leverage or mitigate these.

- Seek out something you can read, watch or experience that will help you focus on your goal.

- Change your physical environment to help you make better decisions (e.g. lay your running gear out for your morning run the night before; write reminders and stick them in prominent places; put money in an account that is hard to access; don't socialise with people that are likely to lead you astray etc…).

Thought-starters

- Think of a negative behaviour or poor choice you seem to keep making. Why do you think you keep doing this?

- What is the emotion present when you are making this choice?

- Why are you feeling this emotion and are you OK with this emotion guiding your behaviour? If not, how can you change it?

Chapter 6

Is it ever OK to go ApeS#!t?

> *"Never wrestle with pigs. You both get dirty and the pig likes it."*
> –George Bernard Shaw

The short answer is: not really. The long and more complicated answer is that going Apes#!t isn't always wrong because it can still lead to desired outcomes—but there's always a better way.

The problem is the better way often just doesn't feel better at the time. Our Ape wants justice, our Ape wants revenge, our Ape doesn't want to feel like it's being taken advantage of or taken for a ride. When someone provokes us, it feels good to react. However, the short-term dopamine hit our brain receives when we let our Ape react is only fleeting, and often we're in the situation where we have to post-rationalise our poor behaviour. Even if we know we can be damaging our reputations or even hurting the ones we love, our instinct to react to perceived provocation is so strong that we can literally lose our heads. I reiterate: this feels good in the moment but never ends well.

With one big exception of course. Love. But we'll come to that at the end of this chapter with a story about how my wife and I first met. First I need to explore another story about my family, and how our brain justifies our reactive behaviour.

The dishwashing incident (justifying reactions)

With love the exception to the rule, when we succumb to our reactive Ape in social situations it rarely ends well for us—even if the short-term goal is achieved. This is something I learned as a parent, particularly when it came to motivating my sons to unpack the dishwasher.

One night, we were preparing to entertain guests for dinner, something my wife and I do often. We enjoy hosting people and chatting over good food and a tidy glass of red. However, we also both live busy lives, which means we're not always as well prepared as we'd like, and subsequently find ourselves doing a mad clean of the kitchen and entertaining areas in the minutes before arrival. On this particular night in the midst of the mad cleaning panic, I asked one of my sons to quickly pack the dishwasher and clear the dishes from the kitchen sink (the usual temporary resting place for any dirty dishes in our house). With only a few minutes left before our friends arrived, I walked into the kitchen to find my son still on his phone texting his mates, and the dishes precisely where they were 10 minutes earlier. In this situation I feel like I'm justified in reacting, even somewhat emotionally. So I do. I snap. I say his name in a sharp manner with a slightly raised voice, and then say, "The dishwasher. NOW. Or I will confiscate that phone for a week!" What I didn't know was he was having a tricky text conversation with a friend, who was also putting him under pressure. On my reactive insistence, he let out an "Arghh!" of frustration, rolled his head back and stomped around the kitchen bench toward the dishwasher in a state of exasperation. Dishes were inserted into the dishwasher with just enough force for me to know he was displeased, but not enough to break anything.

A few minutes later, the dishes were done, the guests arrived with big smiles and my son was back texting again. All was right with the world again. I felt like my emotional reaction was justified. My son wasn't doing as he was asked, and I was well within my rights as a parent to have a little moment of going Apes#!t, given the circumstance. But was my reaction the best reaction? Could I have done something differently that could have resulted in a better outcome? Can I analyse this situation without having to feel bad about the fact I snapped? We'll come back and answer these questions in a minute.

When I write about cognitive bias and Ape behaviour, it's hard for us not to automatically assume Ape behaviour is a bad thing. It leads us to poor decision-making and is the thing that robs us of our future potential, right? Well, what if that isn't entirely correct? Could it be considered OK to sometimes go Apes#!t, particularly if it leads to a good outcome? I mean, even Jesus went a bit nuts upturning tables in the temple when he needed to prove a point to the religious elite of the day.

Part of the problem here is we tend to have a dichotomous view—is an action right or wrong? It seems hard for us to consider there may be a sliding scale between terrible and optimal behaviour—because that means we should be talking about better behaviour rather than 'right' behaviour. So we don't. We think of behaviour as good or bad depending on how well we can justify it. By looking at how we justify behaviour, we can decouple the behaviour from the situation and the outcome, and examine our reactions without guilt or defensiveness. We can start questioning if we could have done things better.

The big question to me is: is reactive behaviour sometimes justifiable? Is it necessary to get a particular outcome? My hypothesis is when people are cycling down, in a negative or violent mental state, the reactive way is never going to lead to the best outcome. It may lead to an acceptable outcome but never the best.

If you can get your head around this, I guarantee it will change your life for the better. Often, it can be hard to look at your past behaviour with a non-emotional lens. We seem to be pre-wired to resolve cognitive dissonance by justifying our past behaviour, and changing our attitudes to match our behaviour.

I have looked at the mental process we go through in justifying behaviour in order to help us look at ourselves in a more objective, less judgmental way. Instead of asking if we were right or wrong, we can ask ourselves if we could have done better in order to get better outcomes. As soon as we think we are judging the 'rightness' or 'wrongness' of an action, we fall prey to our own instinct to justify, and to defend our actions as not bad, evil or unintelligent. So let's look at a formula that helps us decouple the personal emotion from reflection and plan for better possibilities.

This formula is what I call the justifiable reaction bias:

$$JR = (IE<P) + O^+$$

A justifiable reaction (JR) is when the intensity of the emotion (IE) is less than the perceived hostility of the provocation (P) and the resulting outcome (O) is desirable (+).

This equation isn't simply a way of looking at how we justify reactive behaviour. It can be a key to unlocking more critical thinking.

Thinking back to the dishwasher incident with my son, I felt my reactive behaviour was justified (JR) because my emotional intensity (IE) seemed less than his thoughtless inaction (P) and within the limits of social appropriateness for the context, and we achieved a desirable outcome (O+) by way of a clean kitchen. I did not start calling him names or imply he was lazy (which he isn't, by the way) and he didn't storm off or create a scene that wouldn't have been a desirable outcome for the interaction. I consider the intensity of my emotion as less hostile than the provocation (IE<P) so my social justice measure is still intact.

However, there are any number of things I could have said or done that could have led to a better outcome. I could have offered to support him with the crisis he was experiencing with his texting and, in turn, we may have been able to help each other. I could have suggested a time guardrail, like "give me two minutes and then you can have the whole afternoon." There are many options that would have been less explosive and still achieved better outcomes for both of us. Kitchen clean, teenage crisis averted and a smiling son to match our smiling guests. That would be better, right? It's not that my reactivity was wrong, it's just that if I had stopped to respond, rather than react—I could have behaved *better*. By looking at how I justified my reactivity I can decouple my behaviour with my own sense of self-justice or inadequacy as a parent, and reflect on how I can be better next time. It stops becoming about power and who is right and wrong, and starts becoming about thinking of better behaviour patterns that can lead to better outcomes.

If I don't consider the potential to improve my reaction, I will most likely do the exact same thing next time. I mean, it got the desired outcome so it should be fine, right? Until, of course, it's not and my son's Ape pushes back, and then all of a sudden we're in an argument where each of us feels aggrieved and offended. This is the type of self-learning behavioural loop that can get us into all sorts of trouble. By allowing the end to justify the means, we can justify potentially morally wrong actions to achieve morally right outcomes. By looking at actions through the lens of $JR=(IE<P)+O^+$, I hope it gives us a way to explore better actions for better outcomes, and gives us a way to reflect with less emotion on our own means.

Let's see if we can challenge this model by testing it in some other contexts. Here's something I have no experience in whatsoever: an old school bar fight.

The bar fight

I may have grown up in an Australian country town and spent my teenage years as a young muso playing in some pretty disreputable clubs, but I have never been in a fist fight of any kind. If I'm honest, I haven't even witnessed one. Literally, I've never seen a fist thrown in anger that wasn't on TV. But I have seen a lot of fights in movies and series. In fact, it's quite hard to go far in life without watching a movie or show that doesn't depict Apes going Apes#!t in some sort of physical way. And it's very entertaining to watch.

When we do watch a bar fight in a movie, it's interesting to feel our sense of justice and what we think is appropriate behaviour. Let me paint a typical Hollywood fight scene. You know the one… it all starts with a mysterious man, usually a stranger from out of town, sitting at the bar alone. Then four or five frat boys in the corner, obviously drunk and feeling bold, start to laugh at the way he looks or acts, and then turn their attention to harass an innocent (and usually very attractive) female in the bar. At some point, the mysterious outsider tells them to back off but that just inspires the group to get more aggressive, usually as a way of showing the mysterious outsider who's boss.

Maybe then a pool cue gets broken, or a coward punch is landed on the lone soul, or someone gets called 'chicken' by some Howdy Doody cowboy. In that moment, we all start rooting for the mysterious outsider to take matters into his own hands and inflict our own brand of justice on these frat boys. In a self-justified rage, the lone figure knocks all of the attackers to the ground, finishes his drink and walks out of the bar with the girl to the sounds of groaning knuckleheads rolling around on the floor in pain. No-one dies, the knuckleheads learn a lesson about respect and honour, and the smouldering mysterious outsider gets the girl. Positive outcome achieved all around and the emotional intensity of the action pales against the hostility and injustice of the provocation. We have no problem justifying this reactive behaviour based on this equation. Next time you meet a group of knuckleheads, then this may feel like the right course of action—a justified reaction.

Now put yourself in that same situation: where you're as tough as the outsider and sorting it out the old-school way. Your emotional aggression or reactivity was less egregious than that of the knuckleheads, and the outcome was desirable. Your IE was less than the P, and the O was positive. What if someone hit their head badly after being knocked out, and died? It's now much harder to reconcile the emotional reaction. Now the O is negative. Particularly if the provocation was merely that the other person called you 'chicken'. Then it becomes a disproportionate response with an undesirable outcome. You can no longer justify your behaviour based on such inputs. Hang on a minute! The behaviour is the same, right? Why should the outcome, or the provocative actions of others, have anything to do with the ethical judgment of our behaviour? Maybe the behaviour is bad in both cases and we're justifying bad behaviour.

The problem of 'resulting'

We tend to judge the rightness of a decision by the outcome. This is called resulting. Take a look at the picture below.

It's September 8, 2018. Wallabies vs the Springboks in my hometown of Brisbane. This is just moments after Australia's Jack Maddocks made a decision to go for the try line himself, rather than passing to his mates who are visible to his left. I was in the stands watching this game. The game was in the balance and we were all on our feet screaming for Australia to get over the line. With the hope of a nation on his shoulders, was Jack's decision to ignore the passing option a good decision or a bad one?

Most people would say it depends on whether or not he scored the try—but does it? At the time of making the decision, he couldn't take that into account—so did he make a good decision? Yes or no? It's a tricky one when we can't use resulting, isn't it!

Statisticians have looked at this particular play and determined this was the statistically correct decision based on viewing hundreds of other games where a similar decision had to be made. Jack made the right call, with this move resulting in a try 7 out of 10 times in other games with similar contexts. This, from a statistical point of view, means Jack made the correct choice. Unfortunately for him, he was stopped short of the line, much to the dismay of the crowd who were all frustrated at his decision not to pass (myself included). With the result known, we were quite happy to pass judgment with absolute confidence that if we were in that situation, we would have passed. Even though the choice to pass in that situation feels like a different outcome would be likely, statistics tell us we should have been applauding Jack for making the best decision. The outcome should have little bearing on the rightness of the decision. In the split-second Jack had to make a choice, he made the right call and simply got unlucky with a negative result.

The Steve Jobs effect

Understanding the weight we put on the outcome helps us to better look at (IE<P)+O+ as it often plays out in an organisational setting, where the justification of behaviour is hugely influenced by the outcome. Earning lots of money for an organisation or being able to deliver things quickly and efficiently can be a very compelling cover for a rotten culture.

If going Apes#!t's such an opportunity killer, then why are there executives and industry leaders who are verbally abusive psychopaths? I call this the 'Steve Jobs effect'.

Now, I never personally met Steve Jobs or even met anyone who told me a personal account of Steve Jobs. The Steve Jobs I'm referring to in this book is the myth of Jobs—the one where he was said to be an obnoxious bully who randomly tore people to shreds and had little perceivable empathy towards anyone. Whether or not this was a reflection in reality is a moot point, because the myth is stronger than the reality in our minds. I'm playing with the myth.

Anyone who has worked in a large organisation has probably encountered a version of the Steve Jobs myth. You're in a meeting, somebody says it can't be done (usually a technical expert who has to do the work) and the psychopathic, emotionally stunted leader tears shreds off them in a public dressing-down. In a fearful state, the doubting Thomas who received the tirade scurries away to work day and night to get what was asked done in the time dictated. Leaders who sit above the psychopath hear reports of this reactivity and instantly make an intuitive judgment using $(IE+O)<P$. Was the intensity of the emotion and the resulting outcome less than the provocation? The answer from their point of view is obviously yes.

The provocation clearly came from lazy workers who lied about their ability to deliver on time and on budget—proven by the fact they were indeed able to deliver on time and on budget in the end. If it wasn't for our resident psychopath, then the liars would have gotten away with it and we wouldn't have the positive outcome we need to keep the business profitable. So let's promote the psychopath and shun the technical experts who lied. Led by the justified reaction bias, they mistake fear-inducing or threat-based management as strong or effective leadership.

This is how, in high stakes industries like politics, health, investment banking and armed forces, abusive behaviour can quickly get out of hand. The psychopath and everyone around them learns this is acceptable behaviour and continues with this culture (of course, often the reverse is true as well, and some people need some encouragement to stop dragging their heels and do some work). Senior leaders who have limited experience or low EQ won't instinctively ask the question, "Was there a less reactive way to get an even better result?" Instead, they think of the outcome they achieved and conclude that they simply cracked some bad eggs along the way to keep the project on track. When you think about it that way, it seems fine.

Yet despite whatever successes they claim, even psychopaths see their legacy disappear along with them. This is because holding up a legacy after we're gone depends on others liking us enough to do so. If you're an arsehole to everyone, the favour will eventually be returned. Karma. We need better ways to encourage good decision-makers and critical thinkers rather than lucky punters.

An additional note to add to this Steve Jobs effect is there are many more leaders who aren't psychopaths, who have experienced generational success precisely because their Apes don't run the show. It's just there are fewer stories about these people, and they're less obvious than the psychopaths. Think about it: of the hundreds of leaders you've met in your life, are you more likely to remember the ones that just go about their business, or the ones who hurl abuse at people? People who control their Apes are much more likely to succeed.

Steve Jobs was clearly one of the most influential geniuses at the dawn of the digital revolution. He was smart, entrepreneurial and lucky to grow up in the right place at the right time in history. One can only wonder how much greater Steve Jobs' legacy would have been if he could have better controlled his Ape.

So this justifiable reaction (JR) bias may explain good decision-making in social and work situations, but what about life and death situations? What about law enforcement where you may be faced with a drunk or crazy person wielding a weapon. How does this apply then? Well, I'm glad you asked!

JR and the law

Picture this. It's late at night. A woman who's just lost her boyfriend and her job in the same day is in her unit, very drunk and wielding a kitchen knife, ranting about how the world is an unjust place and that, if the world is going to try to kill her, she'll protect herself and kill the world. She has a history of mental illness and her neighbours, clearly disturbed and tired of the abusive language late at night, call the police. All the police are told is that there is a crazy woman in her unit who's possibly on drugs, swearing and threatening to kill people.

Officers arrive and burst through the door yelling. When they see the knife they raise their guns, which have lights on them designed to blind the person the guns are aimed at, and scream at the drunk woman to put her weapon down. They yell and advance in aggressive movements. The tension escalates. Apes are running wild. The officers keep screaming, "Get down!" as the woman roars like a lion and stomps aggressively towards the blinding lights of the officers' pistols.

A policeman uses a stun gun to try to immobilise her. Full of alcohol and adrenaline, the woman keeps advancing. Real bullets are fired this time. The woman is killed with a fatal wound to her upper chest.

The room is quiet, the officers slowly moving in on the woman as she draws her final breath. The situation is resolved. It's not ideal that the crazed woman is now dead, but at least the community at large is protected.

This story is based on a real event—created from the accounts of an incident in New York on April 14, 2019. The obvious question that was asked by the media in the weeks following was, "Why kill a poor woman who was obviously just down on her luck? Was she really that much of a threat to 12 heavily armed officers?" They film empathetic pieces of impassioned relatives and friends, stirring public emotion and creating a controversy. Ask yourself: if you were the police officer, would you have fired the shot? It's hard to know but, given the same levels of adrenaline and fear, the answer may well be yes. Given the same situation later on, the police officers involved would probably do the same thing again. Part of this reason is because they've developed an automatic model of escalation called the 'rule of force continuum', a rule of thumb heavily influenced by their own justifiable reaction bias.

The use of force continuum is a very popular self-defence model used by many law enforcement and self-defence academies around the world. While there are a few variations, the basic model is based on five levels of escalation.

Level 1: Command presence

Make sure you appear in command, unafraid and confident. In layman's terms, try to put the fear of God into them by the way you present yourself. For a police officer or a security guard, this might be as simple as the uniform you're wearing, how you're wearing it, what vehicle you arrive in and how many other team members are with you.

Level 2: Verbal commands

If the perpetrator acts aggressively, escalate through strong verbal commands backed up with body language that gives the impression it's not just a threat. It's important to be clear and direct, often articulating what the desired action is, and what the consequence of non-compliance will be.

Level 3: Controlling force

If verbal commands don't work, show a sign of physical force. This is low contact, light physical force only, or a level of force that has a low probability of causing soft connective tissue damage or bone fractures. This would include joint manipulation techniques, applying pressure to pressure points and normal application of hand-cuffs.

Level 4: Impact force

If somebody moves toward being physically violent, use a non-lethal force like a baton, pepper spray or a stun gun. Intermediate weapon techniques are designed to impact muscles, arms and legs.

Level 5: Deadly force

If someone looks like they could inflict bodily harm, you are to immobilise through the use of potentially deadly weapons.

The important thing here is an officer trained in this model is taught to always be at a higher level of force than the subject.

You can see how this intuitively makes sense. Law-makers have tried to model acceptable reactivity based on assailant behaviour that makes certain reactions justifiable. It's what the law calls reasonable and necessary behaviour. But what constitutes reasonable and necessary? The standard answer to this is whatever the average person does in the exact same situation. Basically, this is saying that if the emotional intensity of the defendants' reaction is perceived as equal to, or less than, the perpetrators' aggression and a desirable outcome is achieved, then we're okay with it.

My problem is the use of force continuum isn't a model for dealing with situations in the best way possible. It's a model that actually helps escalate situations—which our brains then work to justify post-hoc by using the justified reaction bias.

The only way the situations end in a win-win using this model of escalation, is if the perpetrator (who's often drunk or mentally unstable) has the presence of mind to calm the farm. In the use of force continuum, a peaceful resolution is only achieved if the least cognisant person in the room has the mental ability to defuse the situation. This is clearly insane. Surely there's a way the saner people in any given situation can be the ones to control the emotional escalation? Why on earth would you hand control of a situation to a person who's clearly out of control?

I'm not diminishing the difficult situation the officers found themselves in. The stakes for poor decision-making or even hesitation can be high for officers responding to such crises. Speed and quality of decision-making are both important in order to protect their own lives and the lives of those around them. It's absolutely understandable they would react and then work to justify their actions after the event.

Remember, my thesis in this book is, in any situation where you are provoked, you need to ask one simple question: am I reacting or responding right now? If you are reacting, then chances are good you can find a better course of action than the one you instinctively wish to take. In my knife-wielding story, the best outcome would have been for no-one to die, not just that the unreasonable drunk didn't hurt anyone else. So rather than try to point the finger at the officer who delivered the fatal blow and ask whether or not that was a bad decision, we should be asking if there's a better way we can approach these situations so it never escalates to this point in the first place.

Is it possible the decision to shoot can be seen as a good one, given the context, and that better decisions could have been made at many points on the fateful April New York evening to achieve an even better outcome? Pointing out a better decision could be made isn't the same as vilifying the choices that were made. It's simply saying that a better decision could be made.

$JR=(IE<P)+O^+$ should allow us to decouple our justification process and individual defensiveness and explore better decision-making. This is the skill of critical thinking—being able to objectively analyse and evaluate in order to make better judgments. $JR=(IE<P)+O^+$ is a portal to developing critical thinking.

Fortunately, law enforcement and criminologists all over the world are starting to realise this, and some major advancements are being made in the way incidents are being handled to ensure emotional de-escalation is as high a priority in these tense situations as harm prevention. There is a growing understanding that treating assailants as the least mentally clear person in the situation is, indeed, the best way to prevent harm to everyone.

This idea that reacting to a situation was never going to be as good as responding in relation to law enforcement, led me to have a conversation with my close friend and renowned criminologist, Professor Michael Townsley. Mike's official title is Head of School, School of Criminology and Criminal Justice, Griffith University—and his mind is every bit as impressive as his title. Mike and I became friends in our early 20s when I was still a barefoot hippy muso with an attitude, and he was still completing his PhD. What we shared was a love of Ben Folds Five, a noodling curiosity about philosophy and the human condition, and a genuine love of debating ideas and challenging each other's conclusions about life. I remember one night after Mike and his wife, Fiona, left and my wife, Alison, said, "I don't know why they keep coming around—all you and Mike do all night is fight!" "Fight?" I responded, with some disbelief and confusion. "We weren't fighting, we were having a mentally stimulating debate!"

I am very lucky to have a group of friends like Mike. We debate, sometimes drink a little too much, get a little too opinionated, and love the clash of ideas and divergent worldviews—and we have a hilarious time doing it.

So one night, I shared my justified reaction bias idea with Mike to help refine my thoughts. To my surprise, he loved the idea and said it reflected some of the thinking and research that many progressive law enforcement bodies around the world were starting to adopt. So after a scotch or three and a lively debate about something that I can't remember now, Mike suggested that I should connect with a colleague of his, Professor Geoffrey P. Alpert. The next day, he penned an email and introduced us. Professor Alpert, it turns out, is no ordinary scholar—put simply, he is the world's pre-eminent criminologist specialising in high-risk police activities. He recently testified to the President's Commission on Law Enforcement and the Administration of Justice, and has been the 'go-to' expert for the media in relation to any social uprisings, including the 2020 #blacklivesmatter protests around the world following George Floyd's killing by Minneapolis police officer, Derek Chauvin.

To date, Professor Alpert is the only scholar who has testified to Obama's 21st Century Task Force and Trump's commission on law enforcement. He also happens to be the author of the highly lauded force factor model (FFM). Worldwide, the FFM is the most referenced, well-known and influential law enforcement model used when discussing appropriate use of force by officers charged with maintaining the rule of law and keeping the peace. Basically, the FFM is a 6-point scale with three on each side of 0 (-3 to +3). The number you get on this scale is an assessment, or comparison of the force used to control a situation, and the level of resistance encountered. A negative number means the officer used less force than the level or intensity of resistance of the suspect, and a positive number indicates that more force was used and that the level of resistance was significantly weaker than the force used to control a situation.

Derek Chauvin's actions in the arrest and subsequent death of George Floyd would, I imagine, be a +3. A skilled and unarmed hostage negotiator convincing a terrorist holding captives at gunpoint to lay down his weapon, would probably result in a -2 or -3 on the FFM. It's important to note the FFM isn't trying to make any moral judgment about the use of force; it simply gives an indication of the difference between force and resistance. It's a relative measure of force. To quote Geoffrey's 1997 book, *Force factor*:

> *"In situations where the level of police force was greater than the level of resistance, there is no implication that the level of force was excessive or improper. For example, an officer may justifiably use more force than the level of resistance to gain control of a situation. Similarly, it's possible that a suspect's resistance may exceed the level of force used by the officer. A force factor representing such a disparity does not necessarily mean that the officer's level of force was too weak or improper. A weaker police use of force could represent an incident in which a suspect shoots an officer who was unable to respond. Similarly, a positive number could represent a suspect who threatened an officer but who was controlled with a higher degree of police force."*

So the FFM is simply a ratio of force vs resistance, but it doesn't contribute to any moral judgment of the actions of either party. This seems incomplete to me. I love the FFM in that it helps articulate something that could be seen as nebulous. However, it falls short in the usefulness stakes if it can't be used as a guide to assess appropriate behaviour. To me, you should always be attempting to be in the negative number when responding to provocation. $JR=(IE<P)+O^+$ essentially says the only time a positive FFM would be accepted is when the weight of the positive outcome eradicates any disparity in an excessive use of force.

Think of the psychopath 'cracking a few bad eggs' to get a project delivered on time and on budget. Conversely, if the outcome of the excessive use of force on George Floyd didn't lead to his death, would we be as globally outraged at the actions of officer Derek Chauvin? I assume there are other situations when he'd used similar force resulting in satisfactory outcomes, but he would have no way of assessing his actions in those encounters to see if there might be a better way.

If there's anyone on the planet with whom I should test my theory of $JR=(IE<P)+O^+$, then Professor Alpert is surely that person. So, after some banter about the emergence of some good fried chicken joints and cool bars in Brisbane, I asked him his thoughts on FFM. Our emails were quite long, so I'll just pull out the highlights here. Geoffrey's response to my question was:

> *"So funny you ask about the force factor. We developed the force factor in the 90s in response to people using the level of force as an indicator of police action. I wanted to put the use of force in perspective and came up with the idea (on a napkin in a bar) to use a 'relative' measure of force. Fast forward to 2020, I think the force factor has outlived its usefulness and we are moving in a different direction. We used New Zealand and Queensland as our models (in developing these new models). We have moved beyond that ... (to) focus on ability, opportunity and intent and are writing up results from a study we conducted at LAPD and is being replicated in Tasmania on how officers evaluate and respond to suspects' behaviour."*

When I asked him about his thoughts on my justified reaction bias formula as a way of critically evaluating actions, and how this might relate to police controlling potentially violent and large protests, he wrote:

"I like your ideas and agree that our reactions are both instinctive and more reasoned. How we react is complicated and based on a number of individual and organisational factors. What we are seeing with the public reaction to the police shootings and in-custody deaths here and around the world is a good example. In previous years, we have seen collective responses to such police behaviour but it has been localised and short-lived. This year we have seen demonstrations/ riots all over the world based on collective reactions, social media and the political atmosphere. First, the Minneapolis choking of Floyd was so bad it resonated with a society which had been cooped up because of COVID, many were unemployed, bored, scared and really pissed off at the unnecessary police brutality.

"Once the crowds react, the police have to control them. Police have been criticised for being too lenient, taking a knee with the protestors, allowing them to take over a police building (Seattle) and also for being too harsh and using excessive force against non-violent protestors. I don't think there is much the police can do to satisfy everyone. In some communities, the police had built trust and social capital and were able to work with the local protestors. However, many people with no stake in the community came to cause problems and get others to protest—often violently. We have seen examples of crowd members throwing water bottles at the cops but, rather than water in the bottles, there is urine, faeces and harmful chemicals. In a few cities, pallets of bricks were delivered to parking garages to arm the protestors ahead of the demonstrations. As

far as I can tell, in the excitement of the moment, our instinct takes over and otherwise-peaceful protestors turn violent."

When people go Apes#!t, no-one wins.

By looking at the way law enforcement negotiates intense situations, we gain an insight into our own strategies when we inevitably provoke the ones we love. Conflict with people you love is often about power and status, and very rarely simply about the things you are arguing about. Irrespective of the provocation, or the perceived outcomes that may have been achieved in the past (or negative outcomes avoided), we must always seek to find better ways to respond in order to discover better outcomes for everyone.

I'm left wondering that if governments of certain large superpowers learned to ponder decisions using $JR=(IE<P)+O^+$, the world might be a better, safer and more prosperous place for everyone.

But there is always an exception to the rule, and as mentioned before, the one aberration to the negative impact of going Apes#!t is love.

Love, love me do

Finding love is pure Ape behaviour. Choosing a suitable mate to procreate with and live out our lives with is more heart than head. I often say it takes heart to fall in love and head to keep it. Finding love is a pursuit where our Apes and emotion work for us. Of course, there are the horror stories of people finding themselves in poisonous and abusive relationships but, by and large, our Apes don't do too poorly in this department.

It's why children cleaving from their parents to join with another human being can be so explosive. Love is the purview of Apes. The love of a friend, your children, a romantic partner, of a sporting team, of a piece of music. Every expression of love can be a pathway to complete joy and madness, pleasure and pain, safety and betrayal. Love is the language of Apes and you could say it requires a little bit of irrational behaviour to work. There is a moment where we actually have to let our rational brain check out and let love in. Love is the secret doorway to both enlightenment and heartache, and we have no real option but to trust our Apes. Love and strength of connection is crucial to our psychological health as humans, and because of this it's also where we often find our deepest pain and suffering, but it does make for great viewing. The story of humankind is actually the complex tapestry of billions of love stories over thousands of years—and I'm not sure we're much better at it now than we were thousands of years ago. Some might even suggest we're worse!

For all of the potential pitfalls and human complexity that are human relationships, I still think our Apes do a pretty decent job of finding deep connections with others, even in the face of pressure telling you to do the opposite. This is exemplified in my own love story: of how the heck a muso drop-out like me ended up with a smart, educated and highly talented woman like my wife. The ever-patient, loving, thoughtful and freakishly intelligent Alison.

By now, you should have firmly established in your mind that we all have an Ape that helps us navigate and make sense of our complex world. It's not good or evil, it's just the way it is. So, if we all have an Ape, and our Apes have a massive influence on our decision-making, it makes sense we spend a lot of our lives influencing our own and others' Apes toward behaviours that are good for us, and less toward behaviours that are bad for us. We do this all the time. As a child and teenager, I learned how to influence other Apes to like me—in particular, my future wife.

As a teenager, I played piano for our local Baptist church, in a suburb about 20 minutes south of the city, in what could be described as typical suburban Australia. Each Sunday, we'd play three services to congregations of between 800 and 1800 people, depending on the time of day. It's a major operation each week, a random and complex mix of musicians, pastors, tech crews, families, children, programs and people logistics. To an outsider it must seem like chaos but it all seems to work each week and, as a teenager, I loved being involved (and still enjoy being involved to this day.)

One winter's morning at the 10am service, I kicked off the band into our set like we'd done hundreds of times before, launching into each song with energy to help wake the congregation up as they meandered into the building. About three songs in, over the noise and energy that a band and 1500 people in full voice can create, a family of four entered the building. If I'm honest, I didn't see the whole family. I saw one person—one female—as she entered the room. She'd eventually become my long-term partner in life.

Tall, blonde, in jeans and a very 1990s-style jumper, I was gone the moment I laid eyes on her. I was in love or at least my Ape was! Maybe it was the way she looked, the way she moved, maybe it was just a smile or gesture she made as she entered the room. Whatever it was, my Ape brain registered an instant connection and, in that instant, made a decision. As soon as the first set was complete and we were sitting back in the congregation ready for that morning's sermon, I leaned over to my best mate next to me and said, "See that tall blonde girl sitting over there? I'm going to marry her."

Problem was, while my Ape was instantly convinced, Alison's Ape was much less so inclined, and Alison's mother's Ape was even less impressed! There was nothing in the taxonomy of ideal suitor in Alison's or her mother's mind that matched what they saw before them.

I was a long-haired, Hawaiian shirt-wearing, often barefoot hippie-type, "wasting" my life playing music and socialising with friends. Alison, on the other hand, was well-heeled, educated in one of Brisbane's finest girls' schools, sporty, smart, destined to marry a doctor, or a lawyer, or a beau from some other reputable profession. In fact, I'm sure that if you hold a picture of me in your mind and then created a person that was opposite to me in every single way, then that's the person Alison was supposed to marry. It was definitely not me. They were right of course—I was a plucky, hippy teenager, punching way above his weight in pursuing someone like Alison.

One evening at a youth event, I finally gathered the courage to awkwardly ask her to go out with me. You can only imagine the uncontrollable shock and confusion that was reflected in Alison's response. After a few seconds of processing what had just been said, she turned slowly, said nothing, and walked away with a face that said, "If I walk away quietly, maybe he won't see me". It was cold, pure ice cold! But my Ape was not to be deterred. My Ape was very patient. It had made up its mind and was in love.

So what does a love-struck teenage musician do while he's waiting for his true love to see the light? He goes out with other girls, of course. Which is exactly what my boofhead teenage self did.

Over the course of the next few years, I had a number of other girlfriends, all lasting several months. Each time after I broke up with them (or, more truthfully, they broke up with me) I'd approach Alison and say, "So, are you ready to go out with me yet?" Each time, she'd give me the cold shoulder, and I'd then go out with someone else for a time. That was until some serious competition came along. After attending a summer music camp, I started going out with another musician—let's call her Suzie. She was also well-heeled, smart, sporty, tall, blonde and, worst of all, she was very likeable. All of a sudden, Alison had a comparable other, and her Ape didn't like it one little bit. Suzie wasn't one of my usual groupies so easily dismissed as pretenders—she was a serious threat. Something had shifted. The matrix of possibilities for partners that Alison's Ape had built up in her mind was seriously challenged. Here was someone whose Ape resembled her own, who was going out with someone like me, and everyone accepted it as a great match! All of a sudden the hunter became the hunted... or at least that's how I like to think of it.

After years of quiet pursuit, Alison and I eventually did get together, and very soon after were married. Alison's mother took a little more convincing. It is a mother's responsibility to guide their children in the way they think is best and so, right up until the wedding day, Alison's mother's Ape tried very hard to influence a course of action that didn't end in Alison walking down the aisle to meet me at the other end. That, however, is a whole other story for another day. The important thing is the wedding went on and 22 years later we're still happily married and the in-laws are okay with the thought of me being the father of their grandchildren! (Mum, when you read this, know you're still my favourite mother-in-law.)

Now, while my pursuit of Alison was not at all planned out like hindsight might suggest, it's a classic example of Apes and influence. Love, teenage years, family dynamics: they're all a complex concoction of Ape behaviour and, therefore, Ape influence. What's interesting is that the turning point for Alison wasn't anything I said or did (in fact, I'm sure that often worked against me). The turning point was having a comparable other that represented her in-group acting in a way that helped redefine what was acceptable behaviour for someone like her. All of her life, she'd grown up with a very clear image of an acceptable partner, and I definitely wasn't it. She was in an in-group, and I was clearly in an out-group. That was until someone she considered to be a representative of her in-group challenged the expected behaviour and was still accepted by others in the in-group for her choice. Suzie likes Phil. Suzie is like me. Maybe I like Phil, too. I never thanked Suzie for changing my life but if I'd never gone out with her, I may not have ever married Alison. (Suzie, by the way, is also happily married and having all sorts of wonderful adventures with her family, so all's well that ends well!)

This complex love story of mine actually helps to explain a cognitive bias called the halo effect. If someone you consider to be an exemplar of your in-group likes something, then you're more likely to like that same thing. Their love of something creates a halo effect to encompass you.

My Ape wanted to influence Alison to like me enough to marry me, while Alison's mum's Ape wanted to influence Alison to dislike me. Much to my relief, Alison's Ape walked my direction, and has walked with me ever since.

Chapter snapshot

Key take-aways

1. We all have Apes. They are not bad or good, they are simply how our brain helps us navigate a complex world. Instinct and emotion are our allies in the fight to survive.

2. Love is instinctive, irrational, and awesome.

3. Don't demonise emotion. Controlling emotion isn't the same as ignoring or suppressing it.

4. When we succumb to our reactive Ape in most social situations it rarely ends well for us—even if the short-term goal is achieved.

5. JR = (IE<P) + O⁺. A justifiable reaction (JR) is when the intensity of the emotion (IE) is less than the perceived hostility of the provocation (P) and the resulting outcome (O) is desirable (+).

6. JR=(IE<P)+O⁺, gives us a way to explore better actions for better outcomes. It is a way to reflect with less emotion and mitigate our own confirmation bias.

7. Judging the 'rightness' of a decision based purely on the outcome is called resulting, and is a flawed way of assessing if a good decision was made.

8. When groups of people go Apes#!t, no-one wins.

Things I can do to practically apply this insight

- Download the *Decida switch* app and mentally rehearse using switches when you are in your right mind, so your Ape can better control itself when you are emotionally triggered. Switching is simply the term used to flip from your reactive Ape into your more responsive self.

- Every few hours in the day, learn to stop. Take a minute to simply focus on your breathing and notice the small detail of the things around you. This helps reset the chemical balance in your brain and keep in control.

- Learn to step 'outside of yourself' and look at your own behaviour. Don't berate yourself for doing something wrong, just ask yourself if you could have done it better. If so, mentally rehearse what 'better' would have looked like so you're more likely to do it when faced with a similar situation in the future.

Thought starters

- Are there patterns of behaviour, or a particular decision, that you tend to emotionally justify post-hoc?
- Think about shopping, relationships, commercial strategy, business decisions, family, eating habits, mental health and exercise. How can you start making better choices in each of these areas?

Chapter 7

Emotion, spirituality and the group

> "Honour those who seek the truth, beware of those who've found it."
> – Voltaire

In order for me to talk about the impact of emotion, spirituality and group dynamics and not be completely boring, I'm going to offer some of the stories of my youth. As I grew up in a Christian church community and went to a private Christian school, a lot of my stories inevitably involve the church or Christian community in some way. Please note that, although I'm pointing out some oddities of human behaviour through these stories, it isn't my intention to cast judgment on Christianity or the church in any way. These are just my stories, my experiences and my insights as I've come through different trials.

I think this is important because no group on the planet is perfect, and I feel it's all too easy and popular to take cheap shots at the Christian community. In fact, I think the western media can make a bit of a sport out of it. At times, it goes well beyond the noble pursuit of holding leaders and political influencers of the largest religious group on the planet to account, and instead ends up being sensationalist click fodder aimed at point-scoring by taking cheap shots at the biggest kid in the playground.

I'm sure that if I'd grown up in a sporting community, a Buddhist community, a political community or hippie commune that I would have learned the same lessons through pitfalls in those communities—but I didn't. I grew up in a strong Christian community. So please read the following stories with that in mind to hear the lessons as they apply to all our lives. No-one is perfect. We're all just here trying to survive the best way we know how with what we happen to be born with.

Growing up as a musician in a large church paved the way for many great experiences, and I am wholeheartedly grateful for the learning opportunities that this facilitated. Those opportunities included witnessing firsthand how music and emotion played into the human decision-making process—for good and for bad.

In an evangelical church, the musicians play a crucial role in creating a mood that helps people lower their defences and become more open to receiving some hard truths about their lives and how to become better human beings. As a musician, you help to create a pathway directly into their emotions, past the crustiness of their jaded and cold cognitive crust. It's the same role that music plays elsewhere in life—in film or theatre scores, in songs at sporting events, in jingles for advertisements, or even 1990s singalongs after a few wines at a party. Music gives people permission to feel something in a group setting they don't often get to feel in our modern world. It helps to open a window to the soul.

So when you're on stage in front of thousands of people in the context of a religious service, the burden of that responsibility was never lost on me, primarily because people are often asked to make life-changing decisions in a very emotional state. In a way, people's Apes are intentionally being put into a state where they're more likely to make a decision based on instinct. This isn't always bad, of course. Sometimes people really do need to emotionally let go to be released from the mental binds that hold them and see with clarity. It's one of the oldest psychological insights in the book that, in order to get control of your thoughts and emotions, you have to let them go. You can't be an emotional captive to something that doesn't have a hold on you.

However, there are some that will abuse the Jedi mind trick that music and emotion can create. Most people do respect this and do not take the responsibility of people's decision-making in this environment lightly. But there are definitely some who use it for their own purposes. In a church context they may use this emotional feeling and mis-label it as the Holy Spirit when, in reality, what they are doing is just opening an emotional gateway to the subconscious. The Bible actually warns about this type of behaviour in leaders. It's called blasphemy: vainly taking the name of God and attributing it to something decidedly human. Claiming that something is of God when it isn't, in order to serve your own vanity. In biblical terms, it's the only unforgivable sin. Every other sin on the planet is forgivable—murder, sexual misconduct, being a self-righteous snob. All forgivable. Not so blasphemy.

Some preachers seem to have skipped this lesson in Bible college because mis-attributing things to God that are simply man-made emotional moments and group behaviours seems to happen a fair bit. Later in this chapter, we'll explore how music is used in meaningful and positive ways: to inspire, illuminate, motivate and provide emotional healing and spiritual connection. However, first we must travel to the dark side. It's the side I saw in my late teens that rocked my faith and caused me to challenge everything that I knew to be true. Two moments come to mind that happened all in the space of 12 months from 1994–1995. Two moments that helped me understand how the influence of music and social group dynamics can combine to evidence some very bizarre behaviour and decisions. They have to do with drunk teetotalers and golden teeth.

The case of the teetotalers and the golden teeth

In the Christian community I grew up in, I was exposed to all sorts of beautiful, deeply conscientious and completely selfless people. These were honest people who were driven by a deep belief they were called to help others and create a better world. Their devotion, intelligence, compassion and grace were, and remain to this day, a source of great strength for me. However, I was also exposed to some genuine insanity and self-serving con artists. Needless to say, it can sometimes be difficult to tell the difference between the two. That's what makes con artists so good at what they do.

When I was 18, I found myself in the first year of a Bachelor of Teaching at a private college in Brisbane where I met one of my oldest and closest friends, Tim. Tim was a hippy/surfie Jesus type. Easy to talk to and easy to like. He's always had a way of disarming people and telling the truth to them in a way they want to hear it. I don't think I've ever met anyone who didn't like Tim. Tim and I were both searching spiritually, but he was the rock and I was the one who really wrestled with opposing thoughts and doubts about most things.

About half-way through the year, we encountered a most curious social movement. By movement, I mean a kind of social craze that has a way of resonating with people and making them act in some bizarre ways. I had heard of people dancing themselves into trances without the aid of drugs, or fainting from high blood pressure at the mere mention of some rock star's name, but this was something quite different. It was something being called 'drunk in the spirit'. People who'd never had a drop of alcohol in their life—who wouldn't even know what drugs looked like, let alone what to do with them—were going to church services and getting so filled up with the Holy Spirit that they'd either pass out or start acting like they were drunk. There were wild reports of police pulling people over on the way home from church, thinking they were drink driving, only to get blood alcohol readings of 0. It was the oddest thing, but it was a really, really, really popular thing in evangelical circles, and I wanted some of it. I mean, what if it really was a movement of the Holy Spirit? Wouldn't you want some of that?

Tim was amused by my apologetics of the matter. He was a stable, conservative Baptist boy. He believed in Jesus but thought this whole movement was a sideshow for the weak of mind. Being a Christian to him had nothing to do with the selfish pursuit of wanting spiritual validation. I bought that in my head but I was a seeker. I needed to find out for myself.

I started to go to small services during the week where people would go and get lost in songs of worship, but nothing happened. I went forward to altar call after altar call (which is where the preacher calls for people to come to the front of the church to get prayer) and, while people would pass out and start laughing in a drunken manner all around me, nothing for me. Not a stitch. However, rather than doubt the legitimacy of what was going on around me, I started to doubt myself. What was wrong with me? If God is real and the Spirit's really moving in and around this place, why does He keep missing me?

I started to ask these questions of different preachers who were at the forefront of this movement in Australia (being a talented young musician gave you access to pretty much whoever you wanted in those days) and they suggested I might have been overthinking it. They thought my finite rational analysis was getting in the way of truly experiencing something other-worldly and beyond my rational comprehension. Anyone who knows me in real life knows I have a tendency to completely overthink things, so this wasn't a hard diagnosis for me to believe. So all I had to do, apparently, was empty my mind, leave all of my doubts and thoughts behind, and open myself up completely to the process. That sounded easy enough to do.

After a few weeks of practicing complete abandonment of thought and emotion, and still nothing, self-doubt started to creep in again. Hundreds, thousands of people all around me were experiencing this movement of the Holy Spirit. What was wrong with me? Was I so evil that I was detestable even to God?

One day, I was walking past a large church with Tim and saw a poster for a big preacher who was coming to town this Friday night. She was known to be at the forefront of the worldwide movement and was only going to be in town for a few nights. After some begging, I convinced Tim to join me on my quest and, a few nights later, we rocked up to the biggest church hall in Brisbane. It held 5000 people and it was packed. The music was loud, the atmosphere electric, and people had come from all around expecting an experience with the Holy Spirit. Tim, on the other hand, was just hungry. He said, in his very Jesus kind of way, "Mate, I think this is bulls#!t. I'm giving you 30 minutes and then I'm going to Maccas with the other guys".

I was undeterred. I saw a seat right in the middle of the third row from the front. I bounded down before someone else could snatch it and stood there with the most passionate people in the building, singing my heart out. This was going to be it. If ever it was going to happen, it was going to be now. The band started playing a song and I closed my eyes, lifted my arms to the sky (this is normal for these events, in case you're wondering) and gave myself completely over to the moment. I emptied my mind and heart and was focused entirely on the moment at hand, completely unaware of my physical surroundings. That was until I thought I heard the faint cry of Tim from the back of the auditorium yelling, "Phil!"

I thought, that couldn't be right—it must have been my mind playing tricks. But there it was again, over the thunderous noise of the band.

"Phiiiiiilll! PHIIIIIIILLLLL!!!"

"What the heck was wrong with him?" I thought. Then I opened my eyes. Everyone around me—and I mean everyone—had fallen over under the influence of the Spirit. The whole first 10 rows. Probably a couple of hundred people. Everyone except me. In the third row. Right in the middle. I turned to meet 5000 sets of inquisitive eyes staring at me, judging me, wondering what evil must exist in this boy that not even the Holy Spirit would touch. I glanced back at the stage. The preacher shot me that panicked look that suggested I wasn't really helping her cause. A few members of the worship band behind her who I knew well, were smiling from ear to ear. I was so embarrassed. I was spiritually humiliated and exposed as incapable and unworthy of spiritual connection. Then I caught sight of Tim at the back of the hall, pleading with big arm movements to get out of here.

I ducked my head and barrelled toward the door in shame. As I walked out, I noticed the tables and tables of merchandise filled with clothes, CDs, books and sign-ups to exclusive members-only groups. I realised in that moment that this wasn't a worship service, not really. It was an emotionally charged sales event that simply used 'spirituality' and heightened states of emotion to sell stuff.

We didn't go out clubbing that night—just to a friend's house for a couple of quiet beers. I don't remember much else of that night, but even with the insight that this preacher was simply there for sales, the memory of the abject rejection was still pretty raw. I can still feel the ping of it as I write this now. I was pretty low.

Sunday morning, out of habit, I found myself with 1500 of my fellow congregation members in my local Baptist church, still feeling pretty low and questioning everything. I was on the piano every other Sunday. I was assumed to be a spiritual young leader and yet, here I was: hurt, rejected, worn-out and questioning everything. However, for some unknown reason, when the altar call was given, I went down the front for prayer with about 100 others strewn across the front of the stage. It was a last-ditch effort to salvage whatever faith I had left, I suppose.

The visiting minister and his team started to pray for people by the laying-on of hands (again, a kind of weird custom where they put their hand on your forehead and proclaim words at you until you either fall over or they tire). They started to my left and were working towards me through the crowd, one by one praying for everyone who'd come down the front. People were either falling over or going back to their seat after they were prayed for, so it was pretty obvious who was next. Then they got to me and, you guessed it, completely missed me. I had my eyes closed so it wasn't until the preacher had moved on by some distance that I took a peak and, once again, found myself standing alone in front of a large church after being overlooked. The preacher was, by now, down the other end with at least 50 others waiting for prayer.

"This is nuts!", I remember thinking. "There is no way I can be this abhorrent. This is all bulls#!t. It's all just hypnosis on a grand scale. Some sort of mass hysteria that's controlling people."

I was angry. Furious with preachers, the church, God, everything. In that moment, as clear as day, I remember making a deal with God. Knowing that it would take at least 20 minutes before the preacher could get back to me, I thought, "God, I'm going to count to 10, and if that prick of a preacher isn't praying for me, I'm out of here for good".

And I meant it. There was no more journeying left in me.

"One, t…"

And, in that second, I felt a hand on my forehead and the minister praying for me. Well, that was weird.

No, I didn't fall over or start acting drunk—but it did make me think that just because people profess to be of God, it doesn't mean they are.

It also showed me the immense power of emotion and social dynamics to significantly change someone's psychological state. This experience led me on a path to unravel the potent concoction that combines to create spaces where even the most bizarre behaviour becomes acceptable, and the great power of suggestion when people are under a strong influence.

Importantly, this experience made me wary of multi-level marketing sales conferences, self-help groups or motivational speakers at big stadium events promising to release the power of you. It's the same social cocktail of lights, hype, music, group experiences and power speaking that combines to make people act in all sorts of weird ways, and make all sorts of poor decisions as well. Remember, these events are specifically crafted to transfer your wealth to them in as many ways as possible, for as long as possible.

If you find yourself at an event like this, you should absolutely be inspired and motivated and connected. There is great release in the communal act of being emotionally vulnerable and feeling the acceptance of the group. We're scared of our own Ape, and exposing your Ape to a group of people and hearing them say they like it is incredibly powerful.

Just don't spend any money or make any life-changing decisions while you're still in the building. I've heard of people ringing spouses from self-help events to ask for divorces or calling people they have abused in some way (or who abused them) to confront issues and it all ending very badly. Apes should never be allowed to call, email or text. It rarely ends well. Even if it goes well in the short-term, Apes never think long-term or consider any side implications. Walk away, give yourself some time to think about it—then if you still want to do something, give it a crack. At least it will be you doing it, even if it was your Ape that wanted it in the first place.

Years later, I was music director for a touring group said to represent the Toronto Blessing (those in the know will know what this is). Backstage, before the event, the speakers would make jokes wondering if they could get people to think they had gold in their teeth, or snow falling on their clothes (it was 40 degrees at the time), or something equally unrealistic. What really happened? At the emotional height of the service one night, the speaker called out to the crowd that the Lord had said there would be golden teeth in the mouths of believers tonight. Like magic, people started yelling out they could feel golden teeth in their mouths. Even weirder, people around them looked into their mouths to confirm they could see it! Do you have any idea how odd it is to see hundreds of people with their mouths wide-open so other strangers around them can have a good look in?

The point is this: do not underestimate how easily influenced you are.

The sound of hell

We've all experienced a moment when we've heard someone sing a melody that has moved us to our core—a sound or a voice that just happened to cut through all of our defences and touch our soul. There is just something about the human voice that creates tones and inflections that register with our core humanity. David Suzuki, who created the Suzuki music method, refers to this as the universal language. It doesn't matter what language a masterfully written and performed song is created in—if it's done with skill, there isn't a soul on the planet it can't touch.

It's why certain orchestral instruments that mimic the register of the human voice are so popular as solo instruments. The upper range of the cello, the French horn, the violin, the oboe: they all mimic and touch elements of our very humanity, so they get under our defences more easily. It is why the *Gladiator* soundtrack is so moving. Composer Hans Zimmer uses every trick in the book, using the powerful vocal tones of Lisa Gerrard, the weeping nature of the Armenian duduk, the power and melancholy of a massive French horn section, and cellos at every turn of the score. Or why *The Mission* soundtrack by Ennio Morricone has outlived the movie through the powerful use of choral techniques and oboe solos that are simultaneously both beautiful and heartbreaking. These scores are a masterclass in how music can reach into our emotions through vocals and instruments that mimic the human voice.

It is for this reason, as a young composer, I used a small vocal group to replicate the feeling of Hell. What I thought I'd get was something interesting and a little scary. What I got was something so much more, and taught me just how responsible we need to be when we use music as a tool—because these tools can be weapons if we misuse them.

It all started when I was part of an independent theatre group called *Paradigm Shift*. I worked with a wonderful scriptwriter named Abi Hull and toured a musical based on the novel by Calvin Miller called *The Singer*. It's a classic tale of good versus evil. It all sounds incredibly corny now but at the time we were passionate young artists, wanting to break out and do something extraordinary—and in many ways, we did.

As you can imagine, there is no worthwhile story of good versus evil that's complete without a visit to the horrors of Hell. One needs to appreciate the bad in order to feel good about the good. The sweetness of the apple is all the sweeter when you've experienced the bitterness of the lemon.

With that in mind, I decided to have a small choir as part of the orchestra each night. When it came time for the song of the damned, I thought I would get them to vocally improvise the start of the song rather than follow a score that I'd written. This made sense to me because I wanted them to vocalise what Hell meant to them and, in turn, create a cacophony of sound that resonated with the audience. In other words, I wanted to completely freak the audience out. If David Suzuki's belief that sound and music was the universal language was true, then the singers should be able to communicate the horrors of Hell without a single word of English getting in the way.

One evening, about a month before opening night, I gathered the small vocal ensemble to rehearse in the rumpus room of my family home in Brisbane. I explained the concept for the piece. Everyone seemed intrigued and eager to give it a go, so I thought, "Let's really push this concept to the edge and see what we come up with".

I got everyone to lie down or sit comfortably with their eyes closed and then turned off the lights to limit distraction. I then spent a few minutes guiding them through a kind of meditation process to access a memory or situation that would represent Hell if they lived it over and over again for eternity.

I have to say that I really didn't know what I was doing at the time. We were a room full of 17 and 18-year-olds who were experimenting. If I knew then what I know now, I definitely wouldn't have been so blasé about it.

For about five minutes, I got them to travel deeper and deeper into the dark parts of their own psyches—encouraging them to look at all of their fears, emotional scars and deepest secrets to really feel what Hell might feel like. Then I got them to feel the sensation of the room getting hotter and hotter, like being in an oven that's turned up to 100 degrees that you can't escape. Then I hit record on the cassette player and encouraged them in their own time to start to vocalise where they were psychologically. I was seriously not prepared for what happened next.

It was silent for about 10 seconds and then, out of the darkness, came a groan. Not one of pain but one of deep disturbance. And then two other female voices joined, almost a perfect semitone apart at first, but then sliding and weaving in and out from each other. Then the screams came. Not like you hear on the movies from a damsel in distress, but like those of a father mourning uncontrollably over the death of a child. The effect was palpable, eight voices all writhing in one painful sonic tapestry that was spine-tingling… and really, really scary! It was sonic horror. It was almost paralysingly fearful.

After a few minutes, I realised I couldn't just snap them out of it. I got them to slowly quiet themselves and then spend some time visualising a safe place—whatever that meant to them. We sat in silence for at least another five minutes, feeling the warmth and comfort of our happy places before returning to reality. When I turned the lights on, it was clear almost everyone had been crying during the piece. Strangely, everyone reported it had been a truly amazing experience that made them feel incredibly alive. It was like every sense in their body was stimulated and there was an incredible feeling of hope and contentment. I now know that there is a good psychological explanation for this that we're not going to explore here—but I also know that I was bloody lucky not to have opened a serious psychological wound that could have done damage, or even inserted a trauma that didn't actually exist before. Kids, don't try this at home.

The point is: it worked. While we didn't go anywhere near as deep during the performances, the choir would spend a minute each night getting themselves into the right headspace and then proceed to completely freak out the audience (and the rest of the cast, crew and orchestra, I might add). We were using music and sound in their rawest, most human form to communicate a feeling—an emotion that was way too deep for words to describe. This was Apes talking directly to Apes, and it was incredible.

The point here is music really can be a doorway to the far corners of our psyche, with the power to unlock parts of ourselves we're not even aware are there. When we take others there, we need to be super, super careful. When we are in that state, we are dangerously open to the power of suggestion. It's what successful marketers are so good at. Create an emotional experience, and then link something you are trying to sell to that feeling. Cool brands are linked to feelings of acceptance and tribalism, cars are linked to feelings of status and success, and diamonds are linked to the euphoria of love.

I only listened to the recording of that rehearsal night once, and was so freaked out that I destroyed the tape. I was at least smart enough to realise I'd touched on something that I didn't know how to control, and we were all lucky to emerge without psychological damage. Never again would I approach the dark places of other people's psyches so flippantly.

Emotions for good

In spite of all of this dubious emotional manipulation, there are many ways we can use music and emotional states to improve people's lives and inspire good decision-making. Music and emotions aren't the enemy—they're simply tools that need to be used with integrity. Problems arise when people who feel they have been hoodwinked or emotionally manipulated in the past think it's emotion that's the problem. If I avoid emotion, then I should be less gullible, right? Well, maybe, and maybe not. You may avoid some financial and emotional scars but you will also miss out on many of life's great opportunities. Yes, our emotional Apes can lead us astray but we have emotions for a reason.

Emotions are a beautiful part of what makes us human. Emotions are a tool we use to alert ourselves to danger and also to let us know when we are safe. They help us connect to groups and build deep relationships that strengthen our mental resilience and help us through the tough times. They help us to create and commit key experiences to memory so we are more likely to not repeat mistakes of the past. They allow us to communicate and create understanding where there are cultural and linguistic divides. They allow us to sympathise and show compassion for others in need, which strengthens our communities and helps us survive as a race.

In fact, recent discoveries by the neuroscientist, Antonio Domasio, shows us that without emotion we simply cannot make a decision. He describes a particular brain lesion study which is fascinating.

A brain lesion study is simply what we call it when we observe the behaviour of people who have brain injuries to particular areas of their brain. We know, for instance, that certain parts of the brain control the construction of speech because people who injure that particular part of the brain can't speak anymore. This is why you see 'stars' when you hit the back of your head, because that is where the visual cortex is. Hit yourself on the back of the head and you will give yourself a temporary brain injury, a brain lesion, and you lose the ability to process visual information. It's kind of like looking at someone who has no legs and noticing that they can't walk, and then concluding that legs must be critical for walking. Losing your legs in an accident is a body lesion, injuring your brain in some way is a brain lesion.

Domasio observed many people with injuries to the limbic system, the part of the brain that is linked to the generation of emotion and a key part of our Ape brain. These people were otherwise incredibly normal, highly intelligent individuals who had the misfortune of injuring their brain. He explains it beautifully in his recent book *Descartes' error* with the curious case of Elliott.

Elliot was a model father and husband, an executive manager in a large corporation and active in his church. But one day it was discovered he had a brain tumour, and the resulting operation to remove the tumour changed everything.

Elliot's high IQ didn't change, however, after surgery he was simply incapable of making a decision. Normal life became a distant memory. Simple jobs that would normally take a few minutes took hours, with Elliot endlessly deliberating over the smallest and most insignificant of details. He would go into an endless loop about whether to use a blue or black pen, what shirt to wear or which car park was the best.

The most interesting of these decision loops was when Elliot had to choose somewhere to eat lunch. He would look at each potential venue very carefully, considering each restaurant's menu, lighting, seating and how busy it was. After a considerable amount of time, he was completely unable to decide where to eat. A busy restaurant might have better food, but it will take longer to get served. A small café will serve the food quicker, but the small space isn't very comfortable.

A larger restaurant that has fewer people will be more comfortable, but the food might not be as good. On and on and on it would go. He had lost his emotional centre. He had lost the ability to make any decisions.

As Antonio Damasio describes it:

> *"Elliot emerged as a man with a normal intellect who was unable to decide properly, especially when the decision involved personal or social matters."*

By careful observation of Elliot, Domasio realised that human emotions were not irrational as previously thought. If that were the case, a person without emotion should be a better decision maker, not completely lose the ability to make a choice.

When the ability to feel or generate emotion is cut off, when the ability to feel is inhibited, the most trivial choices become impossible decisions. If you can't emote, you can't decide.

One of the more fascinating scientific discoveries of recent years is related to the concept of empathy and how it impacts our perceptions and how we relate to each other.

Have you ever winced at the thought of someone hitting their finger with a hammer, or kicking their little toe on the corner of a table? Ever felt hungry after watching someone else eat or felt sad during movies when you watch someone experience grief? Have you ever found yourself smiling simply because someone else is smiling at you, or felt love when someone else gets a hug? These are all empathetic responses triggered by mirror neurons in our brains and, surprisingly enough, they have little to do with our emotions in the first instance.

Mirror neurons are brain cells that mirror what we see, projecting onto our own experience so we can guess what it would feel like if we were in the observed situation ourselves. In that sense, we're not actually feeling what they feel—we're feeling what we *think* we would feel if we were in their situation. When we see someone eating in an advertisement, we feel the joy of what we would feel, with no idea, really, of what the actor on the screen is feeling. They could be gluten intolerant and hate hamburgers, and be doing all they can to not spit it out during filming. Our brain doesn't care. It sees the smiling, nodding, good-looking young person enjoying a bite of an unrealistic representation of the actual burger that you get in the store, and feel how we might feel if we were biting into this piece of fatty, juicy goodness.

The same thing happens when we feel pain. Every now and then I accidentally injure myself, but I have a pretty high pain threshold. So when, as a kid, I jumped over the fence to retrieve a cricket ball and landed on a piece of wood with a rusty nail, I was more inconvenienced than upset. Struggling into the house with a piece of wood nailed to your foot while looking for your mum is tricky, right? Well, when she saw this she went straight into meltdown, crying and asking me every few seconds if I was OK. I might have been the injured one but clearly Mum was the one in more distress. This was because she was probably feeling more pain than I was. Her mirror neurons saw something which triggered an emotional reaction which was her brain's interpretation of the pain. She wasn't feeling my pain; she was feeling her version of my pain.

This is a good thing. It activated my Mum to help me when I needed it, and her swift actions probably saved me from greater infection. The disparity between what I was feeling and what she thought I was feeling was actually kind of nice—it made me feel loved and valued.

However, this isn't the reaction of most people going through grief. If you were to say to someone who was going through their own personal experience of grief, "I know how you feel", this often invites their Ape to come out and get very defensive. "You can't see the depth of my pain!", their Ape howls. "You can't see the hurt that I'm going through—you have no idea what pain I'm feeling right now!" And they're right. You cannot feel their pain; only a representation of what you think their pain might be like.

A lot of the research on mirror neurons comes from work investigating autism. It is largely speculated that people high on the autism spectrum have poorly functioning mirror neurons. They find it hard to read other people's reactions and, therefore, never really learn not to say inappropriate things. I mean, how do you know if you've offended someone if you can't emotionally relate to the vision of someone you've just offended? You still have feelings—they're just not related to functioning mirror neurons. This research goes a long way to showing us the importance of emotions and the role they play in inter-personal connectedness.

If you want to learn more about research into autism and mirror neurons, I suggest you start with looking up Simon Baron-Cohen, who is Professor of Developmental Psychopathology at the University of Cambridge, and director of the university's Autism Research Centre. He and his team have done some truly remarkable and inspirational work in this area. They are true living giants of science.

So it may be true that unfettered emotions and openness can expose us to suggestion, irrational behaviour and unhelpful mindsets. However, the interplay between our mirror neurons and our emotional reactions also allows us to feel compassion, leads us to commit acts of kindness toward others, and helps us to act selflessly in a world where we selfishness is celebrated. Emotion is not the enemy; it's how we manage and control it that matters.

It is these acts of charity and selflessness that help us become better humans and a more considerate society. Learning to leverage our emotions for good can open our minds to amazing possibilities and unexpected opportunities to grow.

To live a full and bountiful life requires us to feel, to be open to new experiences, to be vulnerable with others so that we know deep trust and companionship. It's part of what makes us human. The trick is to be in control of your emotional Ape and to tame it—not to persecute it and hide it away in shame. Emotions can be the gateway to goodness, cognitive maturity and psychological healing.

The healing power of emotion and belief

'If you believe it, it will happen' is, in my humble opinion, one of the most destructive lines in the history of destructive one-liners.

It's usually said in reference to career aspirations, particularly glamour careers like film, music, theatre, photography and journalism. The truth is this is a self-fulfilling lie somewhat perpetrated by people who have 'made it' in their field. They don't like the thought that chance played a big part in their success. They want to believe they did it their own way: they believed more, worked harder, were more committed, read the signs better. Now, to a degree, that may be true, but just as often we see people not succeed who are even more talented, harder working and more committed.

The idea that you're pre-destined to be a star is kind of bulls#!t.

In the past, I've also believed this to be true of a spiritual connection between healing and your personal health. For years, I've heard so-called healers profess the benefits of a certain tonic, a particular artefact, a method of alternative treatment or the power of words to magically heal your ailments. The additional catch always seems to be belief: you must believe it will work.

I've always seen this as my cue to run quickly in the opposite direction, but it turns out they may actually be onto something. Scientifically, it's more about the power of our *minds and attitudes* that impacts our physical health.

One of the ways we can see this is through experiments they do with things called blister boxes. These are boxes that attach to your body and then gently rub without any pain until a small blister is formed. Scientists then measure the time it takes for the blister to heal, as a way of tracking how well your natural immunity system is working. By using these packs, a number of studies have shown that, when couples are arguing or when people are in the presence of others with whom they have a strained relationship, their immunity levels drop and their body is less able to heal itself. This is a fascinating area, and if you want to read more you should start with the 1997 research paper published in Psychology and Health by Mayne, O'leary, McCrady, Contrada and Labouvie titled, *The differential effects of acute marital distress on emotional, physiological and immune functions in maritally distressed men and women.*

It seems clear from this research that a distressed mental state puts the body in a physically distressed state that has negative implications for our physical health.

This was like manna from heaven for organisational psychologists in the 1990s and early 2000s because to be able to spread the gospel of anything, you need a great evil. The gospel of mental health in the workplace needed an evil adversary with which to battle against, and we found it. Workplace stress. The crusade of the workplace in the fight against evil bosses who put their workforce under too much stress had begun. The word spread to all corners of the globe and researchers confirmed highly stressed people were indeed likely to die earlier and that a lot of what they were dying from was clearly stress-related.

This is all true. None of what they were saying was a lie. But it turns out it wasn't the whole truth. In 1998, US researchers conducted the National Health Interview Survey and linked it to prospective National Death Index mortality data through 2006 (To read more, look for: *Does the perception that stress affects health matter? The association with health and mortality.* Abiola Kelly et al.). They asked around 30,000 adults how much stress they had experienced in the past year and whether or not they thought stress was harmful. Eight years later, the researchers found that high levels of stress did indeed increase the risk of dying by about 43 per cent—but only for those people who believed stress was harmful.

Even more fascinating, the other 57 per cent of people in high-stress jobs who didn't believe stress was harmful were no more likely to die than those in low-stress jobs. In fact, they were the least likely of anyone in the study to die. It seems that stress, and a positive attitude toward it, might actually be healthy for you!

The point is that stress itself isn't actually bad. It's the *belief* that stress is bad that's so dangerous.

If you search for psychologist Kelly McGonigal, you'll find her great TED talk that explores this in some more detail. In her book, *The upside of stress*, she reflects on the research, saying:

> *"Over eight years, 182,000 Americans may have died prematurely because they believed that stress was harming their health. Over 20,000 deaths a year! According to the Centers for Disease Control and Prevention, that would make 'believing stress is bad for you' the fifteenth-leading cause of death in the United States, killing more people than skin cancer, HIV/AIDS and homicide."*

And it's not just attitudes to stress that seem to have an impact. It's also beliefs about your metabolism and self-confidence that seem to affect your ability to lose weight. Indeed, there is a lot on the internet regarding the healing benefits of certain foods or practices to cure everything from skin rashes to cancer and even speed the recovery of broken bones. Turns out, it may actually be the *belief* that these things will work that makes them work—or at least makes them more effective.

If you believe it, it has more of a chance of happening than not, it seems.

Chapter snapshot

Key take-aways

1. Music is a gateway to unlocking the full power of emotion in our lives. It also can be used as a powerful tool of manipulation.

2. Be wary of people asking you to make financial decisions immediately following moments of high emotion.

3. Correlation causation is something we do all the time, and is rarely correct. Be careful when making causal judgments about other people or practices.

4. Emotion is essential to decision-making. Without emotion, we cannot make the simplest of decisions.

5. The key to using emotions for good is balance. Too much of a good thing is rarely a good thing.

6. Stress seems to only be bad for you if you believe it to be bad for you. Our emotions and beliefs about the world can actually impact our physical health, not just our mental well-being.

Things I can do to practically apply this insight

- Create playlists of songs that help you unlock the right emotion for the mental state you wish to be in. You might have a classical playlist playing in the background while you work, an alarm set to wake you up with music that will help motivate you to exercise, inspirational songs when you feel a bit nervous and need a little confidence boost, etc.

- If you are at an emotional/inspirational meeting, always wait a few days after the event to make any financial decisions. By all means commit to be a better human in the moment, just be very careful if you're asked to part with any money.

- Learn to label your emotions. Language is a conceptual vessel, a way our brain helps make sense of things. Once we can label and conceptualise emotion we can better manage it. There is a great emotion wheel on the Decida website you can download for free. A lot of people find very helpful.

Thought-starters

- Are there any moments in your life when you feel you have been taken advantage of emotionally?

- Have those experiences made you wiser, or have you simply hardened your heart toward similar situations in order to save yourself from being hurt again?

- When do you think emotion may be used to inspire better decision-making?

Section C

Apes in packs

The group is more powerful than the individual

Chapter 8

Running with the pack

"Fools give full vent to their rage, but the wise bring calm in the end."
–Proverbs 29:11

The power of belonging and identity

The desire to belong is one of the most basic and strongest human instincts we have. The desire to belong to a group, a pack, a tribe. Knowing your tribe is essential to feeling like your life has value and meaning, and is core to our psychological safety. When we don't belong to a tribe, we get lost, depressed, anxious and often resentful of life.

This makes sense when you think about it from an evolutionary point of view. On the plains of Africa, the slowest, weakest or ones who stray too far from the pack are more vulnerable. They're the ones more likely to be picked off by predators. Over the millennia of natural selection, those who learned to stay with the pack were more likely to survive and pass on that instinct. Our need to belong is in our DNA.

How do we better understand the power of belonging from a neurological point of view? Well, like many psychological studies, we look at the effects of something by studying how we act without it or how we act to avoid the threat of losing it. To study the importance of belonging, we need to look the effects of ostracism.

Studies on ostracism are some of the most interesting pieces of research in all of psychology. One of the best studies was developed by Kip Williams and his student, Lisa Zadro. Search up both of these guys and see some of the videos they've made looking into social exclusion and ostracism. It's fascinating and at times, heartbreaking stuff.

One of the basic experiments had someone wait in a doctor's surgery where two other people were also waiting (who, unknown to the first person, were actually part of the experiment team). Let's call the first person A, and the others, B1 and B2. B1 started a game where he would just throw the ball between the three of them, and then at some point B1 and B2 would exclude A and just throw it between themselves for a bit. I don't know about you, but whenever I hear that situation my heart just feels so bad for A, and so did they. In half the cases, they didn't exclude people, and in half they did. Then they watched how they behaved when they went into the doctor's for a check-up. Those who had been excluded went through their check-up in a significantly less healthy emotional and physical state. Their blood pressure was affected. They were more depressed and much less likely to talk about their hopes of the future.

This was intriguing to Williams and Zadro, so they set up another experiment where they had people play a video game where B1 and B2 were just virtual players. Playing it on the computer meant they could put participants in a fMRI machine (a functional magnetic resonance imaging machine that tracks changes associated with blood flow in the brain) and they could actually see what was going on in the brain when people felt socially excluded.

What they discovered was that each time participants felt excluded—even when it was unintentional or they knew it was just a computer they were playing against—the brain's dorsal anterior cingulate cortex lit up like a Christmas tree (Science nerds can read the full results in *Science*, Vol. 302, No. 5643). This neural cortex area is part of the brain's physical pain detection system. This is huge. This means when you ostracise someone, the brain registers it in the same way as if you are being physically violent with them. It seems sticks and stones are really not the only things that can hurt people.

This is why bullying, break-ups, and being isolated because of sickness or even being the last one picked for a team can hurt so much. They're all forms of ostracism that hurt people as much as if you were physically stabbing them. Or, at least, that's how your brain sees it. And the scars are much deeper and can take much longer to heal.

Psychologists Leary and MacDonald showed (in *Psychological Bulletin*, 2005, Vol. 131, No. 2) that social pain and physical pain use exactly the same nerve pathways in the brain. They stated that "Social rejection and pain serve the same purpose—alerting an organism to a potentially life-threatening risk".

To mitigate this risk, to feel connected, and to have a sense of belonging, we tend to join 'tribes'. We have work tribes, old friends tribes, sporting tribes, religious tribes, cultural tribes, family tribes, tribes born out of socio-economic status, where we went to school, who we vote for, our sexuality, where we live, what music we listen to, games we play or sporting teams we follow. The list is endless. The stronger we're linked to these tribes, the stronger our personal identity is derived from these tribes and the roles we play in them. This becomes what psychologists call our social identity. Its influence on our behaviour and decision-making is massive.

This is a lesson I learned after being lucky enough to land Alex Haslam as my thesis supervisor in my honours year at the University of Queensland. It fundamentally shifted the way I see the world.

What is social identity?

As an undergrad psychology student, walking into Alex Haslam's office for the first time in the newly refurbished social psychology wing of UQ's social science block was interesting. He was (and is) a giant in the field of psychology, one of the superstars of the social psychology unit. I felt like a young muso about to meet Sting. Being nervous, I was a few minutes early. Alex had been called into a meeting, so was going to be 10 minutes late. But there I was, waiting in his office with time to take in the surroundings, to maybe get to know him a bit before he arrived.

As I looked around, I saw a weird under-sized fold-up bike in the corner, which still had wet grass on it from a morning ride into the office. A little eccentric, I thought. There were a couple of magazines on the floor on American politics and the Obama campaign, papers strewn all over his desk, and boxes of books that still hadn't been packed into shelves. A large new Apple iMac was in the centre of his desk with a headset hanging over the screen, which I imagined was to discuss research with his colleagues in England and Canberra, with whom he collaborated. This was, of course, a while before video conferencing became more normal. The only furniture in the odd-shaped room was his worktable, the chair I was in, two whiteboards, his computer and a lone plant in the corner. At least he had a large window to let light in—no doubt other researchers looked at this with some jealousy.

Some people set up their office as soon as they move in. Not Alex, obviously—this seemed to be a rolling work in progress that just wasn't as important to him. It felt like a kind of ordered chaos. It seemed like the office of a man who bounced around between a million thoughts and requests each day but kind of still knew where everything was.

All in all, I thought he was maybe a little 'on the spectrum', distracted by what's important and only in the detail of things he cares about. It occurred to me I'd need to be interesting enough to keep his attention. Although I liked what I saw, this made me even more nervous.

When he finally arrived, I don't think I was too far off the mark. Carrying a hoard of paper from the meeting, it took a few seconds for him to find a place to put it down and shake my hand.

"Sorry about that," he said politely, as he sat down. "Right, now, where do you think we should begin?"

I pulled out his book, *The new psychology of leadership*, with little bookmarks all through the book and pages folded over in the edges to make it look very well read.

"We could start here," I said, offering his book back to him (as a side note, It's an amazing read – an incredibly inspiring book on the social psychology of leaders and teams).

He took a moment as I handed him the thumbed book to have a quick look at the highlights and notes I had made on the edges—possibly a little surprised I might have read it or even understood it.

Then he said, "What do you think about it?"

Panic. I hadn't thought about this question! If I said I loved it, he'd probably dismiss me as someone trying to impress… but who am I to criticise, particularly when I thought it was amazing? So I did what I'd learned from years of training in the theatre when asked about opinions of people's creative work. I made it about me, not him or the work.

"When I finally got to the end," I told him, "the one thing I knew was that I had to go back and read it again—there was just way too much in there for me to absorb in a single read. So I'm in the process of re-reading now."

He paused, looked at me curiously and asked in a light manner, "Am I always going to have to say things twice for you to understand them?"

Oh God, now I'm really panicking, so I respond, "I think I'll be recording these sessions, won't I?"

He smirked. "That does seem prudent, doesn't it?"

From that moment on, I liked him. Smart, witty, competent and yet a bit of a lovable mess. Over the next few months, I did quite a lot of recording. Thirty-minute meetings turned into hours, papers were swapped for reading and comment, and I challenged his social identity theory in every way I could, and couldn't break it. I loved it.

Social identity theory is based on the observation we all have a sense of our own identity that comes largely from the social groups we identity with and the roles we play within those groups to align with, respond to, and strengthen the groups we care about. Your social groups are ones you subscribe to, or they resonate with you, and they help to define who you are. Once you identify with those groups, then you tend to conform to the behaviours and beliefs associated with that group. The stronger your identity with a group, the more likely your behaviour will conform to what is expected to be normal for that group—or 'group norms' as we psychs like to call them.

Group norms are the informal guidelines that groups adopt to define and reinforce what it means to be a member of the group. The informal nature of norms means they're never written down or discussed, they're simply understood and hold an incredible influence over our behaviour and attitudes. As part of his journey to becoming a psychological rock star, Alex and his colleagues published a landmark paper looking at group norms and creative behaviour in artists who strongly identified as part of a creative community.

They found identity salience (which is how prominent or noticeable any identity is in any given moment) was a significant factor in determining normative behaviour. In other words, the people who more strongly identified as artists were more likely to behave in alignment with the expected group norms of the artistic community. Remember, group norms are created by us to maximise a group's social success and to ward off any potential threats to the survival of the group. Therefore, the more an individual derives their sense of self from a group, the more likely they are to engage with attitudes and behaviours that promote or protect the group. The stronger the identity, the more militant the attitudes.

So, let me take myself as an example. My strong social identities at the moment include as a managing partner and founder of Decida, a behavioural economist, a composer for film and theatre, an Australian cricket fan and a family man. At any moment, I can perceive myself as a member of the corporate community (as a company director), a behavioural expert (as a psychologist), a member of the artistic community (as a composer), a crazed, passionate and opinionated supporter (as a cricket fan), a loving father (as a Dad and husband), and so on. This categorisation is really important because, as Alex and his video-conferencing colleagues point out, how I categorise myself at any particular point in time will inform my attitudes, decisions and behaviour in any given moment.

When a particular social identity is more present in my immediate circumstance (i.e. as a psychologist), and I define myself as part of the group that are psychologists, the expected preferences, characteristics and norms of the group will exert a stronger influence on my sense of self and, in turn, my attitudes and behaviour. In this way, our behaviour is guided more by the expected norms that define membership of that group and less by individual characteristics.

I behave differently if I'm in a psychological session than I do at a cricket match, or at a poker game, or at the dinner table. Interestingly, even if the people at each of those events cross over, my behaviour is more influenced by the prevailing identity at the time. That why I'll probably never bring my boys to a poker game because the behaviours and norms attached to the identity of 'Dad' are very different to the group norms attached to my identity as part of the poker guys 'tribe'. If my boys came, then my identity as a father would trump my identity as one of the poker boys, and then I'd be kind of excluding myself from them a little. Which actually feels like a form of self-harm in a way, so I don't do it. Maybe this will change as the boys get older and more independent, but maybe it won't.

The point is the identity you hold at any given moment has a massive impact on your behaviour and decisions.

What is interesting is how quickly we can shift identities. Simply putting on a security guard uniform means we become more authoritarian and rule-following, dressing like a rock star makes us more outgoing and wilder, and putting a nurse's uniform on makes us more caring. Studies after studies have shown this. Probably the most famous of these studies is the Stanford Prison experiment led by Professor Philip Zimbardo in the early 1970s.

In this experiment, uni student participants flipped a coin to see if they were to role-play guards or prisoners in a fake prison. They were initially supposed to play the game for a fortnight, but it got so intense so quickly that some students left only a few days in, and the whole experiment was completely abandoned after six days. Very soon after the experiment was abandoned, it emerged the student participants quickly embraced their assigned roles, with some students playing the role of guards in uniforms being willing to enforce extremely authoritarian rules that in today's society would be seen as psychological torture. Conversely, many prisoners passively accepted the psychological abuse and then played a part in harassing other prisoners who intervened, protested or defied the rules.

While there is some controversy surrounding Zimbardo's role in influencing the experiment (he played the prison superintendent) a lot of key findings of this experiment have been replicated in studies since, including the recreation my mentor Alex did with the BBC in the early 2000s, that was published in 2006 and broadcast on the BBC as the show, *The experiment.* While they did disprove some of the general assumptions made in the initial experiment, this was important to highlight the role leadership plays in the emergence of tyranny, as displayed by Zimbardo's role in the initial experiment.

Want to be a more effective worker when working remotely? See yourself as your own boss. Dress in a suit and play the role of your own manager and see how that instantly changes your approach to decision-making and productivity.

Want to spend less time at work? Then put a family photo and something nostalgic like some of your children's drawings on the wall (even if they're old drawings), so you and everyone else sees you as a parent first, then a worker.

If you have to make trade-off decisions, then changing your most salient group identity at any given moment and reminding yourself of the group's norms and attitudes is an extremely effective tool. If you have a tough decision to make in your business, reaffirming what it means to be a part of your brand, what differentiates you from your competitors and what values are important to the core of your company often makes these decisions much easier. That's because identity drives norms and gives you the sense of psychological safety from running with the pack. In turn, this drives up your decision-making confidence.

Ingroups, outgroups and irrational Ape behaviour

When talking about the groups we belong to, it's important to recognise we're creating ingroups (the people considered in your groups), and outgroups (the people you consider outside your group). There are interesting behaviours that happen when considering ingroups and outgroups.

What often defines the values of the 'ingroup' is what you perceive to be the undesirable qualities of the outgroup. For instance, I am a proud rugby union fan. My ingroup is other fans and players of rugby union. But I define what that means by comparing myself to an outgroup, say fans and players of rugby league, whom I might see as more thuggish, lowbrow or fair-weather supporters. Similarly, rugby league enthusiasts might see us union fans as elitist, snobs, and not as hard or tough as true rugby league-ers.

It's an interesting exercise to think about what defines you, in terms of things that you're not. Are you Pepsi or Coke? Energy drinks or water? Apple or Android? Artist or sports fan? Republican or Democrat? Liberal or Labor? Wine or beer? Craft beer or brand beer? City or country? Anarchist or conformist? Private school or public school? Fashionista or comfort-seeker? Capitalist or Socialist? Spiritual or atheist? Doer or thinker? Beach or bush? Inner city or suburban? Collingwood or anyone other than Collingwood (apologies for a very Australian reference there)? You get the point. We define the values of our group associations, and what it means to be a part of that group, largely by what we aren't. Upholding the image of being a good group member then guides what we buy, who we associate with, and how we act. And it's this last point we need to discuss here: How we act. For instance, consider the below group association questions.

Are you white, black or Asian?

Are you homosexual or heterosexual?

Are you man or woman?

Are you young or old?

Are you rich or poor?

Are you pro-life or pro-choice?

Are you educated or self-made?

Are you a climate change activist or a skeptic?

Are you anti-vaxer or pro-immunisation?

If you draw your social identity too strongly from any one of these groups, then the defence of that ingroup (often at the detriment of the outgroup) becomes vital to our own sense of self. And while it's true that strengthening the pride in the identity of any group suffering from prejudice is essential in rising from a social environment of suppression, at some point the very thing that helps you becomes the thing that holds you back.

This is why losing your job or profession can be so traumatising if your identity is strongly linked with what you do.

It's also worth highlighting your Ape will move to protect the honour and strength of your group associations. Attack my group and you're, in effect, attacking me. The stronger the group association I have, the stronger the reaction I will have. Learning to control this Ape reactivity is essential in a debate of ideas, because as soon as anyone feels like they're defending a position, the focus changes from debating the idea to debating the person. We do this to protect our sense of self—and we usually achieve this protection by attacking an outgroup. This never ends constructively. The best way to manage your Ape in this situation is to ensure you have multiple groups you can flip between at a moment's notice.

If someone attacks me for being a middle-aged white male, then I think of, and draw upon, my identity as a psychologist and respond accordingly. If someone attacks me for my faith, I draw upon my identity as a philosopher and artist and respond accordingly. If someone attacks me for being a musician, I punch them in the nose. Just kidding, I then bring to mind my identity as a father and instantly I feel less reactive. It's a very difficult trick to master because these attacks feel so deeply personal. The more groups you can draw meaningful identity from, then the better you will be at managing your Ape reactivity because the less identity you are drawing from any particular role you see yourself fulfilling.

This strength of identity can also be used for good. It helps psychologists to keep your secrets, doctors to focus on health, lawyers to argue law (most of the time) and priests to help the poor. You'll notice as a student grows into the profession of what she or he is studying, or someone approaches a career change, they start to dress both professionally and socially like the group they want to be accepted by. This is us instinctively changing our attitudes and worldview to align our behaviours with our group associations. We like to think it's the other way around but, for the most part, it's not.

Who am I and who are you?

Humans are complicated beings and just thinking of how we change our own identity isn't enough. Being able to reframe the identity of the person you are talking to is also vitally important.

We actually do this all the time without realising it. Back to rugby as an example. As a fan, think of the way our attitudes towards players can shift depending on if they play at club level or at a national level. At a club level they can be a threat to your group and represent everything evil about the outgroup, and at a national level they can be an exemplar of your group and all that represents. Even for the players, footballers seen as the mortal enemy at a club level may be brothers in arms when playing at the World Cup in national colours. Further to this, fellow club members who happen to come from another country are exemplars of the ingroup when playing at club level but viewed as the outgroup when playing at an international level. Attitudes and behaviour towards others change simply by changing the salient group membership and the context in which group members find themselves.

It's also where the concept of 'leave it on the field' comes from. Deeply emotional bitterness and angst emerge when Australia plays England in the Ashes. While the game is on, it's gloves off, and ferocious mind games are played both on the field and in the stands. However, after the game, we all want to have a beer together because, after all, we're all cricket fans and that's what groups of cricket-lovers do. Anything else and, well, it's just not cricket.

Looking at this was precisely what my thesis under the supervision of Alex Haslam was all about. My big question was: can I change the perceived value of something if I manipulate the identity of the judge and the identity of the person being judged? I wanted to test if how you see yourself and how you see the other person influences your perception and judgment.

I set up an experiment where I took a photo of two piles of bricks laid out on my driveway at home (see the picture below) and called them pieces of 'conceptual art'. I then convinced my brother-in-law, Dan, who is a renowned local builder whose grandparents come from Europe, to put his name to the creation. I then went to people I knew in the theatre community and asked them how valuable, desirable or likeable the artwork was. In a way, this replicated an actual event in London in the 1970s that caused an uproar in the local press. A pile of bricks had been bought by an art gallery for a staggering amount of money, and this was seen by common people on the street as a staggering waste of money and an indication that London's elite had lost touch with reality.

When I approached Brisbane people for my experiment, I either made them feel like an Australian and made that identity salient, or I made them feel like an artist and made

The two pieces of 'conceptual art' that were made out of common pavers on my driveway used in my experiment.

that identity salient. Further to this, I changed Dan's salient identity to be that of an Australian builder, an Australian artist or a European artist. The design is shown in the below diagram.

My research was based on the hypothesis that perceptions of creativity should change depending on the salient identity of the creator, the salient identity of the perceiver and the given context. Previous research by my supervisor Alex Haslam

Identity of the judge

We primed the participants (theatre professionals) to think of themselves as either

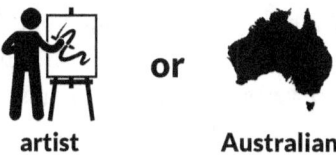

Identity of the person being judged

The participants were told the artist was either

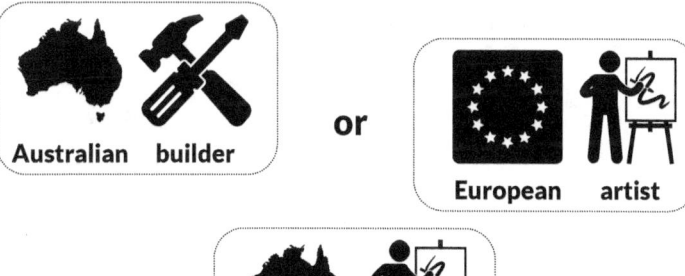

looking at leadership supported this, showing a dynamic interaction between self-categorisation and social identity processes leading to effective leadership. In my study, we manipulated group identities to create numerous group status scenarios within a similar cohort of people (i.e. an artistic community), and examined how the shared or mismatched group status and relevant group norms influence perceptions of creativity.

What we found was super cool—or I thought so, anyhow. The coolest results are shown in the tables below.

What this shows is when my fellow thespians thought of themselves as Australians (the circles) they loved the artwork when it was from an Australian builder and disliked it significantly more it when it came from a European artist. Notes from the survey suggest this is because a key part of the Australian identity is the Aussie larrikin, the joker. With an Aussie identity, I perceive this as a fellow Aussie sticking it to the establishment by presenting a pile of bricks as art but the European was trying to take the mickey out of us. However, when my artist community saw themselves as artists (the stars) the effect was completely reversed. They hated it

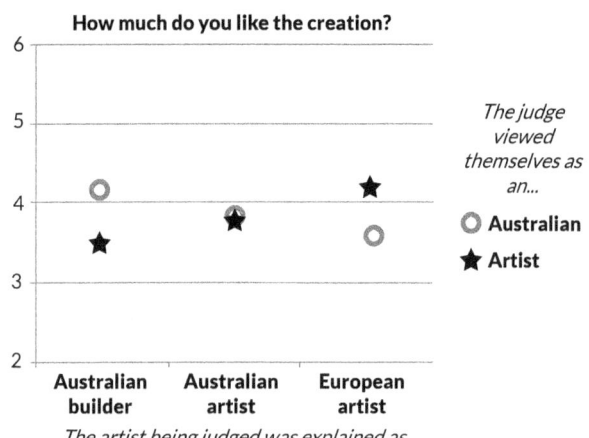

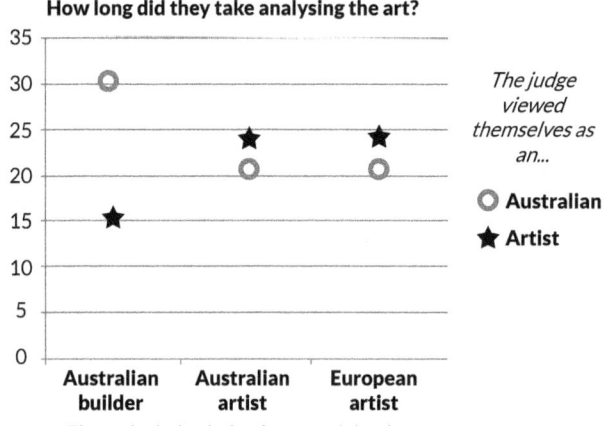

when the art was said to be from an Australian builder and loved it when it came from a European artist. Again, notes in the survey suggest this was because, as artists, they feel disconnected from mainstream Australia and being European has more artistic group norms associated with it. So the sense of an ingroup match changes the interaction effect and the European artist is more liked.

We also timed how long people looked at the artwork. I found it fascinating that artists who thought of themselves as Australian, spent twice as much time studying the art of an Australian builder (30 seconds), than when they thought of themselves as artists (15 seconds). It's funny how our prejudices can shift simply by changing how we see ourselves and how we see the person or thing being judged.

If your Ape is having trouble getting along with someone, maybe reframe the way you see them to be more of an ingroup match. It might make things a whole lot easier.

Chapter snapshot

Key take-aways

1. Knowing your tribe is, is essential to feeling like your life has value and meaning, and is core to our psychological safety. When we don't belong to a tribe we get lost, depressed, anxious and often resentful of life.

2. Ostracism hurts. The brain interprets the pain of being ostracised in the same way as physical pain.

3. We have multiple social identities (professions, family status, sporting club, musical preference, sexual orientation, religion etc.). What identity we have in our mind at any given moment changes the way we think, perceive and behave.

4. If we hold onto one identity too strongly, our Ape is more likely to go Apes#!t when that identity is threatened in some way. The more social identities people subscribe to, the less reactive they tend to be.

Things I can do to practically apply this insight

- Think of a number of identities that you hold. When you are in a situation where someone triggers you, think of an identity not associated with the situation to draw upon. Draw upon an identity in that moment that is not linked to what is being threatened, and the emotional impact seems to go away.

Thought-starters

- How many social identities do you have that combine to make you, you?

- Are some identities stronger than others? If so, what are they?

- Is there a particular identity that you are more sensitive about when you feel it is threatened or put down in some way? Why is that?

- When this sensitive identity is attacked and you are triggered, which identity can you practise bringing front of mind to mute the impact of the confrontation?

Chapter 9

Are Apes tribal?

"Stop. Collaborate & listen."
– Vanilla Ice

Our individual worldview (the lens through which we see the world) is created and defended because, at its core, it's about survival and how to make sense of the world in order to live a meaningful and successful life. Interestingly, in my travels and experiences across many cultures and when I look at the stories relayed by history, these three worldviews seem to be at the core of every conflict, every clash of ideas. This is pretty powerful stuff. Whether it be nation to nation, group to group, or person to person, these three worldviews are at the heart of every debate, whispering lines of logic in the ears of the different actors to challenge ideas and provide brilliant moments of comedy or drama. I like to call each of these groups of people who share similar worldviews, tribes. Psychological tribes.

If you're of the same tribe, you'll seem to intuitively get someone and bond more naturally. Apes of similar tribes hang out, communicate more easily, empathise more effectively and employ each other more often. For me, diversity of thought is much more important than other forms of diversity in teams. If we're truly recruiting for diversity of thought then we will have a diversity of race and gender as a natural by-product. However, simply diversifying along race and gender won't guarantee diversity of thought.

These psychological tribes are emotion-driven. When you meet someone from the same tribe, your emotionally reactive views of the world seem to align. This does not mean you agree on everything—far from it—it just means the emotional drivers that lead you to your choices seem to have a similar emotional logic to them.

You're more likely to marry someone in your own tribe, trust people in your own tribe, and do business with people in your own tribe. This is how cultures are formed in nations and in business. They might look similar on the outside but the core logic-driving decisions differ between companies and nations. At a more personal level, it's interesting to note all your children won't necessarily be from your own tribe. This could be because of a deep need to cleave from the parents to make their own mark, or because our human instinct leads us to develop different psychological perspectives for ongoing survival, or because of some yet unknown driver. Whatever the reason, children from the same tribe tend to be favourites, which spurs the conflict between people's different mindsets.

While these psychological tribes seem to be at the heart of most conflict, I believe society as a whole is stronger when all tribes are represented. This is because, as humans, we grow and learn through conflict. We know this from developmental psychology—we can only progress through stages of development when our mind is able to reconcile psychological conflicts. Looking at Piaget's or Vygotsky's theories of cognitive development is a great place to start exploring if you want to deep-dive this further. For now, the point is that for individuals and society to grow and develop, these three tribes need to be able to thrash it out. It's actually in the struggle between these tribes, and the overcoming of conflict and adversity, that we mature as a species. It's a very human thing, but our group consciousness seems to have evolved the very mechanism for conflict that stimulates psychological maturation. Fascinating stuff.

Core to the comedy or drama of most great stories is the conflict between key characters. Whether it be an episode of *Seinfeld* or *Friends*, a Shakespeare play, an Italian opera or a tribal folk tale, comedy and drama are found in the human conflict. If you dig into the psychology of these stories you'll find there are three schools of thought or worldviews that different characters seem to share. Stories that resonate with us do so because at some level they touch on the conflict between these psychological tribes. They resonate because they're reflecting how the world works. It doesn't matter whether the story is a hero's journey, like *Indiana Jones* or *Les Misérables*, or absurdist storylines like those found in a Seinfeld episode, comedic and dramatic stories only really work when this conflict between perspectives is exposed.

So, we belong to physical tribes (race, nationality, sporting team, socio-economic status and so on), and we also belong to emotionally reactive psychological Ape tribes. What are these three tribes? I call them the Groupies, the Purists and the Authoritarians.

The first tribe is the Groupies. Groupies are concerned about their impact on others and are constantly looking for social validation and group connectedness.

The second tribe is the Purists. Purists are driven by the right way to do things and what the perfect ideal is we should all be striving for (irrespective of popular opinion).

The third tribe is the Authoritarians. Authoritarians believe relying on the group or idealistic notions is flawed, and actions and opinions should only be based on data. Data is truth and used as power to bring everyone around to that point of view.

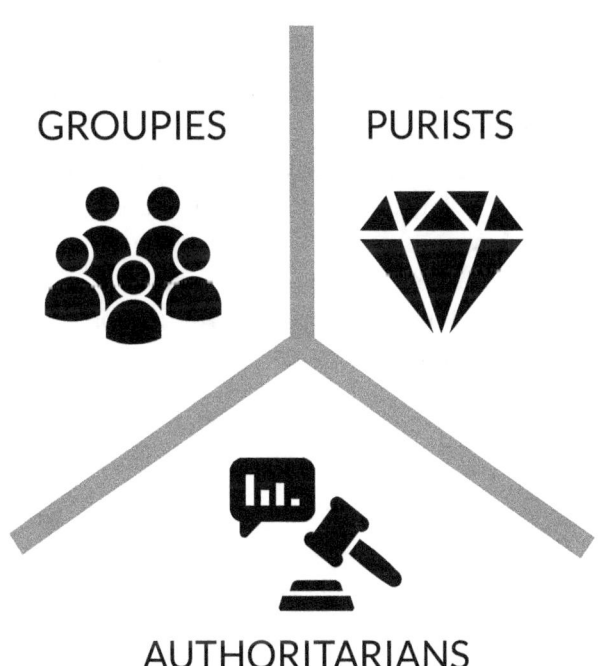

So to which tribe do you belong? Read through the three short paragraphs below and see which one you most resonate with.

Paragraph A

I think you should always do what you believe, no matter what people think, even if that means others may be hurt or you may become ostracised from the group. In the long run, staying true to your beliefs in every moment will always mean you will be better off. People who seem to flip-flop between different values seem weak. I respect others who live by their values—even if they're slightly different to mine.

Paragraph B

Evidence and facts are important, and it's imperative to make decisions based on empirical evidence. I also see indecisive people as somewhat incompetent and lacking in vision and conviction. To effectively live by your values, you have to be able to influence those around you. The system is what it is, so knowing how to understand and control the system is how you get ahead. You have to have influence or know someone who is influential to get things done. When something goes wrong, it's because some information was missed.

Paragraph C

I think it's important to know your values and to stick to your beliefs, but sometimes you have to be aware of how your behaviour impacts others. There are times to stick to your guns and times to compromise based on what's best for the group at the time. Our survival and success largely depends on the strength of the group.

So, which one resonates most for you? If you're struggling to pick one, ask yourself why you are struggling and carefully observe your own thought process. The very process of spending some time thinking through the why will help you to identify which one resonates strongest.

If you picked A, you're likely a Purist. B, an Authoritarian. C, a Groupie.

Whether or not you correctly identify your own Ape tribe isn't the point here. Simply becoming aware there are different tribes is a mind-opener for many people. It's the start of the journey into individual differences that will help us to collaborate more harmoniously with those around us. Living with everyone's Apes for a lifetime means we all appreciate and understand, to an extent, where the different tribes are coming from. So it can be hard for some people to choose just one tribe. However, we are all mostly one of the tribes. Choose the one tribe that resonates with you most, and then try it on for size as you read this chapter.

In my view, mastering the identification of Ape tribes (and differences within those tribes themselves, as we will explore later on) is the starting point to true emotional intelligence. I like to think about it as three levels of mastery.

1. Tame your own Ape and recognise and help tame others' Apes.

2. Understand Ape tribes and how they interact with, and react to, each other and our more conscious selves.

3. Detect the individual differences that exist within each tribe, and what gives them energy.

So we are currently at the second level, looking at Ape tribes. If you are having trouble working with someone or someone just seems to trigger you constantly, chances are you may be experiencing a disconnect between tribal worldviews. A fundamental disconnect in the very nature of what you see as common sense. So what are some of the basic differences between tribes?

Authoritarians need to see the data to change their mind or have confidence in your opinion. They will be adamant you need to be one way and then completely flip when you show them enough evidence that points to a different way. This isn't disingenuous at all (which is how Groupies and Purists often see it). It's actually just smart. Change your mind based on the available evidence at the time. Arguing conceptually with an Authoritarian is a fool's errand, as they won't listen to simple opinions that aren't backed up with evidence. This doesn't mean they're closed-minded. Our level of openness seems to not be impacted by our tribe. It's just that, for an Authoritarian, a position in an argument needs to be backed up by evidence, or you'll be disregarded as irrelevant or mentally deficient.

Purists, on the other hand, are driven by ideals. They look for purity and beauty in what they do, how they do it and what experiences they have. When talking to a Purist, it can be all about recognising the nobility in their views or recognising their superiority or artistry in their chosen field. It's not that they know everything about their field like the Authoritarians—it's that they're the best at it. Talking in ideals is often the way to challenge their thinking. Tap into their ideals and show how doing something will be a better representation of those ideals. If you are seen to cave in to social pressure to compromise your own ideals, or cut corners or do shoddy work simply to achieve something, you'll be seen as lazy and incompetent, and then disregarded.

On the other hand, Groupies cut corners and create ways around frustrating and irrelevant processes to get stuff done all the time. This isn't lazy, it's just smart! Groupies gain confidence and are heavily influenced by the views of trusted others and social data they pick up from social interactions. You could have many experts advising to go with option A, and fewer saying to go with option B, but if Groupies have a better relationship or connection with one of the B team, then they'll often go with this choice in order to preserve the trusted relationship. The social connection of their group is more important to maintain than the right option (which, in the mind of the Groupie, is often a grey area, unlike the Purist). They also respond well to hearing about what most others are doing. This doesn't mean they're mindless followers—it's just that social data is as important to Groupies as hard facts. If you want to resonate with Groupies, talk about things like social impact and how the decision will affect other people.

Just a side-note and an admission: I'm a Groupie. Now you've read a description of this tribe, if you went back and examined how I've written this book, you'll notice I explain concepts by looking at how my actions impact me and others around me. Even my tone of voice is intentionally inclusive and Groupie—I can't switch it off, and nor do I need to.

We'll continue to unpack each of these tribes and individual differences within the tribes in a moment. However, I feel the need to state the obvious, which is this is all starting to look and feel like personality typing—a term, I admit, that makes me cringe a little. I try to avoid terms like personality or types because they conjure up notions of immutable mindsets that cannot change or adapt over time. This simply does not reflect my experience and it isn't a useful matrix when you're trying to predict or influence your own Ape. It's also important to note this is just looking at your Ape, your reactive self. There is another whole side of you and how we use conscious logic, which interacts with your Ape to predict behaviour. Your Ape is a significant part of the story but it's not the whole picture.

The history of personality typing is filled with characters who are more akin to star-sign readers and mystics than scientists. Even in the hands of credible scientists, the research into personality and individual differences isn't infallible. We have much yet to learn about this area of our behaviour, which is precisely why it fascinates me so much.

During my masters studies, I had the great honour of studying under Professor Arthur Poropat. A lovable and rather scattered character who doesn't have much time for the bureaucrats you often find littered throughout universities, he is a thinker, a philosopher, an artist and an intellectual. You can see why I like him so much.

Arthur had spent a lifetime looking at different theories of personality and whether or not these perspectives on personality actually predict human behaviour. I learned many things from him but two things stand out: most personality tests aren't highly reliable, and even fewer personality assessments predict future behaviour. Most really are no better than astrology in simply highlighting different aspects of anyone's behaviour in a way that makes people believe it must be something specific to them. Making people believe star signs have validity is one of the oldest mind tricks in the book, so it's no wonder something as vague and difficult to observe as personality would fall prey to this same deception. At their best, most personality tests rely on the notion that past behaviour will predict future behaviour. Something that sounds good but isn't actually a reliable predictor. Even the most cited and statistically valid personality test, the *Five factor model* of personality (openness, conscientiousness, extraversion, agreeableness and neuroticism—the first letter of each of these spells the word OCEAN, which always makes it easier for me to remember) seems to rely on past behaviour to predict how you will behave in the future. Many companies like Facebook and Amazon have been trying unsuccessfully to apply this to their search algorithms to show you things you're more likely to buy or trust.

In my experience, using past behaviour as a predictor of future actions is flawed and illogical. I mean, did the way you behave as a teenager predict what you would be like after getting married? Or predict what house you would buy? Or what you would be like as a manager 30 years later? Of course not. Your behaviour and attitudes aren't consistent over time. They change based on experience, relationships, circumstance and social influences. They're connected to your past, of course, but assuming causality would be to fall prey to the causation correlation fallacy.

Humans love finding patterns and correlations where none exist, particularly when it helps to explain a mystery. Our brains do not cope well with things that seem mysterious or chaotic, so we make things up and see connections where there are no connections to be made in order to feel safe. Our brain rewards us with a little shot of dopamine to make us feel good when we make sense of chaos, even if there is no pattern or sense to make in real life. We're hard-wired to find explanation and tend to latch onto things that perceivably illuminate a truth. There are many examples of personality typing tools that initially feel insightful but are useless when predicting or influencing actual behaviour. Personality is a dim torch to help illuminate the part of our humanness that helps us to think differently, develop pathways to increase empathy and critical thinking, and make better decisions.

Our desire for clarity and truth makes us susceptible to sales pitches and philosophies that feel like they bring order to the chaos, that explain the nature of things. So, as we dig deeper, hold it lightly. Use this insight as a tool—and if it works in your life, then fantastic. It'll be the best thing that explains how we're individually different until something more insightful comes along.

What I am discussing here isn't personality—it's emotional reactivity, the way you intuitively make sense of human interactions. I can't stress how important this point is. You aren't the total sum of your emotional reactivity but your emotional worldview does drive most of your decisions. Whether it be your choice of career or what to eat for dinner, your emotional reactivity doesn't just drive your decisions, it's how you can make a decision at all. As mentioned in an earlier chapter, there are many scientific studies investigating people who have injuries to areas of the brain linked to emotion, and these show they're unable to make decisions at all. We think that getting rid of emotions will make us better decision-makers but, in fact, we need emotions in order to make any decisions. It's our ability to understand and control—not suppress or try to eradicate—our emotional reactivity that leads to better decision-making.

The way we process information dictates how we make sense of it, which in turn triggers our Apes in predictable ways and leads to predictive Ape behaviour.

The theatre of thespians

Let's continue to unpack our Ape tribes by travelling back in time to when I first started to recognise them myself. My first insight into the three tribes actually harks back to my time as a wide-eyed, twenty-something developing composer in a world of artistic giants and celebrities.

While I was a good composer, I don't think I was ever the best. I often won jobs over people I felt were more talented for two reasons. The first was my ability to meaningfully connect with the director, and the second was my reputation for the way I could work with people to get stuff done in that high-pressure, five-week rehearsal period. The latter was no small task. Combining high levels of narcissism and big, fragile egos in a high-stakes, high-pressure environment makes for an interesting mix. I saw plenty of people's Apes go Apes#!t and it was, at times, funny, dramatic and tragic. Theatre music was interesting, but navigating the intensity of human interaction was the real drug. It was here I started to observe people and characters tended to fall into one of three worldviews. At times, you had a clash of people with different Ape worldviews, and I found I could better connect with people if I changed the way I spoke to people to better resonate with their Ape's worldview.

Where it all started was learning to recognise when an actor or creative went Apes#!t, and what I had to do to help switch them into their more rational state.

For some people, I needed to give them a barrage of facts and figures, use hard data and statistics to prove a point and make them feel smart, powerful and respected (Authoritarians). For others, I needed to argue the truth of something, explore the essence of what they were doing and why it was important, and look at the honour and rightness of what they were doing and the stand they were taking (Purists). For others, I would just need to go outside and smoke a cigar with them and give them a hug—connect with them in some tangible human way so they felt supported and accepted. I could then move the conversation to what we could achieve if we all stuck together (Groupies). This was how I broke through all of the negative Ape behaviours and defences so we could get creative crews working again when the wheels seemed to fall off.

These three tribes represented the lenses through which people saw the world. By speaking and interacting with the same tribal lens as the person going Apes#!t, they felt less threatened, and better heard and understood. All of a sudden, the chaos of the moment felt less threatening and their Ape would calm down. Knowing which lens to put on at any moment was the trick.

If this theory of psychological tribes is real, surely I'm not the only one to see it. If it's actually real, then there should be other psychologists, scientists and practitioners around the world that have also discovered the same patterns. If I am alone, then maybe I am just making a pattern out of the white noise. While I was pondering this a few years back, I happened to be sitting in a presentation where a marketing firm referred to the research of a German-based market research group. The insights from this research seemed to bear a striking resemblance to my own observations. On the other side of the planet, someone else had indeed identified very similar psychological patterns of emotional reactivity.

The sheer fact that on the other side of the planet there was someone else observing this psychological phenomenon was super exciting for me. It was validation of the patterns

I was observing: that there were three different emotional worldviews driving our decision-making. The research and marketing company identified the three tribes as Stimulation (Purists), Dominance (Authoritarians) and Balance (Groupies). To this day, I can remember sitting in that videoconference listening to the consultant running through each of the definitions of each group as if he'd been looking at my own research notes! Confirmation bias it may have been, but incredibly exciting, nonetheless.

Understand the tribes and you start to understand their reactive logic, why they get easily offended at certain things, how you can better communicate with them, and how you can better predict what they will think or do in different situations.

My time in management consulting in my 30s really helped me to refine and apply these theories in practice. As a young psychologist, I was fortunate enough to be mentored for a time by a very influential management consultant and advertising executive who had drawn upon an incredible body of research and experience to arrive at his own personality profiling system. The short time I worked with him definitely helped to consolidate my thinking and stretch my understanding of human nature.

The type of consultancy we were involved in meant I was advising many leaders of teams in many different organisations on any given day. It was common to have a portfolio of three or four large clients, as well as many lighter-touch clients, where I was attempting to help with rolling out a major change initiative or influencing human behaviour in some way. Often our clients came to us because failure meant they became front page news. I was there to help them stay off the front page by helping to make sure people didn't go

Apes#!t. In these situations, you learn pretty quickly what works and what doesn't. Science is great but there is no better teacher than that of experience.

This is why I try to write stories that hopefully you can translate into your own history. Understanding Ape tribes and the individual differences between people within these tribes is powerful stuff. So powerful, in fact, that many people get lost in the enlightenment and good feeling that learning about our Ape naturally brings. It's probably worth reminding you here that it's how well we control our Ape that predicts success, not how much we worship it. Learn about it—but learn to control and change it. Don't let yourself fall into the trap of thinking that your Ape is who you are, or worse still, use it to explain away your own poor behaviour.

As we continue to explore the different Ape tribes, it will help you to embed the information if you can relate what we are talking about to your own situation. To help you work through this, we have even designed a simple five minute survey at decida.co to see what your tribe might be, where on the thinking-doing scale you might get your energy from, and how this changes your social perceptions and interactions. It's pretty cool, if I do say so myself! Doing this will help you personalise it, test it and apply it.

> *It's how well we control our Ape that predicts success, not how much we worship it. Learn about it—but learn to control and change it. Don't let yourself fall into the trap of thinking that your Ape is who you are, or worse still, use it to explain away your own poor behaviour.*

We're all individuals... kind of.

Ever notice how who you are tends to change depending on your social context and your physical environment? That, in different situations, you'll be the one to jump to action or the one who is more considered? How sometimes, when you hang around some people, you're the life of the party—yet around others you tend to go along for the ride? Sometimes you need to be alone with your own thoughts, and sometimes you need the energy of others.

This is because while our Apes tend to remain in their worldview-based tribes, we all move up and down the scale of flight or fight, between introversion and extraversion, between thinking and doing. There is a natural point on this scale that we tend to gravitate toward, a natural resting place where our Apes draw energy. Theory suggests this is because it's the point when as a child we learned to survive and thrive; it's where nature has determined we feel most comfortable and safe. This concept of feeling safe is important because fear is a strong driver of Ape behaviour. It is why, at the centre of our brain, we have what is commonly referred to as the 'fear centre' that drives our fight–freeze–flight instinct.

By now, we all know we have a neural fight, freeze or flight instinct linked to our amygdala—the place in our brain where chemicals are produced that influence our emotions and panic mechanisms. What is less obvious is that this fight–freeze–flight instinct is two ends of a continuous scale rather than dichotomous categories. Your Ape will have a degree of fight or flight when faced with a threatening situation. Halfway between the scale of fight or flight is freeze, which is the act of playing dead when faced with a predator (a very effective survival tactic in many circumstances).

In real life, I find talking about these responses as thinking (flight) and doing (fight) more helpful because it starts to speak to where you get your energy from. Plus, we're rarely attacked by wild animals nowadays. Everyone likes to muck in and do at times, and we all also have moments of introspection where we retreat, contemplate and recharge. However, there is a point between these extremes where your Ape will be in its happy place, a place that gives you energy, and a place where you seem to more naturally fit.

It is my current view, influenced heavily by cognitive development psychology, that the selection of our tribe and where we sit on the thinking and doing scale are socially directed. We form them in reaction to the world around us as we experience life. They're how you make meaning, and inform what needs to be done in order for you to survive in the future. Without a cognitive appreciation of your Ape, you basically let it run riot—unable to control or influence what you don't understand.

Let's have a look at the tribes and how people tend to differentiate within them.

In the diagram on the next page, you can see the sliding scale between thinkers and doers, and between flight and fight for each tribe, with the midpoint on the scale representing a freeze state. Remember, you tend to slide up and down this scale, depending on who you are around and the context you find yourselves in. What we are looking for is the point on the scale where you feel more comfortable, where you get your cognitive energy—a point on the scale where you go to rejuvenate and find motivation. Where you find yourself on this scale and what tribe you belong to changes the fears that drive behaviour, and what we do when we feel under threat in order to survive.

Are apes tribal?

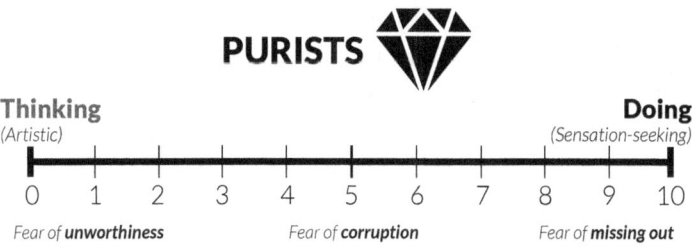

Let's go a little deeper and pick apart each of the tribes and what it might mean for you.

Tribe 1: The Groupies

The first tribe we should look at is the Groupies. Groupies process information and make meaning as it relates to or impacts the group, or how the group impacts them. Achievements are seen as worthy because the group says it is so. Peace and group harmony are more important than anything, unless of course that comes at the cost of achieving something the group deems important. For instance, a mild approach to climate change might be appropriate unless it's seen as imminently impacting individuals. Then, even if it causes discord, an aggressive approach to climate change feels right. The way you help most Groupies cycle up into a more positive mindset is by increasing interpersonal connectedness, and a sure-fire way to cycle them down into negative and destructive mindsets is to talk about power (or the loss of it).

Being a Groupie is all about social cohesion with the central value that we are stronger together. People who don't actively work to connect with the group are seen as weak points, outliers to be excluded in order to strengthen the core group. Social norms are rules to be strictly adhered to because they make the group stronger. Injustice is felt strongly when their efforts go unrecognised or others take credit for their work. Divergent opinions are encouraged, as long as you don't attack valued members of the group or value your own opinion over group consensus.

This is democracy in action. Hunt in packs. Allies are more important than experts or truth. Win on the measures we see as important. Hold the integrity and strength of the group as important. Individualism can flourish as long as it's not weakening the group or undermining its goals. Sometimes individual sacrifices need to be made in order to keep the group together. At a meta-social level, Australia and Ireland have very Groupie cultures.

For a Groupie, doing means achieving things that are relevant to the group. If others don't see it as something worth achieving, then it takes all the fun out of achieving it. Thinking means reconciling the many social paradoxes of the universe around us so you can keep the peace and navigate the complexity of life so others enjoy the ride as much as you. Because if people enjoy the ride, then the group will stay together. For someone with equal parts thinking and doing you realise the impossibility of being everything to everyone, so you make many contingency plans to account for different possible scenarios that could happen when people let each other down. You start to question everything, and I mean everything— yourself, others and the system—in order to best make plans for any eventuality.

The fear driving those at the thinking end of the spectrum is being seen as incompetent by others. This fear drives them to gather as much information about people and data as possible before siding with anyone on an argument. They seek pleasure and love food and big, comfortable things that help make them feel good about life. If they feel like they're being made to look stupid, they will react with anger—often quite explosively. Because they tend to take in all sides of an argument, they can be seen as peace-makers, so people often don't expect such explosive anger when it does erupt. Competence is seen as the way they get love and acceptance from the group. Guilt and shame are often hot on the heels of anger. Making them feel loved and comfortable, and recognising their intelligence in front of a group, helps them regain confidence.

The fear driving those who sit in the middle of the thinking–doing scale is of deception. They're fearful of being taken advantage of or used in some way, so they tend to question people's trust and motivations. This distrust of the future and others tends to make them good contingency planners, with many alternate plans ready at a moment's notice. Loyalty is paramount, and being betrayed by a friend is literally the most painful thing that can be experienced. When they cycle down mentally, they show lots of anxiety and start demanding to know the truth—but only believing it's the truth if their worst fears are confirmed. Random acts of kindness and thoughtfulness help them to regain trust and confidence.

The fear driving those toward the doing end of the scale is the fear of mediocrity. If you meet a G10 (a Groupie who is 10 on the scale of thinking–doing), they'll be highly driven to achieve goals that are determined to be valued by the group. They like to achieve and be rewarded for achieving. If you don't achieve goals, then you aren't recognised and life becomes less meaningful. The greatest pain you can feel is when someone does something you believe robs you of an achievement you think is rightfully yours. If you're helping to achieve their goals, you are their ingroup. If you're not, you become insignificant and somewhat tiresome to be around. When they cycle down, they get depressed and need to tick some things off their list to regain their confidence.

Tribe 2: The Authoritarians

While Groupies tend to focus on the strength of the ingroup, Authoritarians have an intuitive sense of the hierarchy of the group. They tend to be the people who can walk into a room and instantly know the influencers and the pretenders. Instead of holding the opinions of allies as important, they will refer to experts and data. If experts cannot produce data, they're no longer considered experts. Favours are traded—helping someone creates a credit that should be able to be cashed in at a later date at the discretion of the person holding the credit. Failure to come good when this credit needs to be cashed is considered betrayal, and fundamentally undermines trust. Power isn't a dirty word and society is stronger with strong, powerful leaders who aren't distracted by the complexities of human emotion or relationships. Safety of the group stems from the maintenance of order. As a general rule, this tribe is at its noble best when talking about justice and goes into a tailspin when focusing on control (which, to this group, is a very different construct to power).

It's all about system stability with the central value that we are stronger with a system that isn't broken. People who actively work to disrupt the order are seen as renegades, cowboys and threats that need to be extinguished for the safety of the group. Social norms are simply rules to maintain social order. If the system is broken, or data show social norms need to change, then fix it and move on. Injustice is when data are ignored and a decision flies in the face of evidence to the contrary. Divergent opinions not supported by evidence are discarded. At a meta-social level, England and China are quite Authoritarian cultures.

For an Authoritarian, doing means dominating your world in business and life generally, and thinking means analysing all of the data possible to dominate a particular field of expertise—to become an indisputable expert. For someone with equal parts thinking and doing, you know it's too hard to dominate the world around you and yourself, and therefore you spend time helping others to become the power in the system. In this way, you dominate through influence. You don't have to be the expert or the power. You just have to have influence with others who are.

The fear driving those at the doing end of the spectrum is of enslavement. This word feels strong (particularly to us Groupies) but this simply means people at this end of the spectrum fear being trapped or controlled by others. Shows of power and force become very important as deterrents for other bullies, and therefore they can be mistaken for bullies themselves at times. I guarantee courtrooms were designed initially by authoritarians. Everything about the intimidating physical design of a courtroom seeks to maintain order and seek justice. Intimidation is simply a tool of the powerful, and people who crack under pressure are either weak, unintelligent, guilty or liars. In a negative mindset, Authoritarians on the doing end of the spectrum display dominance. Helping them to feel strong and powerful again cycles them back up.

Towards the middle of the spectrum, the focus on being the overtly powerful authority shifts to be a more behind-the-scenes influencer. This comes from a realisation that, to get anything done, you work with the people who have influence and power, sometimes irrespective of their official hierarchical position. You help others and they help you. Help, therefore, is a form of influence. The real fear here is a fear of insignificance, but not in the eyes of others, which haunts the groupies—just living a life that does not significantly influence the world for the better. Power with a small group of allies is more important than being popular.

Data and information are collected and traded like currency, particularly information about people and projects, all with the goal of being an effective influencer on the system. If this feels a little evil, then you're probably not an Authoritarian. If it simply feels like this is the way the world works and you're somewhat dispassionate about it, then you might be an Authoritarian. When they feel threatened, Authoritarians will often look proud and a little patronising, but trust them with a little information and a feeling of inside influence, and they'll quickly cycle up again.

At the thinking extreme of the spectrum, the driving fear is that of loss—loss of assets, loss of key people, loss of financial security. If you feel under threat, you'll retreat and protect the things that you feel are yours. You conserve and preserve energy, and spending time building relationships with random people can be seen as a waste of time and resources. Hard data is the most powerful ally in any decision-making process, and anyone who ignores the data is simply a fool. This is a transactional approach that can come across as heartless, but it's not personal. It's just the way it is.

Tribe 3: The Purists

Being true to your ideals is more important than group cohesion or social order. In fact, chaos and anarchy can be necessary instruments to shake up a repressive system or buck a regime that holds different values to the ones you feel are more correct. It is more important to be right than popular, and sometimes being unpopular can be seen as validation that you must be right. Injustice is someone being forced to do something against their will and people compromising in order to get ahead are seen as weak and characterless. There is a right way to do things and people who try to diverge from what is seen as the right way are just arrogant or of low intelligence. Beauty is truth and appearance is important. Being controlled by others is seen as the ultimate betrayal of self. Social justice is more about equality and what's right, than reward for effort or evidence-based decision-making.

For a Purist, it feels illogical, infuriating and debasing to work with people who don't seem to have a position on something. You tend to give respect to people with strongly held opinions, even if they diverge from your own. You may despise people who hold views that offend your ideals, but you prefer them over those who seem to be people-pleasers. Purists value what they perceive is ideally right over relationships. In a Purist mindset, society will perish if we don't hold or aspire to ideals. At a meta-social level, America, Japan and France are quite Purist cultures.

For Purists, doing means experiencing all there is to life—sucking the marrow out of life as Henry David Thoreau put so eloquently in his poem. Thinking means becoming a master artist of whatever pursuit you pursue. The artisan cabinet maker, the most revered graphic artist, the most idealised leader. For someone with equal parts thinking and doing, you are torn between becoming the master of one thing and experiencing all that there is on offer, so you rely on perfecting the way to do things. You desire the perfect system, the perfect order, the perfect environment.

People who tend toward the doing end of the spectrum are driven by a deep fear of missing out. New or emerging ideas are incredibly attractive because you don't want to miss out on something that could be right. You seek sensations, and look to get the most out of every moment. Often spontaneous and prone to not finishing things, you'll find more energy in following your curiosities than in finishing projects.

People who gravitate more to the middle of the spectrum fear corruption. That is why we have a right way of doing things, so people (especially Groupies) don't game the system to create inequalities and unfair advantages. Fairness is equality, and injustice is when people win by not doing things in the correct way (which is interpreted as cheating or carelessness). Perfect quality and cleanliness are energising (even if hard to maintain at times). Pointing out when others have not lived up to your high standards and ideals is essential to upholding good standards. If standards slip, then society itself is at peril of crumbling. People who don't understand or don't care about the right way of doing things are less intelligent and untrustworthy. To move these people out of a reactive state, usually agreeing with them or letting them know they're the standard-bearer isn't a bad start. To a Groupie or Authoritarian, this will feel like ego-stroking. But to the Purist, it'll feel like they're being heard and respected.

Purists down at the thinking end of the spectrum are driven by a fear of being unworthy. A Purist musician may be unworthy of the craft, a religious person may be unworthy of the love of their god, or a Purist child may fear being seen as unworthy in the eyes of their parent. This fear of unworthiness to a higher ideal drives them to beaver away at things until they're worthy to be shown, and rarely does anything they do rise to the lofty ideals to which they aspire. When they cycle down, they can become indignant, which usually is the precursor to manic depressiveness. To cycle up, you often need to tell them you love what they do, because they won't love it. Because they see themselves as unworthy, they will often withdraw from, or even hurt relationships in order for the other people to fight for them. When they push away, they want to be pulled closer. It is in this effort they know they're loved.

Chapter snapshot

Key take-aways

1. It is important to know how different Apes react. Knowing how we see the world, and how the world interacts with us, is key to living in a more harmonious and collaborative way.

2. There are three main worldviews, or 'tribes of thought' that our reactive Ape tends to belong to: Purists, Groupies and Authoritarians.

3. Purists are driven by the right way to do things and what the perfect ideal is we should all be striving for (irrespective of popular opinion).

4. Groupies are concerned about their impact on others and are constantly looking for social validation and group connectedness.

5. Authoritarians believe relying on the group or idealistic notions is flawed, and actions and opinions should only be based on data. Data is truth and used as power to bring everyone around to that point of view..

Things I can do to practically apply this insight

- Go to decida.co and do the SDMF survey to explore what Ape you might be, and get some hints and tips on your possible strengths and blindspots.

- Think of someone that you find difficult to communicate with. To which Ape tribe do they belong.

- Practise changing the way you communicate with them by either focusing on the group dynamic impacts, the 'right' or ideal way of doing something, or find data that support your request or opinion. Find the thing that helps you communicate with them better.

Thought-starters

- We develop our dominant Ape tribe primarily in our childhood. The way we learn to survive and thrive pre-puberty tends to stick with us for life. What are the things that you think may have contributed to you developing into your Ape tribe?

- Are these experiences something that you value? Why?

- Are there others who are close to you who you suspect may belong to a different tribe? If so, does seeing their 'Ape logic' from the view of another tribe shed light on some of their behaviour and reactions?

Chapter 10

Living with your Ape

"Be yourself, everyone else is taken."
–Oscar Wilde

Switching between you and your Ape

We know identifying, labelling, understanding and then dealing with your Ape are essential to making sure you avoid poor decision-making and maximise opportunities. However, it's also worth exploring the times your Ape really does work for you, in your best interests. How do we know when to trust our instinct when it's our purpose-built survival mechanism? The very reason we have evolved with a reactive Ape is to help us navigate the complexity of the world around us. This has been key in helping us to become the dominant species on the planet.

Examples of our Apes working for us are present all around us. For example, the 10,000-hour rule Malcolm Gladwell popularised in his book *Outliers*—where he looked at the real difference between geniuses and the rest of us—identified ways we can train our Apes to help us win. Simply put, we can practise different activities enough to become expert. In fact, the description of 'talented' often relates to our Ape's ability to do something well without us having to really think about it. In this way, Apes can be our friend. This was highlighted in a story I ran across as part of my psychology undergrad class—a story about one of New York's finest.

In newspapers in the late nineties, it was reported there was a team of New York firefighters who showed up to an apartment building that was ablaze. This particular crew was a relatively young crew led by an experienced captain. They had trained hard for situations just like this, and they were a confident and tight-knit group. The captain and his team ran into the apartment, like they had done many times before, to look for survivors. This time, however, something didn't seem right to the experienced captain. Something seemed off. Much to the surprise and disappointment of his young crew, and despite a few protests, he abruptly turned around and ordered everyone out of the building. Moments after they had cleared the building, there was a loud explosion and the ground floor collapsed. Unknown to the crew, the blaze had been burning for some time in the basement and all of the supports for the ground floor had been compromised. If they had spent any more time in the building, they surely would have been killed.

The media present at the time had a field day with the story, hailing the captain as a sort of messianic figure. When the captain said he just sensed something was wrong, they wrote stories of ghosts who were whispering warnings in his ear, protecting angels released by relatives across the country who had sensed they needed to pray at that exact moment, and even dead residents of the building in ages past yelling warnings from the fire. Anybody with any sort of crackpot theory had their five minutes of fame. It was the talk of the city for months.

There were also some psychologists who took a real interest in the story, convinced there may have been something else going on, something that better explained this instinct of the experienced captain. With the city officials tired of the media circus and wild theories, the psychologists were granted time to interview the captain to get to the bottom of what seemed to be an intuitive call. What they concluded after their investigation changed the way we look at memory and cognitive capacity forever, and gave us another key insight into the way humans can put an immense amount of information into the implicit side of the brain to quickly make life-changing snap judgments.

What they found through some intense sessions and scenario-testing was that every event the captain had ever experienced had created a memory. These memories were then filed into a bank of sorts in the long-term, unconscious part of his brain. When we capture a memory, it's not lost or forgotten—just organised into a deep part of our brain that only our Ape can access. When the captain walked into that apartment, his Ape instinctively and instantly compared that room to every other memory of similar fire-ravaged rooms he had ever been in. And when that fast comparison was made, his Ape saw something was off, something was different—and Apes hate anything that's different. Difference or change is interpreted as potentially dangerous, so his Ape started to feel uneasy. Fortunately, the captain listened to his Ape and got himself and his team out of harm's way, just in the nick of time. *If you want to deep dive in to the fascinating science of the hippocampus and memory, start by searching for neuropsychologist Morris Moscovitch.*

This is why experience is so essential in all areas of life. It is the very conflict between the enthusiasm and counter-culture nature of youth and the experience and cool-headedness of our elders that helps us to move forward as a human race.

The difference seems to be that, in the face of imminent danger or threat, the Ape plays a crucial role in helping us to be decisive and confident when it matters most. However, the feeling of going Apes#!t is different from the intuition of experience. In fact, our fearful Ape can rely too much on experience when the noise of the youth or disruptors is inconvenient (we'll look at the status quo effect later). The key is to learn what is feels like when you're about to succumb to your reactive Ape. Identify it and train yourself to use different tricks to switch yourself out of your reactive Ape state, and more into your responsive state.

Remember former US Treasury Secretary, Robert Rubin, and his insights on reacting and responding with the prisoners? One technique he suggested to tame your Ape is simply to ask yourself in the moment of decision: Am I reacting, or responding right now?

This is something that's supported from my own experience Simply by asking this question you can 'switch' out of your Ape state into a more rational mindset. We want to respond to situations rather than react. When we are in a more responsive headspace, we are more likely to consider probable outcomes, assess the situation with a clearer head and make a better decision. This is one of many switch techniques that you can try.

We have also included below a list of the most common switch techniques we find individuals use to tame their Apes. These are just some of the more than 50 techniques you can find in our *Decida switch* app.

Not all of these techniques will work for you. The trick is to pick a few that resonate with you and practise them so you learn to apply them before your Ape goes a bit ballistic. If applied with some tact, these can also be used to help others calm down when they're going Apes#!t.

Name it

When you mask your emotions, you limit your cognitive capacity. Use the 'Name it' switch to free cognitive capacity for the task at hand.

1. Stop. Recognise the emotions that are triggering your Ape (if it helps, use the emotion wheel below).
2. Acknowledge the emotions and call them out by name, "I am feeling ___"
3. Rate the intensity.
4. Recognise the trigger that caused the emotions. Re-look at the situation without these emotions.

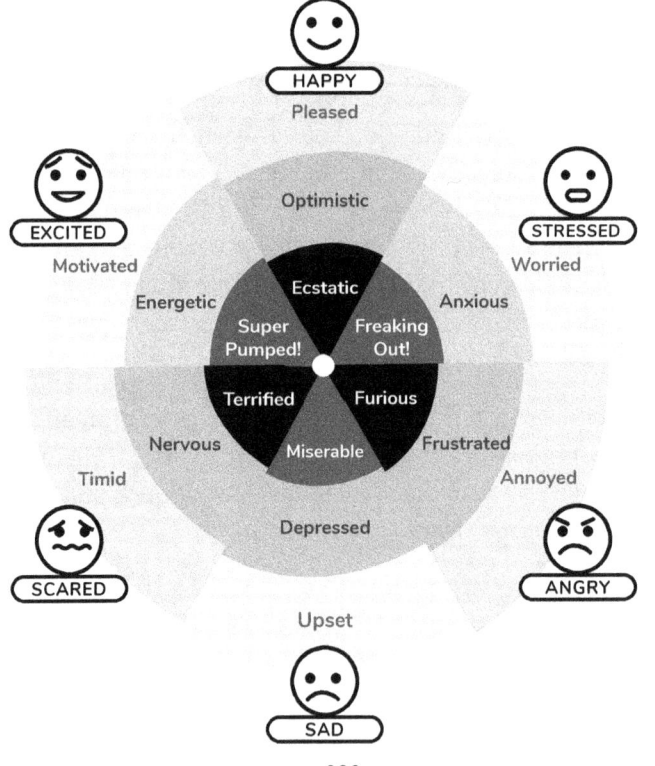

Box breathing

In yoga, this is commonly called square breathing. Controlled deep breathing lowers your stress hormones by 30 per cent, which has an instant physiological impact on your body and increases your ability to perform competently.

1. Sit comfortably in a chair with your hands resting on your knees.
2. Close your eyes and focus only on the rise and fall of your stomach as you breathe.
3. Breathe in while slowly counting to four. Hold for four. Breathe out for four. Hold for four.
4. Repeat at least 10 times.

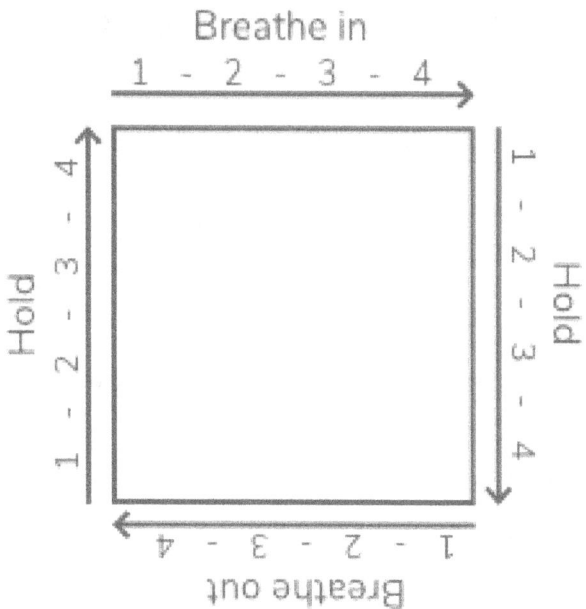

Time

Giving your Ape some time helps to create distance between the cause and any effect, and can allow you to become more mindful of context and circumstances. Time allows the chemicals and emotions that overwhelm the brain to dissipate.

1. When something triggers your Ape, don't react. No texts, no emails, not even a phone call—nothing.
2. Choose a time frame to wait to respond (e.g. 24 hours) in order to give your Ape time to calm down.
3. Go for a walk or try some other switch to distract you until the time has elapsed.
4. Once the time limit is up, reassess how you are feeling. If your Ape is still triggered and will react and not respond, give yourself more time.
5. Repeat this process until you are back in control.

Role Model

Creating cognitive distance by externalising gives perspective. Identifying with a role model focuses your attention on constructive problem solving.

1. Bring to mind a mentor or respected role model.
2. Think about what they would do in this circumstance and what their advice would be?
3. Be the person you respect. Do what you think they would do.

Significance

Our Ape only really considers short term or immediate impacts. When we are controlled by our Ape, it's difficult to see issues with the perspective of time, but doing so can help us return to our rational selves.

1. Ask yourself "Will this matter in 10 years' time?"
2. If no, let it go.
3. If yes, find a way to address this situation constructively, simply, and without emotion. The APSI templates at decida.co are helpful tools.

Reframe

Our brain is hard-wired to make snap judgments on little and often incomplete information. Changing the story allows us to see other possibilities and motivations, which changes our immediate emotional responses. We bombard our minds with negative thoughts, and terrifying reasons not to do things. These self-limiting beliefs just prevent you from becoming the best version of yourself.

1. Write down the story you are telling yourself, or the meaning you are making from someone's action.
2. Rewrite your thoughts, changing the language and removing the personal judgment to be less emotive.
3. Challenge whether this is assumption or fact. What evidence is there to support this story you're telling?
4. Now consider the story you should be telling yourself, that is constructive and not destructive, and what you can do about it.

Fake email

Important note: Apes should never send emails! Simply by writing your Ape thoughts down, you are more likely to focus on the responding in a more measured way rather than reacting to the individual.

1. Open up a note-taking app or word document and write the email or text you want to send.
2. Once you have finished, delete your writing.
3. Then, compose the email or text you should send.

Walk

Walking releases feel-good chemicals in the brain, making you feel better and allowing for a broader perspective to be considered. Additionally, taking some time to yourself allows you to calm your body, separate yourself from the situation, and think clearly.

1. Stop what you are doing and quietly go for a walk in nature.
2. Pick something to focus on during your stroll (e.g. plant, animal, art) and be intentionally curious.
3. As you are returning, use the quiet time to think about what triggered you and why it had such an impact.

In order to give you the tools to best switch out of your reactive state and to help others switch out of theirs, we have created an app you can find in the different app stores called *Decida switch*. This will take you through the most commonly used psychological switches and enable you to save your favourite ones to practise in real life. If the thought of an app doesn't work for you, we also have physical switch cards you can order at decida.co.

Sex and money

It's impossible, and probably irresponsible, to talk about Apes and emotional decision-making, without talking about sex and money. No two concepts are more wedded to our emotions than these two. Power, fear, status, self-worth, trust and identity are all enmeshed with sex and money, with confidence, familiarity and learning to delay gratification all playing a huge part in the quality of our decisions and our ability to cope with the accompanying social complexity and maturity in these areas. These areas are complex. Sex and money speak directly to how loved, accepted and needed we are by others. These are very human, core psychological survival constructs. What people often underestimate is how financial or sexual traumas in the past can impact the decisions we make in the present—even when the link between the two things may seem illogical or, at least, unobvious.

Part of this is because trauma, whether it be financial or sexual, is often a collection of interwoven experiences over time. Yes, there can be some major events that have a significant impact on our psyche and need to be specifically explored in a safe way to understand the hidden influence they exert on our thoughts and behaviour. But we aren't about to do that here.

These matters are incredibly individual and sensitive, and to pick at the wounds of the trauma you've experienced in your life without due care, support and attention would be reckless. This is why we have psychologists who can help explore the impact our past has on our present. Wounds don't tend to heal in the dark. Light needs to be shed on them in order for healing to take place, and this needs to be done with care, in a safe space, and in whatever time it needs to take.

However, with this firmly in mind, my continued view on these matters is, irrespective of past trauma, learning to control your Ape means these experiences can have a significantly reduced influence on your perception and decision-making. In fact, controlling your Ape is the first step to healing in a lot of cases. Many times, we come to love the story that defines us, and sometimes the more tragic it is, the more we love it. Changing the story is scary, and we've talked about how much our Apes hate change. Sometimes the chains that bind become more comforting than the world without restraint.

Control your Ape and become the master of your past experiences, rather than having them master you.

I know this to be true of myself because I was one of those people who found themselves taken advantage of sexually while I was still underage. By no means is this a secret, and I've spoken on these experiences many times very consciously to aid in my own healing and in the healing of others who have shared similar experiences. However, it was only later in life when I learned to control my Ape that I realised my Ape-taming reduced the impact of these experiences on my decision-making. It was me learning to recognise the moments I was going Apes#!t, examining why those moments made me go Apes#!t and controlling them more in the future that actually improved my decision-making. It wasn't so much that my experience was making me a poor decision maker, but that controlling my Ape reactions made me a better one.

The same goes for financial trauma. I've travelled with many people going through bankruptcy, getting scammed out of savings, having a co-investor run off with money, giving sizeable loans to friends in good faith that never get paid back—even receiving unplanned bills or the humiliating experience of being chased by debt collectors. Even simply being born into poverty can be a traumatic experience, particularly in western society.

Many people have to navigate these harrowing experiences, with their Apes picking up all sorts of scars along the way. Learning from your past experiences in a way that maximises your future opportunities is hard, it's painful and it often feels unjust. But it's crucial. Your Ape's primary function is to protect, but sometimes the very same mental processes you put in place to protect can turn into controlling inhibitors. At some point, the hard crust that forms to heal scars needs to fall away for the new skin to emerge.

The reason these topics feel so personal is because they speak to our deep need to belong and our general fear of rejection. Experiencing a breaking of trust in these areas, or trauma, can create fractures that not only echo throughout our own lives but in the lives of those around us and through the generations that come after us. Due of the severity of these traumas, our Apes often strive to protect us in ways that can be highly illogical and sometimes even hurtful.

Our Apes push away the ones we love so they won't hurt us. Our Apes hold on to those that hurt us to confirm our own poor beliefs of ourselves. Our Apes get anxious and smother the people we should trust with panic and doubt. Our Apes avoid confrontation and become resentful of those we should be journeying with. Our Apes inflict similar pain onto other people so they might understand what we've had to go through. I guarantee one of these statements resonated with you. Why? Because, deep down, we're all human and the human story is filled with patterns of behaviour that repeat throughout the ages. It's up to us to stop the cycle and rise above reactive decision-making.

To do this we must at least acknowledge that our Apes often hurt us and those around us, and rob us of amazing opportunities and beautiful experiences out of fear and shame. Avoiding repeating traumatic experiences isn't ignoble, but at times it becomes more important to your Ape than the people or prospects right in front of you. Sometimes this is compounded by us creating self-fulfilling prophecies based on the meaning we make from past experiences, which harden our hearts toward people and situations and therefore results in similar outcomes, confirming your initial bias and hardening your heart even more. It's really difficult, and sometimes painful, to be vulnerable in the face of traumatic past experiences—but a soft heart and a gracious mind are keys to unlocking your true potential.

Just because it's happened one way in the past doesn't mean it will happen that way in the future, particularly if you have more control over your Ape this time around. In the words of one of my childhood rock legends, Bob Hartman:

> *"Don't let your heart be hardened,*
> *Don't let your love grow cold.*
> *May it always stay so childlike,*
> *May it never grow too old."*
>
> *-Bob Hartman*

Grieving Apes

There are some circumstances where we shouldn't try to switch our Ape on or off—where we actually need our Ape to go through a neurological process in order to make sense of what is going on. One of these processes is when we experience change or grief. Whether it be the loss of a loved one, loss of a process or loss of a capability, it all requires us to experience grief. Trying to suppress Apes during this process can have horrible repercussions later in life.

Managing grief or change can be simple or complex, but it always requires us to help Apes through the grieving process—not around it.

Grief can be as simple as the loss of your normal way to work due to roadworks, as complex as the loss of a life partner or as painful as the loss of a friendship. The time the process takes, and the strength of the emotions felt throughout the process, depend a lot on the individual involved and the circumstances of the loss. However, we all experience loss, and when we do, the process we need to go through is as predictable as the sunrise. What we need to do is all be aware of this process, and then allow Apes to do what they need to do in a safe way in order to get to the other side, stronger for the experience.

I had a recent experience which grieved me considerably. It was a situation where trust was undermined and I was forced to explore the difference between my perception and reality.

Bear in mind: I don't simply have colleagues at work. I make friends with them. I build deep trusted relationships, and if I can't seem to make you a friend, then I tend to stop working with you. It's not as harsh as it sounds because I do make friends easily, and I tend to be a trusting sod. My Ape values trust and loyalty, and what is a friendship (or indeed a good working relationship) that doesn't have these qualities?

My story of grief involves one of these work relationships. I'd been working with Dave for a few years and considered him to be a very close friend. We were allies in the political reality that you often find yourself in with any organisation. Dave and I worked together, laughed together, shared experiences together and trusted each other. We were friends, true mates as we would say in Australia. When it came time for Dave to leave the organisation, I expected we'd remain friends like I do with most people when we go separate ways. We might not see each other much but we'd still be trusted friends. I have lots of relationships that I have built up over time as I have traversed many diverse industries in my career, and I keep and value them all dearly. My Ape likes to be liked and is very loyal to people when we create lines of trust.

A few months after Dave left to find greener pastures, I missed out on an opportunity to speak at a small conference that I was really looking forward to. It wasn't a major event by any stretch of the imagination, but for some reason I really wanted to do this particular conference. I had been sharing with Dave for many years about my desire to speak at this event, but the stars never really aligned for numerous reasons—one year I wasn't in town, and another year I had a conflict of interest that ruled me out. This year I was available but my topic wasn't seen as aligning well enough to the theme of the conference, so once again the opportunity slipped out of my hands. Soon after, I had lunch with Dave and articulated my disappointment. We had a great lunch together and went our separate ways again.

However, a few weeks later when the speaker line-up was announced, I discovered Dave was on the list, and my Ape couldn't help but feel the pang of betrayal. It wasn't that he was speaking and I wasn't. His acceptance had absolutely nothing to do with my not speaking—there were many speakers on the list and I was genuinely happy for him. The reason for my feeling of betrayal was he hadn't even mentioned he'd applied for the conference, let alone been offered a slot. I had the crushing feeling that, while I'd seen Dave as a friend, he'd only ever seen me as a contact. In that moment, I felt our trust line had been betrayed. In that moment, I felt I'd lost a trusted friend, or at least realised the friendship I thought existed may never have been there in the first place.

To some, this will seem like a childish reaction, and reading back on it now, it doesn't seem too seismic. That's the thing about Apes. It never usually makes sense. It is reactive and often illogical. I was hurt by the loss of what I'd considered a trusted friendship. Even if I didn't really have it in the first place, I thought I had it and that's enough. It was as if the ally

I thought I had simply disappeared. My Ape was grieving the loss of a valued relationship. And it hurt. Dammit.

Many of the situations we've discussed regarding going Apes#!t are in contexts when you feel angry, frustrated, tired, fearful, or when the situation is something you've had a lot of experience in, and something goes against what is expected. However, this is a situation where my Ape was guiding my reactions without any possibility of my more rational self being able to exert control. For all of us, this is simply the process our Apes go through when dealing with loss.

Of course, the magnitude of the Ape's reaction changes wildly depending on the circumstance of the loss, but what doesn't seem to change is the process that our Apes go through in order to process and deal with the loss. This process is often called the 'seven stages of grieving' because it was first discovered by carers who were helping families impacted by loved ones who had terminal cancer. What we see is we go through the same psychological process whenever we experience loss of any kind. We can't stop the process but we can reduce the impact it has on ourselves and others, and sometimes even the speed at which we can navigate the journey.

Almost as influential as Kahneman and Tversky's behavioural insights were the incredible observations first made by Swiss-American psychiatrist Elisabeth Kübler-Ross in her 1969 book, *On death and dying*. She noticed people all go through common stages when dealing with grief. While this observation was made during her time of looking after terminally ill patients and their families, it's become more obvious in recent years that this is more than just about helping people through the loss of a loved one. It's the brain's way of processing any loss. The brain needs to grieve any loss—the only difference is the magnitude of the grief, and the speed at which people tend to move through the stages.

Kübler-Ross's initial five stages of grief have been expanded upon over the years with most practitioners agreeing on seven stages:

1. Shock and denial
2. Guilt and shame
3. Anger and bargaining
4. Depression, loneliness and isolation
5. Turning the corner
6. Reconstructing the future
7. Acceptance and hope.

You can even see this mental process play out with the smallest of losses, like hitting roadworks on the way to work and being asked to take a detour. Instantly, you can feel your Ape kick in, usually with a second of shock, a hint of anger and frustration and a moment of depression as you

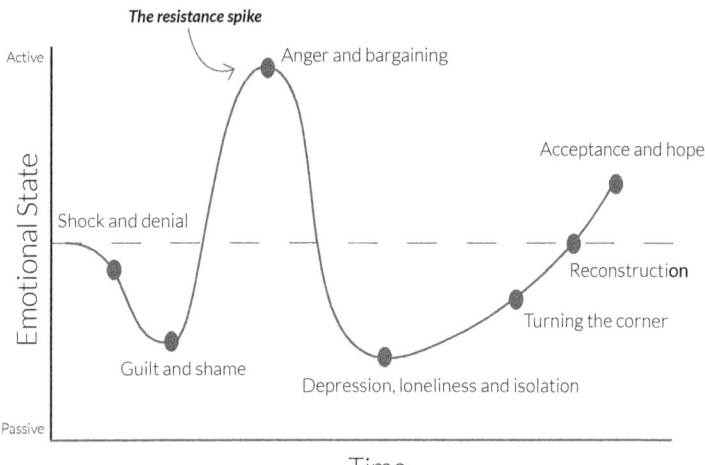

The emotional states of the seven stages of grieving change over time.

realise you'll be late. Once you accept the new situation, you realise it's actually not as bad as you thought and you head into the day, back on track. This may have only taken a few minutes but you actually went through each stage. Even if outwardly you didn't show much of this, inwardly these are the psychological stages you need to go through.

The way to manage change has a lot to do with recognising and managing people through these stages of grief. There are many ways to do this, depending on the nature and context of the change. Ultimately though, Apes are running the show in times of change, and to ignore or dismiss them only leads to chaos and distress. During change, you will want to know the what, why and how, but your Ape needs time and space to grieve. Your Ape is less fixed on what it could gain and more concerned about what it could lose.

When I first heard about Dave and the conference, I think I went quite quickly through shock into a state of self-blame. I obviously wasn't friend-worthy. I was untrustworthy. It was my own openness and enthusiasm that led to this. Or maybe I'm just being stupid. I'm making a mountain out of a molehill—we were never that close, obviously I'd misread our friendship. It was my fault I'm feeling this way. I tried to suppress these thoughts, but they just seemed to keep niggling in the back of my thoughts and draining my energy. It was only after about a week of this self-deprecation that I realised I was in grief and rang my colleague, Roshelle, to vent. I know I needed to push through feelings of anger and to get to a space where those around me didn't let me become too depressed. At the very least, I realised I might need a bit of TLC to quickly turn the corner.

After I spent some time journaling—literally venting and articulating my grief on a page—I was able to turn the corner and stop looking at the grief, reconstruct the new reality and accept the trust and friendship I have with so many other close friends. This is the great thing about understanding the grieving process. It doesn't stop it hurting, or avoid the pain, but it can help us navigate the process much quicker so we don't get stuck and it enables us to rebound quickly. In a way, this is the essence of emotional resilience.

I should quickly mention here that, when it comes to organisational change management or having difficult conversations, sometimes you need to communicate or negotiate in a way that avoids triggering people's Apes and the grieving process. I deal with this situation directly when we talk about APSI, which we won't elaborate on in this book. For now, let's look at an easy way to memorise the stages of grief.

Memorising the stages of grief

I can't iterate enough how helpful it is to memorise the stages of grieving and what they mean. I use it almost every week in my life to deal with any sort of change, or to help others through the change process. But we're all human and trying to rote learn the stages simply won't work for something that you don't think about or practise every day.

If I need to remember or understand something, I tend to come up with simple stories or analogies to help me remember it. To remember something slightly complicated like this, I use a simple location-based visualisation trick. It is the same trick magicians use to memorise whole decks of cards or long sequences of numbers.

All you need to do is think of a physical journey or space you know very well. It could be the regular route you take when running, walking through your house, entering your place of work or going to your favourite shop. The point is it's a journey or space you know very well with imagery already burned into your brain. Once you've decided on a journey or space, take that journey in your mind and place objects along it that trigger other information. This way, you not only remember the information but also the order it should go in. If you choose a meaningful object, it can even remind you of other nuances of the things you are trying to remember.

To help explain, let me take you on the memory journey I created to help me memorise the seven stages of grief. It's the journey I take at the beginning of my morning run. It's part of my regular routine, the images of which are very, very familiar to me.

In my mind, I walk up to my electric gate and see a monkey sitting on top of the fence being given an electric shock. I stare in disbelief and there you have the first stage: shock and disbelief.

As I open the gates to keep going, I walk through the middle, still looking at the monkey. I accidentally stub my toe on the small metal gate stopper that sits in the middle of the road. I hop around in pain and tell myself that was a stupid thing to do and how could I possibly be so silly as to stub my toe on something that has always been there. Here's stage two: pain, doubt and blame.

Once the pain has subsided, I continue on my journey down my long driveway. After about 20 metres, there's a point that indicates the end of our property and the start of my neighbour's. As I approach that point, I see my neighbour there and he's furious at something. He won't let me pass unless I agree to something. (I should point out, my neighbour is one of the most pleasant and mild-mannered men I've ever met, which makes this make believe scene even

more memorable.) This is the third stage:
anger and bargaining.

Once I'm past my neighbour's property, I see a small natural gully or depression next to the road, which takes the water away during a heavy storm. As I approach their driveway, I see three monkeys like the famous 'hear no evil, see no evil, speak no evil' monkeys. One monkey is sitting in the natural depression in the land. Another monkey is looking at the other monkeys, but their backs are to him. The third monkey is a little distance away. Welcome to the fourth stage: depression, loneliness and isolation.

I finally reach the end of my driveway and turn the corner and look down the road. Stage five: turning the corner.

As I continue down the road, I walk under some scaffolding two or three stories high, with some workers working furiously on something buried within the scaffolding. Stage six: reconstructing reality.

Finally, I walk past the Lutheran church that's on the corner of my block and I see a big sign out the front that says, 'Jesus is hope'. I walk into the church and I'm greeted by the minister with a big hug. I've reached the final stage:
hope and acceptance.

Now, while it's a story that's taken some time to explain to you in written form, it only takes a couple of seconds in my mind to complete. Since I've created this mind journey narrative, I have never forgotten these seven steps, their order and what they mean. And, in the moment when I'm deep in conversation and watching someone go through this cognitively painful grief process, I have found it invaluable to draw upon this information to help clarify my own thoughts and understand what's happening.

I encourage you to try this now with the stages of grief:
1. Shock and disbelief
2. Pain, doubt and blame
3. Anger and bargaining
4. Depression, loneliness and isolation
5. Turning a corner
6. Reconstructing reality
7. Hope and acceptance.

Pick a familiar journey or space and make up a story to help you remember the stages. Then test yourself tomorrow and see if you still remember it. You'll surprise yourself with how much information you can retain this way after a little practise.

Chapter snapshot

Key take-aways

1. You are NOT your Ape.

2. Your ability to tame your Ape and switch from your unconscious, reactive Ape to your more conscious, responsive self is what is important.

3. Switches are simple activities or thought changers that help tame your Ape, and stop you from going Apes#!t when triggered. They don't stop you being triggered—they just help you be less reactive to the trigger.

4. Grieving Apes go through the seven-step process of:
   > Shock and denial
   > Guilt and shame
   > Anger and bargaining
   > Depression, loneliness and isolation
   > Turning the corner
   > Reconstructing the future
   > Acceptance and hope

Things I can do to practically apply this insight

- Start practicing different switches to identify strategies that particularly resonate with you. Consider getting some *Decida switch* cards, or download the app for more inspiration.

- Talk about how you are using switches with those around you. This will help them know what to do when you are going Apes#!t.

- Journal your experiences (again, the *Decida 10 minute journal* is a great guide if you struggle to do this) so you can better track and reflect on your experiences over time.

- Use the visualisation memory trick to help you memorise the stages of grief. You will never regret this, and will find yourself applying it to so many conversations about loss (not just the loss of a loved one).

Thought-starters

- What are the things that often trigger your Ape? Why do you think you're so reactive to these triggers?

- Think of a time when you have been overly reactive in the past. Have there been any long-term consequences for that reactivity?

- Do you tend to trigger someone else in your life regularly? Why is that?

Section D

Influencing Apes

Being the better Ape

Chapter 11

We're all going Apes#!t!

"Those who are offended easily should be offended more often."
–Mae West

Helping others switch

It's one thing to manage our own Apes. It's quite another to help manage other people's Apes. Having a team member or colleague who is going Apes#!t kills collaboration, undermines the creative process, and creates a host of lose-lose outcomes for the individual and the team.

Ironically, when we let people go Apes#!t without managing it, we can often feel like it's the right thing to do because we've avoided the pain of conflict (and our brains tend to not like the pain of conflict). Meanwhile, the person who went Apes#!t has had their ego fed because they feel justified in their Apeness. Avoid conflict and keep your problem children happy. Right? Wrong. This never leads to good outcomes in the long run.

The trick is to calm Apes in a constructive way and focus people's energy on the correct pathway without inflaming the situation. In trying to do this, sometimes we swing too far the other way—we match conflict with conflict, thinking there is nobility in attacking things head-on. Unfortunately, while this sometimes does work in very limited contexts (usually where there's a very clear hierarchical situation and the person in the higher power situation is calling out political gamesmanship of clearly unethical behaviour), a large portion of Ape behaviour can be brought under control by employing some simple switch techniques.

What won't work is talking rationally. You can't engage rationally with other people's Apes. Apes are instinctual, not rational. Trying to argue logic to an Ape will, more often than not, inflame the situation. If you recognise someone is going Apes#!t, you need to talk to their Ape to calm them down before being able to talk logic. These switch techniques are practical things you can do to help switch others out of their emotional, instinctive Ape state and into their more rational mindset.

Below are four of my favourite switch techniques I use to tame other people's Apes. It's important to note not all techniques will work for you. Just pick a couple that resonate and then practise them so you train your Ape to use them instinctively when you see others' Apes going crazy. If the switches you choose don't seem to work for you, come back to the list and choose a couple of others to try.

Parking lot

If you are in a group meeting that is being hijacked by Apes, a parking lot reassures Apes their view is heard, allowing the meeting to move swiftly on without appearing rude or brushing aside a point that might escalate Ape reactions.

1. Allow people to briefly articulate their thoughts.

2. Capture their thoughts somewhere visual (i.e. write a note or scribe on a whiteboard).
3. Put the note in a place where everyone can see it, and make sure they know you will come back to it later.
4. Refocus the conversation on the objective or key task at hand.

Active listening

When you listen to understand, you demonstrate that you comprehend the person and care, reducing their reactivity and building trust. People calm down when they can tell their story and know that it's heard.

1. Pause what you are doing and without blame, judgment or distraction really pay attention.
2. Don't interrupt, just be attentive and hear them out.
3. Use the last three words of key sentences and reframe them as a question (i.e. If they say, "I just don't feel that Dave respects my true talent", you would then say, "Your true talent?" This shows you're listening and allows them to further explore their feelings.
4. Summarise what they've said back to them and allow them to nuance if they don't feel you've summarised correctly.

Respond

When you're confronted with an angry person, it's easy to react, often making the situation worse. If you respond calmly and stay in control, you can often defuse the situation quickly.

1. Ask yourself, "am I reacting or responding right now?"

2. Let go of your own ego and don't take things personally. You can't reason with someone who's angry.
3. Acknowledge them and how they are feeling so they know you are paying attention.
4. Be generous and patient. Wait until they've calmed down. You may need to give them time and space.
5. When the time is right, ask what you can do to support them.

Experience nature

Research has shown that spending time in the great outdoors lowers our blood pressure and eases muscle tension.

1. Go for a walk together.
2. Go somewhere green and peaceful such as a garden or park.
3. Get outside into the fresh air, breathe deeply and observe the small wonders in nature.
4. Let them drive the conversation. If they want to talk, that's OK, but if they don't, that's fine too. Just being present will be helpful (especially for Groupies).

Sometimes, simple switch techniques aren't enough. In complex situations with history, high emotion or political complexity, you may need to go a little deeper to calm the farm. Remember that Apes are tribal. If your Ape is of a different tribe to the person you're helping, there are things you'll need to do that will feel silly or weird to you but will help them to control their Ape. Similarly, if you try to calm their Ape in the way that works for Apes in your tribe, you'll actually inflame the situation, triggering their Apes to go even more Apes#!t.

Debating Apes

In my time, I've found that trying to argue against religious or political beliefs with logic is like trying to recite Shakespeare with a mouth full of marshmallows. It will never work. It's not that people with certain religious or political beliefs are stupid. It's that religious or political beliefs are Ape decisions, and using apologetics to change their mind is the irrational bit. If you decide to be a Christian, an atheist, Buddhist, agnostic, Muslim or a follower of the magic rahjah-baha of the far eastern marshmallow people of ultimate enlightenment, it's your Ape that decides and defends that position (and we then use our own logic to defend our Ape's choice).

When you see two people hotly debating two philosophical beliefs, what you're usually witnessing is two people's Apes going at it. This can be really fascinating and mentally stimulating to watch but it rarely changes someone's point of view. When Apes get into defensive positions, logic and rational thought rarely comes into the argument.

No matter how high someone's IQ, influencing their religious or political beliefs is all about influencing Apes and not about logic at all. Even when someone thinks they're convinced by a logical argument, what you usually find is their Ape had already made its mind up to change and they'd simply found a voice or argument to help them feel OK about their decision. This can be confusing when you first think about it, so let me explain the absurdity of this behaviour with a story. It's one of my life-long close friend Hawko (not his real name but he really is one of my closest friends of the past 30 years) and me.

I am a psychologist who believes in evidence-based practice, while Hawko is a strong advocate of a local self-help group that uses little or no evidence. On the other hand, I am a faith-based Christian and Hawko is a hard-core atheist who derides religion based on a lack of empirical evidence. You can imagine the discussions we get into after a glass or three of scotch! I love this guy—I am a better human for being around him. It's just that he's so hilariously wrong most of the time. Or at least my Ape thinks so.

Hawko had gone through a pretty rough patch in life, in both work and marriage, but he was getting things together now and looking better than he had in a long time. One of the reasons he gave for getting his life back on track was a so-called self-help group he'd contributed quite a chunk of finances to, through different learning modules and resources. Now, this could totally be worth the investment if it's turning lives around but, to me, it smelled more like a cult. It felt like something that could be helpful on the surface but then would catch you in a loop of dependency and financial loss.

One of the red flags for me was that the group preached psychologists have it all wrong. They claimed they'd found the only truth and their framework was the only way to truly remove things that block someone's progress to success. I don't know about you, but I always find that when someone tells me they have some magical insight that no-one else has, it's a sure sign they're bulls#!tting. It basically says: "Don't worry about testing whether or not this is right. We've already done all that and it turns out we're right!"

For anyone who's going through a really tough time and is emotionally burdened, the offer to lighten cognitive load in any way is hugely attractive—and Hawko was no exception. He was definitely at a major low point in his life. He'd found solace in the group, which was awesome, but I was concerned they were leveraging this emotional crutch to take advantage of him financially. As a friend, I wanted to be supportive and, as a friend, I equally felt I had to let him know of my concerns. But whenever I did, I felt like I was just reinforcing this idea that modern psychologists represented the enemy.

One day—in a bid to quell my suspicious and somewhat poor assessment of his group—Hawko invited me along to an open night. It was basically a 'bring your friend' night designed to sell the program to those you think would benefit from it… like a church seeker service without the organised religion bit.

So I went along with my identities as both friend and psychologist firmly in place. I was convinced I could listen and dissect the event rationally and, if I presented my thoughts and arguments back to him, his intellect would see through the bulls#!t and be less likely to be taken advantage of in his vulnerable state. Boy, was I about to be disappointed.

Undeterred, I sat in the very front row with my iPad on my lap, furiously typing notes as everyone around me was caught up in the hype of the event. I noticed as I glanced up that many of the organisers were giving me concerned looks, probably because I must have looked like a reporter, or even worse, an academic! Still I persisted, making detailed notes of what was being said and pointing out any inaccuracy, half-truth or trick being used to sell the program to other vulnerable people in the room.

One trick is to use success testimonials. If 20 people do something but it only works for a few, get those few people to get up on stage and tell their story. It will seem like they're a representative sample of the group and people will think that it works 100 per cent of the time. This is an information fallacy that people are tricked by all the time. We're just not built to notice the absence of something or to be good at probability. We just take the information we have and then generalise it to what we like to think we already know.

Let me show you this effect by asking a simple question.

Bob is an opera fan who enjoys touring art museums when he's on holiday. Growing up, he enjoyed playing chess with family members and friends.

Which situation is more likely?
> Bob plays cello for a major symphony orchestra.
> Bob is a farmer.

Most people intuitively say that Bob is likely to play cello for a major symphony orchestra. Our Ape brain takes the small amount of information given about Bob, and then pattern-matches it to our preconceptions of a farmer or an orchestra player to come to an instant conclusion about likelihood. Bob sounds artsy, so he's more likely to be an orchestra player.

Statistically, that would be incorrect. In 2014, the National Endowment for the Arts reported there were 1224 professional orchestras in the US. With an orchestra employing an average of 10 cellists in each orchestra, this makes 12,240 professional cellists in a population of 320,878,310 nationwide. That's a 1 in 26,215.5 chance that Bob is a cellist. However, with the Business Insider putting the number of employed farmers in the US at 2.6 million, you have a 1 in 123 chance that Bob is a farmer. Bob is much more likely to be a farmer.

Our intuitive Ape brains just aren't built for probability or likelihood analysis—it's way too complicated. We much prefer to look at case studies that we think are indicative, which is why testimonials work.

Sitting in the audience of the self-help show, I knew of hundreds of reported cases where their system had not worked for people, where the result of following their advice had ruined families and caused great trauma, even suicides. The process of cutting family off, 'removing those who would seek to block your true potential', or 'ripping the band-aid off your wounds and ringing people to confront the injustices of your past', sounds good to Apes in the moment. This reactive Ape behaviour has many unintended and potentially devastating consequences. Instead of isolating from one family member, it often isolates them from their whole family. Instead of healing wounds, it often forces people into defensive positions where memories of events may differ dramatically between people, creating even more distrust and trauma. Most devastatingly, when it doesn't work, people think it works for others and so consider themselves the problem—that there is something in their core DNA which makes them unlovable, unwanted and unsuccessful. You can only imagine where this thought noodle often ends up.

What I was seeing at the event was a self-confirmation loop for people for whom it had worked—the program had unlocked relational and financial success. No mention of the potential pitfalls to be aware of or the idea these people may have been likely to be successful anyhow. The program just got lucky that it happened to be a part of their story.

This problem of statistics and self-confirmation was one of 36 major issues I had with the program. Thirty of those practices, I concluded, would put my own registration as a psychologist in jeopardy if I promoted them.

Proudly holding my list and assessment, I thought I had him. Surely he'd see the error of his ways and renounce the cult for what it was—taking advantage of (and money from) good people when they were at their most vulnerable. However, it didn't work like that. Hawko simply dismissed my evidence as the influence of the flawed thought processes of modern-day psychology, and said it worked for him in a great time of need where many other things hadn't. That was all the information he needed to know; it was true enough for him.

This was a great lesson for me. I had appealed to his intellect but he had responded with his Ape—calmly, I might add, but this was his Ape's reasoning. He couldn't care about the science because the group satisfied his Ape's need to belong and feel accepted in a time when his marriage and work were being torn apart. In his time of trauma, they were there for him. He didn't care if their intent was good or if their methods were psychologically sound. It worked for him. And that was enough.

At that moment, I realised all I should do as his friend was be happy for him that he felt safe (which he did) and remain close enough to him to help him avoid some potential negative side effects, and just be there for him (which I was). Holding my ground and debating intellectually with him would only have served to distance our own relationship and push him even further into the arms of the cult, who were to him the only ones to 'truly' understand. This is why many families lose family members to cults. If a family member starts to be lured or attracted to a cult, become friends with their new friends rather than the advisor. Accepting their new friends says you accept them and their choices as individuals and, in time, they'll come back. It's really hard to watch, but travelling with them means you'll have a much greater chance of giving needed advice when the *right* time arises. Influence through love, not intellect. Make them feel connected and valued, not gullible and stupid.

This is why political debate around the world is so corrupted. People of differing opinions are made to feel gullible and stupid, which entrenches them in their views irrespective of the validity of those opinions. Apes get triggered and respond to intellectualist jargon, which triggers other Apes and the level of rational political discourse drops to non-existent. All of this is entertaining to watch, of course, so the media encourages it because it leads to more advertising money.

Politicians and seasoned campaigners know this very well. That's why politicians say things that trigger your Ape, that inspire fear, ostracism and other ingroup and outgroup psychological mechanisms. They know when people are running around like Apes they're more likely to disregard rational thought, accept poor ingroup-enhancing propaganda, stay with the status quo, and disregard differing opinions as irrelevant or stupid. Many of them want people to argue rather than debate. This is why incumbent governments are more likely to stay in power in times of crisis. Create a crisis that you seem to be solving and you'll stay in power. I am wary of those preaching the message of hellfire and brimstone, of crisis and doom.

If we started by loving our enemies and valuing diversity of thought, we may find ourselves being much more effective influencers and may just be influenced ourselves in ways that are most unexpected and positive. Tame our Apes rather than trigger the Apes of others and we'll all be better for it in the long run, I believe.

However, while the previous statement might be true for positive debate, social harmony and public respect, there is one major problem with it. As much as we tame our Apes, most of our decisions are still made by our Apes. We cannot ignore the ultimate role our Ape plays in our decisions, even when we have it under control. Its influence is significantly less, for sure, but it's still there. Added to this, smart people are often very good at post-rationalising poor Ape behaviour. This then becomes Ape decision-making dressed up as rational decision-making.

So, despite our best Ape-taming skills, many of our political, social, environmental and financial decisions are heavily influenced by our instinct and automatic assumptions, our rules of thumb. So how do we influence Ape decisions without triggering them and driving people away from the very behaviour or decisions we are trying to encourage? Well, this is where the concept of nudging comes into play.

Nudging

The concept of nudging is basically the practice of using simple cognitive and environmental mental tricks that leverage our cognitive biases and influence our choices. We call this the art of designing better choice architecture. Putting chocolate bars at the eye level of your children when you're lining up to pay for groceries, putting a flashing light on a sign, photographing a sexy woman wearing not much at all, making a task list of the day's activities, sending out notifications in an app with a little 'you're missing out on something' message… these are all simple little nudges that talk to your Ape and suggest behaviour. Understanding the cognitive biases our Apes use to navigate the world allows us to better design nudges that will better influence behaviour.

One of the very earliest examples of nudging to improve decision-making was road markings. When cars and roads first came into being, there was no concept of the side of the road. There were just smooth tar paths you could drive on easily. Where there was a blind corner, and when cars got faster, these corners became death traps for unsuspecting commuters. One of these corners in America became so notoriously dangerous it was known as dead man's corner. That was until someone had the idea of painting lines on the road to suggest where the safes place to drive would be, as shown in the picture below.

Here you can see the painting is very rough, and even arrows had to be put on the road to indicate which side you

should be on. To this day, most road and lane markings around the world aren't road rules—they're actually just road suggestions; very good nudges that help keep us and everyone else safe on the road.

Governments all around the world have been very interested in nudging, particularly when it comes to good health and financial behaviours, economic stability and market negotiations. I know talking about governments and psychological influence inspire Machiavellian thoughts of mind control and big brother surveillance but this isn't how it works out in real life. Lines on a road are less about control and more about safe behaviour. Of course, there is no personal data collected with lines on a road, so digital nudging does need to be monitored with a high level of transparency and ethical regulation. For the most part, governments really are using nudges for the benevolent benefit of the people they serve.

However, what if what we think is best for us differs from what the government thinks is best for us? Well, this is the great thing about nudges. They keep free choice in place. You can still choose not to do something. It's just a little more obvious what is considered a good choice. If you want compliance, you create a law that is policed and has consequences for breaking it. Nudges aren't laws. They just show us a better path and we can choose to follow it or not. This is called paternal liberalism—the idea a government may have a paternalistic view of what's best, but that there is still a liberalism in the ability for the individual to make a choice about what's good for them.

The superannuation program in Australia is a classic example of this. We all know putting away savings for our retirement is a good thing to do. It's not only good for us and our families, it's also good for the long-term health of the economy. Problem is, we have a strong cognitive bias to problems or opportunities in the present and, therefore, trade off future benefits for short-term relief or gain. Ever noticed how saving doesn't necessarily get easier as you earn more? Our ability to expand and contract our expenses in relation to our income is quite remarkable. Therefore, in Australia we have an element of forced savings that's linked to tax and income law. Before your pay even hits your account, your employer by law has to put money into your superannuation. Do we suffer because of this? Not at all. We avoid the temptation to spend by not even seeing or feeling the pain of loss in the first place.

This system recognises the impact of loss aversion and short-termism, and designs a choice architecture accordingly. This makes it simple and painless to put money towards retirement saving, and hard and painful to draw on it before we hit retirement. We can then choose to add more to super if we want. We can also choose to self-manage our super to have more agency in the way it's invested. And, under certain circumstances, we can also still draw on it. It's heavy-handed paternal liberalism but it's transparent, benevolent and works to the best interests of the people the government is elected to serve and represent.

There are, of course, governments who use these types of schemes for their own corrupt purposes. The current government of Chile comes to mind. That isn't paternal liberalism. In that case, it's controlling dictatorship. They aren't using nudges. They're just finding ways to keep the lion's share of the nation's wealth in their own pockets. This type of Ape behaviour won't last forever. As mentioned earlier in the book, the herd will eventually prevail and rid it of the poison that's killing the group. The herd will survive.

Superannuation in most countries of the world is starting to follow a similar system, but it's not just superannuation. In many countries, people separate their own rubbish into general waste and recyclables, something that was unheard of 30 years ago, all because of small nudges like coloured bin lids, the use of icons and pictures, and the fact that having two bins collected means your rubbish won't overflow into the street like it did with one bin. All nudges, all leading to better behaviour without Apes going Apes#!t, and all with the power for people to not comply if they really don't want to. Paternal liberalism.

A friend of mine, Isaac Baker, also a behavioural economist, started up a great social media campaign to take photos of all the different nudges in the wild. His general observations of the world around him are really fascinating—some of his photos are below.

We're all going ApeS#!t!

But nudges aren't only used when you want other people to think about their choices and make good choices more likely. I set up nudges for myself all the time for the benefit of my own finances, social connections and health.

In chapter five we've already explored the nudges I use to motivate me to go running and improve my health. Let's take a look at how I use nudges with my personal finances as well (I have a whole other set of nudges for business finances).

- I set up a password on my bank login that's actually a goal I'm saving for in the next 12–18 months. For example, when we did a Europe trip a few years ago, it was Euro2018!. This reminds me of what we're saving for and makes me less likely to dip into those savings for other things.

- I follow an 80–20 rule. Whatever my income, I live on 80 per cent and save or invest 20 per cent at a minimum. If I can't live on 80 per cent, then something needs to go.

- Weekly direct debits go to separate accounts. I work out what essential and predictable bills need to be paid over the course of the year and then set up weekly instalments to smooth bill shock.

- Calendar reminders pop up a month before I need to buy presents for people. This allows me to think, plan and shop for good value items. Whenever I leave presents to the last minute, I always spend more and the gifts never seem as good.

- I've set up multiple sub-accounts with titles like kids' school expenses, entertaining money and gifts. This allows me to budget unplanned expenses. It also lowers the overall amount I have in any single account. Having five accounts with $500 in them will make you thriftier than having one account with $2500 in it. The lower overall numbers make us feel intuitively like we have less to spend.

- I do not have a credit card. I spend money I have now, not money I hope to have in the future. This also means I don't use services that spread out payments over a month but allow me to have the goods now. Getting it now and paying later isn't controlling your Ape. This is your Ape controlling you.

- I focus my debt on appreciating assets. Debt isn't a bad thing but we try to limit it to large investments—most of which are high-value assets that will grow over time. I definitely limit the amount of debt on depreciating assets like cars, electronics and household appliances.

- I cap our subscriptions and memberships. For instance, we love great wine and visit great wineries and wine-makers. However, we cap the number of our cellar door memberships. If we find a new winery we love, we need to choose a membership to drop before signing up to another. The same goes for entertainment streaming services. If the kids want to sign up for another service, we get them to choose which other service they wish to drop.

- I donate to a cause I know is helping others. Consciously giving a portion of my income away to help others to maintain a healthy attitude toward finances.

- I talk about money with our kids. Being open about finances with the kids not only means they'll be better at managing finances in the future but it also helps to keep us accountable. Sometimes it's in the teaching of something that you learn the best lessons yourself!

- Delay gratification. The more I can think of how I will feel in the future, the better decisions I will make in the present. How will I feel about shouting a round of drinks for everyone tomorrow? How will I feel about this new car in three months' time? The bigger the expense, the bigger the time gap. Again, this isn't about being frugal—it's about being in control, rather than being controlled.

These are all just simple rules of thumb and ways I design my choice architecture to nudge me towards better decision-making.

Your choice architecture needs to suit you. A lot will come down to recognising your own weak spots—when your Ape is running the show—and putting in conscious guardrails to help you when you're less able to tame your Ape.

Chapter snapshot

Key take-aways

1. Knowing and practicing how to help others switch their mindsets will help everyone become more productive and successful.

2. When people hold a deep-seated and passionate belief (often about philosophy, love, religion or politics) you cannot convince them out of these beliefs with reason and logic. It is their Ape that is the holder of these beliefs, so you need to speak to their emotional Ape, not their more responsive selves.

3. Nudging is basically the practice of using simple environmental devices that leverage our cognitive biases and influence our choices.

4. Nudging someone does not mean taking away free choice. Liberal paternalism is when we 'nudge' others to do things we think we know are best, but still allow enough freedom for them to ultimately decide what they want to do.

Things I can do to practically apply this insight

- Write down a list of some behaviours that you would like to change in yourself and others, and then think of some environmental 'nudges' you can implement to encourage those behaviours.

- Similar to the points in chapter 10, download the switch app and start practicing different switches, talk about your switch techniques with your close friends, and journal your experiences (again, the *Decida 10 minute journal* is a great guide if you struggle to do this).

- Practise debating ideas without getting emotional or feeling like a divergent view is a personal attack. When you feel your Ape start to kick in during these debates, find and practise a switch that will keep it in its cage.

Thought-starters

- What are some of the things you, or others, are doing and what 'nudges' may be in your environment encouraging this behaviour?

- Can you change the environment to remove some of these negative nudges?

- When do you think 'nudging' becomes manipulation?

Chapter 12

Creating new habits

"In any situation in life you always have three options. Change it, accept it, or leave it."
  -Naval Ravikant

Whether it be creating new habits for yourself or trying to help others create new habits, the rules generally seem to stay the same. It is, after all, just human behaviour. Let's go back to some of my health nudges to see how I've used them specifically to form habits, in particular, going for a regular run.

In my senior years at school I was an avid runner, rising at 5.30am most days full of energy and busting out a tidy 10km jog before breakfast. However, as time passed, I became more of a night owl, and got married and had two kids. The warmth of my bed became very alluring and my passion for running subsided considerably. In my mid-thirties, I looked in the mirror one day and disliked the way I had let things go. It was time for a change. Time to get back into running.

I'm not sure if being a long distance runner in high school helped me or not. I have vivid memories of being able to tackle hills with pace, glide past other runners on a downhill stretch, and have the time to take in the beauty of my surroundings as I ran. I was super motivated and excited to get back into shape. I bought new running shoes, downloaded an app for my phone, got my running music playlist sorted. I was on my way! That was, of course, until I actually started running.

I remember being about 100 metres out of my driveway at Rochedale South and I was completely shattered. Every bone in my body was screaming at me, "Why would you do this?! Stop! For the love of God, stop!"

But I pushed on. I think it took me almost 30 minutes to get around the 2km block in a running/stumbling/crawling fashion. I must have resembled someone who'd been walking in the desert for days as I burst through the front door, desperate for a drink of water and a rest. The super light long distance runner of my school years had well and truly disappeared. They were just memories, taunting me about how far I'd regressed. This was not going to be an easy habit to pick up again. My Ape and my body were most displeased.

After a few days' recovery, and groaning whenever I had to get up to do anything, I decided to give it another go. But today turned into tomorrow, and before I knew it, a month had gone past and I had only run once. I needed a plan.

I knew that if I didn't run first thing in the morning, I was unlikely to get out on the road at all when I was mentally exhausted from a day in the studio. So the first thing I did was just to set my alarm for 5.30… and get up. But that didn't quite work. As my alarm went off, I found that if there was any excuse not to get up, I wouldn't. If I didn't know where my running clothes were, if my toenails felt too long, if the night before was too big, if my phone wasn't charged… literally, the smallest hesitation seemed to keep me tucked up in bed.

So (like I briefly mentioned in chapter 5) the night before, I would go to sleep in my running shorts, make sure my phone was on the charge and lay out all my running attire right next to the bed so all I had to do was roll out and I was on the road. I also stuck a calendar in the kitchen and put a big X through every day that I did exercise, with a big note next to it that said, 'Four days every week'.

That seemed to work better but I was still missing that extra push that I needed to put my body through the agony of an early morning run. So I thought, "I'm recording an album at the moment with some guys who also like running. Why don't we make it a competition?" So we did. For the next two months, as we were recording the album, we'd track who'd gone out for a run that morning and who'd decided to be a lazy so-and-so. This finally worked. After that album had finished, I was back in the habit of going for a run at 5.30am every day. In fact, the days I didn't go for a run, I felt annoyed. My Ape was actually agitating for me to go for a run, rather than screaming for me to stop. Running had become a habit.

I love to tell this story when talking about habit-making, because it has the four main elements to motivating people to change behaviour and create habitual patterns.

1. Create simple rules.
2. Reduce resistance.
3. Keep it front of mind.
4. Share it.

Let's unpack each of these.

Simple rules

Creating simple rules is really important because the simpler something is, the more likely your Ape will come along for the ride. In my exercise example, my rule was to get up at 5:30 every morning to go for a run. It was a simple rule and it worked for me. I didn't have to think about it, and it was easy, memorable and practical. Other simple rules might be look before you cross the road, never pick up hot coals, leave work at 5:30pm every day, or never eat yellow snow. All are rules we don't have to think about that help us through life. They make life simpler and our Apes love simple.

There is a great book called *Simple rules: How to thrive in a complex world* by Donald Sull and Kathleen M. Eisenhardt. In it, the authors lead a fascinating dive into the world of simple rules, and land on six types of rules: three that help to determine what to do, and three that determine how to do something. Below is my take on the types of rules they outline.

First, the rules for what to do.

Boundary rules

These are rules which have a yes or no answer. They can be values-driven but are often much more simplistic. For instance, never go swimming in an electrical storm, or never be the first, or last, to leave a party, or, if shares drop by X per cent in one day, then sell.

Stopping rules

As the title suggests, these are rules to help your Ape stop something. This helps buffer status quo bias and the tendency toward instant gratification. For instance, stop eating after 7pm, only have one glass of wine a night or don't buy drinks after 10pm.

Prioritisation rules

This is simply putting things into a hierarchy so you can determine which activity trumps another in importance. For example: When the budget is tight, look to reduce spending before selling assets like shares. Or a classic: If your oxygen mask falls from the ceiling, put it on yourself before helping your children or others. Or: My partner comes first, then my children, then my colleagues. These are simple rules that help you to prioritise when conflicts arise.

Now, the rules for how to do something:

Coordination rules

These are rules that help us to navigate the complexity of human interactions. For instance, don't call others after 9pm unless it's an emergency. At work: Always text team members back within the hour, and answer all ideas with 'yes, and…' instead of 'no, but…'.

How-to rules

These are guardrails that help to direct our focus without being so restrictive they suppress creativity. For instance, a rule of never writing more than 300 words in a blog guardrails the activity without dictating what you should say.

Timing rules

When you do something can be just as important as *what* you do. I personally like a rule of choosing one thing I'm procrastinating on and do it first up in the morning. Or, in my exercise story, get up at 5.30am and go for a run.

I like looking at these types of simple rules because they prompt me to think about areas of my life where I can reduce complexity by setting up some simple rules. If we're aiming for a goal, or helping others aim for a goal, creating some simple rules or guardrails can really help the process.

In the theatre we had lots of simple rules that helped us to get a show on the road and make fast decisions. Putting limits on budgets, clearly defining roles and responsibilities, agreeing on ways of working, and even making rules on overall style were ways we implemented simple rules to improve decision-making. Often before we started creating a show in the theatre, the lighting designer, director and I would get together and agree on a colour and sound palette we knew would work together and suited the tone of the show. This was a set of simple rules that would help us in our creative decisions in an extremely complex environment.

Simple rules by themselves aren't always enough to change behaviour in the long term and create new habits. This is why New Year's resolutions don't often last. We make new rules and commitments that are too easy to violate or relax. After a very short period of time, our Ape goes back to what it was doing before and the resolution isn't any more than the punchline to a joke at next year's Christmas party. Once you have some simple rules in place to guide the new behaviour, you must reduce resistance, or the friction, required to do the new behaviour.

Reduce resistance

In my running story, the way I reduced resistance was to wear my running shorts to bed, and lay out my socks, shirt, earphones and shoes on the floor next to my bed. This meant I reduced the time spent in the cold morning air between getting out of my warm bed and my body heating up on my run. I was able to be out on the road running about two minutes after rolling out of bed. The night before, I also made sure there was nothing that could introduce resistance in the morning. I made sure my toenails were short, that the dog food I would have to put out was made, that the spare door key was in my key pocket. I reduced as much of the friction as possible between the alarm going off and me taking the first step of my run.

The power that reducing resistance has should never be underestimated.

Another good example of this comes from renowned behavioural economist, Dan Ariely. The story goes that Dan received a letter from a group of pharmacists one day, who were upset that one of the behavioural economic principles, 'the allure of free', didn't seem to work. The allure of free is simply the observation that if you want someone to try something new, free is better than cheap. You can discount a new energy drink to 50c and you'll get a few more people buying it, but if you offer it for free, then everyone grabs a can.

The pharmacists protested they'd tried to get patients who had long-term health conditions and who get their medications delivered to them to switch to generic drugs, which were about one-third of the price of the branded ones. Sounds perfect, right? Why wouldn't someone who is on long-term medication, and often a low income, take up an offer to slash their medical expenses by a third? But people don't—most still buy the more expensive brands. The pharmacists, after hearing about the allure of free, decided to do a mail-out saying that, if people signed a consent form and sent it back, they'd get their medicine free for a year. Free for a year! Now, to the rational side of any human, this sounds like a deal that's too good to be true. But not to your Ape, apparently. After months of sending out letters, hardly anyone had taken up the offer. It was at this point of frustration the pharmacists penned their curt letter to Dan.

Dan responded to the group with an observation this might actually be a problem of friction. The letters of the new amazing offer were sent to patients, who then had two options. They could either read the letter, make a choice, sign their consent and then post it snail mail back to the pharmacists, or they could just keep going like they are doing now. The ease of keeping the status quo was just too strong. Dan suggested, despite the new offer being amazing, they may have to solve this problem of resistance to see any impact.

Knowing that changing it to an opt-out (do nothing and we'll make a change on your behalf) was illegal, the pharmacists created a forced choice junction. They sent letters to patients alerting them that, if they didn't send the letter back, their medication would stop being sent out. On returning the letter, they could choose whether to go for the generic meds for free or the much more expensive brand. They hadn't lowered the resistance of change, they'd just made the friction equal between either choice and created a kind of choice T-intersection. With this new offer, the vast majority of patients chose the new offer. This is the power of resistance and it should never be underestimated when attempting to change behaviour.

Keep it front of mind

Salience (/'seilienns/)
noun
The quality of being particularly noticeable or important; prominence. The state or quality by which it stands out from its neighbours.

Salience, or doing things that help something stand out from the crowd, is a principle marketers and sales people have known for millennia. If you want people to buy or do something new you have to get, and keep, their attention. You need to be front of mind when they think of something. As a consultant, whenever clients have a problem they need help solving, my name is the one I want to pop into their mind. To this end, I keep doing things on social media and catching up for coffee, just to keep myself front of mind, to increase my salience.

The same goes for remembering and being motivated to repeat an action over and over again until it becomes embedded as an unconscious habit. You need to keep the why and your progress front of mind. Grab and keep your attention focused on what you want to do and you have won half the battle. This is why so much money is poured into branding and packaging. As you walk down the aisle and you pick up something you wouldn't normally buy, what made you pick it up in the first place? Something had to grab your attention—it had to have high salience. The more interesting or novel it is, the more likely it is to keep your attention so you buy it.

Good examples of increasing salience in influence behaviour include:

- Yellow or light green recycling bin lids
- Response rates from an Irish postal survey jumped from 19.2 per cent to 36 per cent simply by putting a handwritten sticky note on the front of envelopes
- Highly effective emotional marketing campaigns to change attitudes toward HIV, smoking, drink driving and being SunSmart

- White road lines being painted on black tar, with metal ribs embedded in the lines to make a loud noise if you stray out of your lane.

In fact, most of the nudges in the wild mentioned earlier are activities in increasing the salience of something in the environment in order to attract your attention to what is important.

There are so many ways to increase saliency and keep things front of mind. This includes using bizarre images, the human face in ads, catchy or emotional music, scare tactics, scarcity effects, loud noises or bright lights, white space in graphic design and count-down clocks. All are examples of ways ad agencies and organisations increase saliency. Individually, this might mean putting a photo of your goal on your wall (in my case, a marathon runner), changing passwords to use words that remind you of your goal, or making your web home page a company that reminds you of your goal (like Decida.co perhaps!). Make it visual and obvious so you keep front of mind the behaviour you want to repeat.

Of course, one of the ways we increase salience and motivation is through the use of incentives. That's why on most wanted posters in the wild west the reward was more prominent than the people they were after. Even I did it with my exercise. If I ran four out of five days during the week, I would treat myself to something on the weekend. It tended to change each week—one week it would be a Sunday sleep-in, another weekend it might be going out to the movies with the boys, and another week something else. The important thing was that I rewarded myself when I met my weekly goal, and denied myself of a reward if I missed it (usually by going for a run instead—which I ended up enjoying, so win-win right!)

It might be interesting to note there is an interesting quirk about financial incentives and how our brains are wired to interpret numbers. It's this: the size of the overall number is more important than the individual benefit. Lotteries are a good example of this. Lotteries know that people tend to notice the size of a reward rather than the chances of winning it (remember, our Apes are terrible statisticians). So, rather than incentivising the purchase of multiple tickets with discounts or cash-back for anyone who buys into a scheme, it's actually cheaper and more effective just to raise the money on the overall prize on offer.

There are also times where we see social incentives working in direct opposition to financial incentives. A great example of cross-purpose incentives was when we were hired by one of the big four banks in Australia to observe the behaviour of staff in bank branches. There was a big focus in Australia at the time on responsible lending, and there was a fear that sales targets attached to particular products were causing staff to push products that customers didn't need. Targets had therefore been abolished and a new incentive scheme had been cooked up to incentivise right product fit, so the incentive was attached to a range of products rather than any single product. It was assumed this would increase staff ability to match a better solution to customer needs. This sounded intuitive, and it really resonated with the staff as well, who wanted to do the right thing by customers.

Very rarely do you find anyone going to work saying, "I'm going to be terrible to someone today!" Yes, those people are out there but we didn't find many of them in these bank branches.

What we did find was even more interesting. In these branches, customer service is a big deal. When a customer left the bank, they had a big screen next to the exit where they could rate their experience at the bank. Managers could very easily track who was delivering a good customer experience and who wasn't, and staff were financially rewarded or penalised based on these ratings. It had a huge impact on the way staff treated customers and all seemed to be working brilliantly. A customer who's had a good experience is a win for everyone. What we didn't initially think of, though, was the way this impacted the behaviour of staff during the lunch-hour crush.

People who have day jobs get very little time to go to the bank (this was before we could do so much online like we can nowadays). So while the bank was relatively empty most of the day, it was manic from midday till 2pm. Staff at tellers had to deal not only with customers in a hurry, but with customers who were frustrated they'd wasted so much of their precious lunch time. In this context, when customers finally got their turn with the staff and asked for a credit card or a personal loan, challenging the customer about their capacity to repay and refusing them the credit they came in for—particularly if they had waited for some time to get served—was not a great experience for the customer. What they did was storm out of the bank and hit a single star on the rating screen, and the staff member responsible for the low rating would feel penalised for doing the right thing.

With the customer service score so salient in the whole experience, it became a much stronger behavioural nudge. The next time a customer came in with a sketchy-looking application, the staff member would convince themselves that it should be fine, and approve the application. There was even some instances where we witnessed staff helping them with the form so as not to raise flags internally and get the loan or credit card approved. Product sold, customer happy, seems like a win-win in the moment. Problem is these customers were actually often poor with their repayments, would get themselves into bad debt cycles and became liabilities for the bank. What felt like a win-win in the moment because of the salient incentives, was actually a lose-lose.

The first thing we did was change the ratings system at the door. Instead of a star rating, it was just a thumbs up, a thumbs down or a question mark. If the customer hit the thumbs down, then a follow-up question saying, "Was one of the below reasons why your experience was not great?" which was followed by a short list of things like, "I didn't get the credit card I need" and a simple yes or no button at the bottom. If they hit yes, then the score wasn't added to the staff member's customer service rating, and a little email was sent to the staff member encouraging them for having the courage to do the right thing by the customer, even if it didn't feel so good. This had an amazing effect. A recent check-in at the bank not only reported an increase in market share, but the staff have the lowest turnover in the country and the culture is reported by the staff to be the best it's ever been.

This was all because we fixed an incentive that had high salience but was perversely nudging good people toward not-so-great outcomes.

However, back to me building my running habit. The calendar in the kitchen was my salient reminder. Originally, it was just to keep me focused on exercising at least four days a week, but it also had the act of curbing my late-night eating and drinking. One look at the calendar and I would remember the pain of the runs and the weight I was trying to lose. In my head, I was thinking, "don't make all that bloody effort be for nought!" It was me making my new exercise habit more salient. I also changed the background picture on my phone to a marathon runner, so every time I used my phone I was reminded of my goal to build a habit of running.

Making your goals salient so they remain front of mind also means others become aware of your goal as well. This naturally leads us to the final element, the final type of nudge that really gives us the best chance to form new habits: social accountability. This is sharing your progress and activity with people you care about, and having them hold you to account.

Share it

As we've explored in an earlier chapter, we all like to be part of the group. Being accepted and celebrated by the group is a core emotional driver that has been evolutionarily honed since the beginning of consciousness. This is why sharing your goals and your desired new habits with your friends, and them helping to hold you to account, is so powerful. Want to reduce your drinking? Get your friends you often drink with to help enforce a two-drink rule (or whatever rule you feel is appropriate). If you do the cooking in the household and want to start eating healthier, maybe create a closed chat group with friends where you can upload images of healthy meals you've cooked each night for a few months until your taste buds learn better habits. If you're wanting to get ahead financially, set up an alert to your partner whenever you spend more than a certain amount (this can be done with some banks). It's not just the transparency of behaviour that's important here—it's the accountability that comes with not wanting to look less in the eyes of your peers. It's much easier to disappoint yourself than it is to disappoint someone you respect and whose opinion you care about.

Whenever I think of using social dynamics to influence behaviour, I'm always reminded of a concept in behavioural economics called pre-commitment. Multiple studies have shown that, if you allow people to determine their own deadlines, they'll be less likely to procrastinate, their individual performance on tasks will improve (as long as you're spacing deadlines out), and they'll feel more in control and responsible. In a way, you're telling people to be their own boss. This is a technique I use all the time to great effect. By asking people to be their own boss, you increase their buy-in and get them to pre-commit to deadlines. In turn, they will perform better, feel more in control, and feel more satisfied with the work they have done.

If you want to investigate more about pre-commitment, behavioural economist Dan Ariely has done lots of studies in this area. A good paper to start with is titled, *Procrastination, deadlines and performance: Self-control by precommitment*, or just do a search on precommitment and you'll find a whole range of interesting reads.

Key to this idea of precommitment seems to be the act of signing your own name to something you've come up with. We use this all the time when we are working with fractured teams in organisations. We get them to co-create a social contract they agree to and sign their name to it. We then scan and print out a small (but still legible) version, which they keep somewhere visible around their workspace to keep it front of mind. This is a powerful tool that really does help teams move from political infighting to building trust and working together productively—as long as they genuinely contributed to the social contract.

This idea of precommitment also works when you're trying to get employees to take more responsibility for the quality of their own work. A great example of this came one day when I received a call from Dennis, a friend of mine who owns a successful cabinet-making business in New Zealand. He was frustrated his company had four levels of quality control on the cabinets before they were sent to customers, and with increased wages and increased competition on household items driving down prices, the heavy bureaucracy and high cost of the quality control process was eroding any profit. His frustration was, "If we just got it right the first time, then surely we wouldn't need all these levels of quality control". The challenge was to streamline the quality control process without undermining the quality of the product.

Dennis was a big fan of Alpha Romeos, and mentioned he always liked the fact the vehicle technician personally signed the engine of each car they helped construct. Dennis saw this as a sign of pride for the mechanic and would ensure the quality of the build, because he'd personally branded his name on it. His idea was to get the craftsmen that were building the cabinets to sign their names on the underside of the benches. He knew the cabinet-makers took great pride in their professions and thought this might motivate a higher level of quality checking in the first place before they signed their name to the work. It's a great idea but I thought we could take it one step further. Drawing upon our success with social contracts, I suggested he get his chief craftsmen to write a paragraph about what it means to be a master cabinet-maker and personally sign it. Then I asked Dennis to frame it with the photo of the master cabinet-maker and hang it in a prominent position where clients and fellow workers can see it. This acted as a kind of social contract. It wasn't precommitment to a specific task completion date but to the quality of work.

Due to the recency of the conversation, this particular intervention is still in its early days— but, as you can imagine, the impact of general motivation, culture and overall pride and engagement in their work is palpable. What's even more interesting is when you extend this beyond the quality of craftmanship to the integrity of a salesperson, to the conduct of a manager, or the quality of care for a health worker. Not only does it build pride in the work, it builds trust in the customer, and uses social accountability to keep things on track.

The way this is used to build better habits is when it's linked to a specific goal or ritual you want to repeat. I committed to my business partners that I'd run at least four times per week, and so, at our daily stand-ups, they help hold me accountable to that.

Sharing your experiences has been made a lot easier nowadays with a range of technology encouraging transparency and accountability. My running app is a great example of this, sending push notifications if I haven't run for a while, and using social reinforcement by getting my fellow runners to celebrate key achievements and encourage me when I need it. It also allows me to see what my friends are doing and I use this to motivate me to keep up.

I must say that, now running is a habit, I don't really need all these prompts anymore. But they were really, really helpful in creating the habitual behaviour in the first place.

If you want to create an environment where you're most likely to repeat something enough for it to be a habit, then create simple rules, work at reducing resistance, find ways to keep goals and the desired behaviours front of mind, and share it with people whose opinion you care about.

Simple right? I challenge everyone reading to just pick one habit that they want to change or create, think about each of these elements and then see if you can keep it going for a month. You've got nothing to lose by giving it a crack.

Transparency and the nudge dilemma

I think one of the most exciting areas for the future of nudging is in the area of health and rehabilitation from trauma or injury (both mentally and physically). The reason for this is that when you're in pain, or frustrated, or feeling mental fatigue in some way, your ability to make good decisions is dramatically reduced. Add to this the fact these scenarios don't come around all that often so patients have low familiarity with what to do. That means simple processes often feel complex just because they're unfamiliar. This leaves us vulnerable to all sorts of people and industries that are more than happy to free you of your finances to help. It becomes very hard to know who is genuine and who is a predator.

In an age of digital transformation and big data, it becomes possible to create systems and environments that encourage better decision-making for everyone in the process. This is about getting the right information to the right people at the right time, simplifying unnecessarily complex processes, and increasing transparency when it helps, and speed when it doesn't. This last point is particularly interesting because we all intuitively think transparency is one of the keys to better decisions and arrangements between multiple parties—but this doesn't actually seem to be the case in many situations.

My good friend, Uwe Dullech, is one of the titans in the field of behavioural economics and one of a great group of scientists, economists, management experts and psychologists at the Queensland University of Technology. He and his fellow researchers were intrigued by the idea of whether transparency of commissions paid to brokers would influence a client's choice of provider. The common thought was that if a broker was being paid a higher commission by provider A than provider B, then broker X would sell more of provider A's product, irrespective of whether it was the best choice for a particular client. In a way, the broker in this situation becomes a salesperson for provider A but it looks to the clients as though they're an independent advisor. It was hypothesised by some financial big brains that if the client knew of the commission arrangement between the broker and the providers, they'd be less influenced by the broker's advice and more likely to make a rational decision.

However, what Uwe and his team found was something quite different. Their research revealed commission transparency engendered more trust between the client and the broker. The client saw the broker as more open and honest and this increased their confidence in the advice given. The proportion of provider A's sales increased along with the commission transparency, rather than decreasing. It was like there was a reciprocity of trust being exchanged; You've trusted me with this information, therefore I'm going to trust you more as well. Transparency in this situation actually led to lower conscious decision-making from the client.

From a health perspective, this raises some pretty interesting questions, particularly if a patient is needing to make decisions while they're recovering from an accident or serious injury. General practitioners, lawyers, allied health professionals, hospitals, insurance companies, chemists and a range of other trusted people and professions often gain some form of incentive when they recommend a particular product or service in the rehabilitation pathway. Attempts have been made to make this complex web of incentives more transparent to improve health outcomes for patients by encouraging decisions more in the interests of the care-receiver than the care-giver. The reciprocity of trust theory suggests this may not be the case.

There are, of course, instances where transparency has dramatically improved outcomes and decision-making. For example, the internet arriving in the early 1990s dramatically increased the transparency of the property market, greatly reducing the opportunity for some unscrupulous real estate agents to use misinformation or to withhold crucial information from buyers and sellers. In this industry, information is power and, back then, the real estate agent held all of the cards. Increased transparency improved buyers' and sellers' real estate decision-making because information wasn't controlled by agents. It wasn't transparency of incentives as such but easy access to relevant information that made it simple to spot the bulls#!t.

It's interesting to see how differently people act when certain private information is made available. For instance, do you think you'd behave differently at work if everyone knew everyone else's wage? This was the exact situation another friend of mine faced after he was hired as CEO of one of India's largest and fastest-growing technology companies. On his first day, he walked into the foyer of the building in Bangalore to find a massive poster welcoming him to the company. The interesting thing was this poster also announced his yearly salary, his bonus package, the KPIs that would trigger his bonuses, and the key accountabilities he had in the company! He hadn't even met his team yet and the usually very personal and private details of his employment were advertised for all to see.

When talking to him about this 12 months later, he actually remembered this moment with great fondness. After the initial shock and slight embarrassment, he actually felt great relief and confidence. It turned out everyone in the company knew what everyone else was paid and how they were being incentivised, so it wasn't really a thing. People who were paid more were less able to hide inactivity and the group held them more accountable. For him, it allowed him to lead with confidence and helped others around him know where they could assist in ways that were actually meaningful to both the company and him. Transparency in that context, with that company, in that time and in that culture, actually improved behaviours and decision-making right across the organisation. It's fascinating to wonder if it would have the same impact in other organisations around the world.

What this company was doing was designing the decision environment to nudge people toward better behaviours and decisions. What I loved about this was it wasn't a control mechanism at all. Actually quite the opposite—it was a nudge. This is the beautiful thing about nudges. They're simple environmental changes that cause significant shifts in behaviour. It's putting food out for our Apes to lead them in a certain direction. In a way, we could call nudges, bananas. It's not the whole story of how to influence your behaviour but it does play a significant part. And the reason it plays a significant part is because of a weird quirk of our brain when dealing with 'cognitive dissonance'.

Cognitive dissonance is the term used to describe the feeling we get when our attitudes and behaviours don't align. It's the feeling you get when you don't stick up for a friend but you wish you had. It's the odd feeling you get if you sell something dodgy to an unsuspecting buyer. It's the feeling you get when you're working late and you're missing your child's birthday party. It's the feeling you get when you've paid an amount for an item that far exceeds its actual value, particularly if you don't believe in excessive living. It's the feeling you get if you drive around in an obviously very expensive car when you don't think it's right to be a show-off. It's the mental pain you feel when your attitudes and your behaviours are out of alignment.

As mentioned previously, your brain is hardwired to avoid pain, so it will always look to resolve this pain as quickly as possible. The thing is, once you've done something, you can't change it, so if your brain is suffering the pain of cognitive dissonance after an action, the only real option it has is to change your attitude toward that action. This makes your brain feels good! We like to believe our values and attitudes drive our behaviour but a lot of the time, it's that the other way around. Change your behaviours, and your attitudes toward those behaviours will shift as well.

Don't like exercise? Start exercising and you'll change your attitudes and beliefs about the benefits of exercise. Think sugar is poison? Start eating sweet things and see how your attitude softens. Think a certain country has draconian and scary attitudes toward privacy and surveillance? Decide to live in that country and see if your attitudes towards surveillance change. Nudging is so important because small changes in our behaviours can lead to significant changes in our attitudes. It is why organisational culture is so important. Behaviours shape attitudes. When we aren't in control of our Ape and our Ape goes Apes#!t, we will post-rationalise and justify our Ape behaviours to make us feel better. The smarter we are, the better we are at making rational arguments to justify poor behaviour. This is why high IQ has no correlation with good decision-making.

It's easy to see how nudging is often used in our digital lives through our devices and different advertising campaigns. There have been literally hundreds of books, thousands of videos and millions of articles written about these areas, with each offering great insight into the ever-fascinating topic of how we get sucked in. One of the most entertaining shows around at the moment is *The Gruen transfer*, which does a great job at pulling apart different ad campaigns and the psychology behind them. If you can find it online, it makes for very entertaining viewing.

What is less obvious, and less talked about, is the way nudging and psychological prompts aid in creating better work environments. Particularly when managing a large group of people through a complex, and sometimes painful, change process.

Chapter snapshot

Key take-aways

1. There are four main elements to creating new habits
   - ❯ Create simple rules (a list of the rule types can be found on pages 267 to 269)
   - ❯ Reduce resistance (removing anything that could be stopping you)
   - ❯ Keep it front of mind (keep obvious reminders around you to help your Ape remember that it's important)
   - ❯ Share it (social accountability is one of the strongest behavioural nudges we have).

2. Simply by making things transparent does not mean that you will encourage the correct behaviours—sometimes it helps reinforce negative ones.

3. Cognitive dissonance is what your brain feels when your actions and your attitudes don't align. Ninety-nine percent of the time you will change your attitudes to match your actions—not the other way around.

4. Change people's behaviour, and their attitudes will follow.

Things I can do to practically apply this insight

- Pick a new habit you want to create.

- Go through each of the four elements of new habit creation and list everything you can do to give yourself the best chance of effectively creating the new habit.

- Now just do it. Even if your Ape doesn't want to. Your Ape's attitude will change once your behaviour is embedded. You are not your ape. Control it – don't let it control you!

Thought-starters

- What bad habit do you have, and why do you think you continue to do it?

- Can you remember a time when you felt cognitive dissonance? Did you change your attitudes to justify your behaviour?

- What does your Ape love to do? Why do you think it loves to do this? Is there a way to use this love to help create new, better habits?

In conclusion

*"You have brains in your head.
You have feet in your shoes.
You can steer yourself any direction you choose."*

–Dr Seuss

Managing our reactivity in a highly reactive world is critical to the ongoing success and development as a human race. With rapid and relentless advancement in digital technologies, scientific discoveries and new sources of data, taking a moment to pause and look at the way we interact, develop and use these new tools is needed. We must increase our decision-making maturity to match the maturity of the systems, tools and processes we interact with every day in our modern digital lives.

If there were six big things I would want you to take away from this book, it would be the following.

1. Respond, don't react

When you let your Ape react, rather than responding as a human, know that you are likely making bad choices and hurting your future self. Learn to recognise what your Ape feels like as it's getting ready to react so you can intervene before it does. Be aware of what is making you react and ask yourself why it's so. Once you think you know the why, use switches and other nudges to reduce your reactivity to this trigger in the future. This will open new opportunities and life will be immeasurably better for you and those around you that you care about.

2. The number and strength of your identities matter

Choose who you associate with carefully. Make sure you aren't drawing too much self-worth from one single identity. When you're too invested in a single social identity you are easily blinded by fear and protection of the group and your role in that group. Live a rich multi-faceted life with multiple identities and roles, and learn to switch identities at will in order to stay objective and in control.

3. JR=(IE>P)+O⁺

Remember this equation when you are reflecting on how you handled a situation, or when thinking about an appropriate response to a provocation. This is core to developing critical thinking, to be able to step outside of yourself and your circumstances to constructively evaluate your past or future courses of action.

4. Hold it lightly

Life is hard, and we pick up many scars along the way from traumas that our Ape wants to help us avoid in the future. Even though it might feel right to harden yourself against life, to hold on to bitterness and unforgiveness—to sit with the pain you know rather than get even more hurt—this isn't good for us. Keep your heart soft and mind open. We only have one life, and it's a shame for it to be filled with missed opportunities. Remember, holding on to unforgiveness is like swallowing poison and expecting the other person to get sick. Let it go, people, let it go.

5. Be present with your emotions

Emotions are a beautiful part of what makes us human. They give us the ability to empathise, connect, create new memories and communicate. However, incorrectly applied, they can leave us open to suggestion, lead to irrational behaviour and trap us in unhelpful mindsets. Learning to be present in the moment and not allowing suppressed emotion of the past to explode in the now will mean you use this amazing tool for good, not bad.

6. Nudge yourself

Give yourself the best chance of success by consciously designing your choice architecture to help you and those around you make better decisions. The more psychological and environmental nudges you can put in place, and the simpler rules you can live by, the better habits you will create, and the better attitudes and mindsets that will develop.

*****

I trust that reading this book has challenged you and given you some tangible tools to make better decisions and improve your life.

By mastering our Ape and improving our decision-making capability, even by the smallest increments, we will solve the big political, social, economic and environmental challenges we are facing today.

Added to this, by understanding ourselves, others and how we interact better, we will be able to collaborate more harmoniously and live a more successful and fulfilling life.

Thanks for sticking with me.

Reading list

If you are up for more, I would highly recommend the following (after reading this book of course). Internet searching has made the mindless listing of references completely redundant in my mind, so a reading list of the books that have contributed to my own knowledge and journey of insight relevant to the content of this book is something I thought would be much more useful.

This is by no means an exhaustive list, but hopefully there is something that resonates with your curiosity.

- *Thinking, Fast and Slow*, by Daniel Kahneman
  - ❯ Along with Amos Tversky, Kahneman is the father of behavioural economics and this book is considered by many to be a bit of a behavioural economics bible.

- Anything by Shakespeare or Marlow, Particularly *Macbeth*, *Hamlet* and *Faustus*.
  - ❯ In my mind, playwrights were the first true psychologists—and Shakespeare remains the king of all for me.

- *Nudge*, by Cass Sunstein and Richard Thaler
  - ❯ Easier to read than others, and also authored by pioneers and giants in the field of behavioural economics.

- *Tipping Point, Outliers, Blink,* in fact, anything by Malcolm Gladwell
  - ❯ Malcolm is a journalist who loves to write about science. For this reason, his works are very entertaining, insightful and thought-provoking, and much easier to digest than some of the other tomes on this list!
- *Descartes' Error: Emotion, reason, and the human brain*, and *Looking for Spinoza* by Antonio Domasio.
  - ❯ A great exploration of emotions and feeling, and how they impact our decision-making.
- *Misbehaving*, by Richard Thaller
  - ❯ This is almost like a 'part two' of *Nudge*.
- *The Man Who Thought His Wife Was A Hat*, by Oliver Sacks
  - ❯ A world-renowned neurologist who has a lovely way of communicating through the stories of his own patients. I read this every couple of years and I still get insight on every read.
- *Mindsight*, by Daniel J. Siegel, M.D.
  - ❯ This is where I first encountered the hand brain, and is a wonderful, approachable book that walks us through how we can design our own neurology.
- *The New Psychology of Leadership*, by Alex Haslam
  - ❯ An extremely practical and insightful book from a pioneer in the study of social identity and social psychology.
- *The Abolition of Man*, by C.S. Lewis.
  - ❯ I think philosophy and psychology should never be too far away from one another, and this book has stood the test of time as a relevant challenge to our humanity.

Reading list

- *Authentic Happiness*, by Martin E. P. Seligman, Ph.D.
  - ❯ The pioneer of positive psychology and a great inspiration for the advancement of human kind.

- *A Real Girl's Guide to Money: From Converse to Louboutins*, by Effie Zahos.
  - ❯ One of my favourite collaborators, and a wonderful human being to boot. Effie has a real knack of making complex financial concepts clear and simple. All her books are great, but this is my personal favourite.

- *Telling Lies*, by Paul Eckman.
  - ❯ At uni this book and Eckman's work utterly captivated me, and still does to this day. Emotional leakage, deception detection and the meaning of what it is to be human all wrapped up in one. Love this book. Can be heavy reading though.

- *Snakes in Suits: When psychopaths go to work*, by Paul Babiak, Ph. D. & Robert D. Hare, Ph. D.
  - ❯ I love all of Hare's work, but I think this is the best book on how to deal with psychopaths in the workplace that I have ever come across. Just brilliant.

- *The Mind of a Mnemonist: A little book about a vast memory* and *The man with a shattered world: the history of a brain wound*, by A. R. Luria.
  - ❯ One of the giants of psychology, these two books are

stories of Luria's case work with some of his patients that led to many of the great insights into the texture of human thought, perception and behaviour.

- *Bono on Bono*, by Michka Assayas.
  - › Rockstar, poet, activist and deeply normal human being in many ways. This book is a very insightful and easy read. Assayas meets with Bono (lead singer of the band U2) and recounts their conversations in this book. Lots of moments of insight and inspiration.

- *Creativity, Inc.: Overcoming the unseen forces that stand in the way of true inspiration*, by Ed Catmull.
  - › Fantastic book written by the president of Pixar and Disney, articulating the principles that have kept them creative and profitable for so long. I have many regular sayings that have come from here.

- *Sapiens: A brief history of mankind*, by Yuval Noah Harari.
  - › One of those books you can read every couple of years and it still feels as insightful and refreshing as the very first time you read it. This book takes a step back and examines who we are and where we are going as a species.

- *A Short History of Nearly Everything* by Bill Bryson.
  - › This book is curiosity on steroids, from one of the most brilliant and curious minds of our time. You need to set aside quite a bit of time to read this one, as each page is jam packed with amazing goodness, and it needs time to absorb!

- *The Happiness Trap: Stop struggling, start living*, by Russ Harris.
  - › The book that started a movement and challenges the very essence of the concept of the pursuit of happiness. Harris' writing helped me as a student focus on living a meaningful life and I've never looked back.
- *Six Thinking Hats*, by Edward de Bono
  - › de Bono was one of the first writers that got me interested in psychology, and the concepts of the six thinking hats is as useful today as it was when it was written in the 80's
- *Good to Great: Why some companies make the leap... and others don't*, by Jim Collins.
  - › If you're starting or running a business and you haven't read this book, then what have you been doing?!? A fascinating and in depth look at the difference between successful and unsuccessful companies across the last century, and what the difference is between good companies, and great ones.

You'll notice these books are a mix of psychologists, neurologists, philosophers, artists and journalists. This is by no means an accident.

I'm mindful of the old Indian folk tale about six blind men describing an elephant while feeling very different parts of the animal. One man holding the foot declared with absolute confidence: "The elephant is like a tree trunk". Another, holding the tail, scoffed and said, "It's clearly more like a rope". Yet another, who was holding the tusk, laughed and said, "You're crazy. It's clearly more like a spear". In fact, each of the blind men had a completely different description of the elephant depending on their experience, and passionately argued their point of view was more correct. The moral of the story, of course, is they're all correct in their own way.

If you want to learn about a topic as broad and complex as human psychology and behaviour, you should learn through as many experiences as possible. It's certainly what I've tried to do over the years.

Decida

www.decida.co

At Decida, we are driven by a fundamental belief that if we improve the decision-making capability of people all around the world, even by the smallest increment, we will solve most of the political, social, economic and environmental problems that exist today.

To do this, we develop and deliver a range of products and services that help you in your personal and work life.

At a personal level this means developing products like:

- the *Decida switch* app to help manage your reactivity and build stronger relationships

- the *10-minute journal* and *AnDi* the digital coach to help you reflect and focus your energy and time

- the *sDMF* survey to help you better understand you, and how you can more harmoniously collaborate with those around you
- and a range of products in development to help improve your performance, increase your resilience and improve your leadership and decision-making capability.

At a work level, this means:

- helping organisations turn innovative ideas into reality, to help create systems and structures that unfreeze the 'frozen middle' where fear, politics and a lack of confidence in decision-making undermine progress
- creating and running webinars, workshops, and blended learning experiences that increase critical thinking, communication and individual decision-making maturity
- helping create better decision architecture to improve the decision-making of staff and customers
- helping design and embed agile, design thinking and behavioural economic philosophies so the right things get done in the right way at the right time.

If you want to know more about everything we do, then sign up to one of our webinars and check out the myriad of other resources on the website.

We learn and grow every day, and it's our hope that you can come along on that journey with us.

That's Decida.

Phil, Pete & Roshelle

www.ingramcontent.com/pod-product-compliance
Lightning Source LLC
Chambersburg PA
CBHW070248010526
44107CB00056B/2383